Defining Ourselves

Black Writers in the 90s

Edited by
Elizabeth Nunez
and Brenda M. Greene

PETER LANG
New York • Washington, D.C./Baltimore • Boston
Bern • Frankfurt am Main • Berlin • Vienna • Paris

Library of Congress Cataloging-in-Publication Data

Defining ourselves: Black writers in the 90s / edited by
Elizabeth Nunez and Brenda M. Greene.
p. cm.
Includes bibliographical references.
1. American literature—Afro-American authors—History and criticism.
2. American literature—20th century—History and criticism. 3. Afro-Americans—
Intellectual life. 4. Afro-Americans in literature.
I. Nunez, Elizabeth. II. Greene, Brenda M.
PS153.N5D38 810.9'896073—dc21 98-43060
ISBN 0-8204-4261-5

Die Deutsche Bibliothek-CIP-Einheitsaufnahme

Defining ourselves: black writers in the 90s / ed. by:
Elizabeth Nunez and Brenda M. Greene. –New York;
Washington, D.C./Baltimore; Boston; Bern;
Frankfurt am Main; Berlin; Vienna; Paris: Lang.
ISBN 0-8204-4261-5

Cover design by Andy Ruggirello

Defining Ourselves

PETER LANG
New York • Washington, D.C./Baltimore • Boston
Bern • Frankfurt am Main • Berlin • Vienna • Paris

Acknowledgments

First, we thank the writers and literary critics who so generously participated in the Fourth National Black Writers Conference and, equally generously, permitted us to publish their papers and remarks in this book. We are grateful to the National Endowment for the Humanities for providing the major source of funding not only for NBWC '96, but for all previous National Black Writers Conferences. We are thankful for support from Local 372, AFSCME, AFL-CIO; The Nathan Cummings Foundation; The Reed Foundation; InterAmericas; Putnam Penguin; W.W. Norton and Company; Ballantine Books; Arts Wire of The New York Foundation for the Arts; the Africana Studies Program and the Institute of Afro-American Affairs at New York University; Con Edison; Brooklyn Union Gas Company; Long Island Links, Inc. and Olympic Vision, Inc. We thank the president of Medgar Evers College, Edison O. Jackson, who encouraged us throughout this project and made available to us the many resources of Medgar Evers College. We thank the administration, faculty, students and staff of the college who helped make the conference a success. Darcel Turner Green has our deepest appreciation for tirelessly transcribing audio tapes of panel presentations and retyping manuscripts. We thank Daveida Daniel for her assistance. Finally, we thank our publisher, Owen Lancer, for his faith in this book and his patience as we tried to balance our demanding teaching schedules with the work involved in editing the conference presentations.

Contents

Panel C2
Black Literature: The Politics of Publishing

Introduction

The National Black Writers Conference

Elizabeth Nunez

I was chairperson of the Humanities Division at Medgar Evers College of the City University of New York when the distinguished novelist and essayist John Oliver Killens joined the faculty as writer-in-residence. Killens brought with him a burning agenda. It had lain in cobwebs for over ten years, not through any fault of his, but because he had found it difficult to ignite interest in his dream to convene a conference of writers, literary critics, and readers.

He had convened such conferences before in the 1960s at Howard University and at Fisk University, but as the excitement that followed the Civil Rights Movement of the 1960s waned, so did interest in literature by black writers. When Killens came to Medgar Evers College in 1983, however, Alice Walker had galvanized attention again on black literature with her Pulitzer Prize–winning novel, *The Color Purple*. That novel, and the subsequent blockbuster movie, triggered heated discussions on a controversial issue in the literary community, one that remains controversial to this day: Should the black writer be held responsible for rectifying distorted images and stereotypes of black people? Should his/her work be judged in the light of such criteria?

Killens argued that as "the harbingers of truth, black writers have a responsibility to expose to the world the evils of racism, sexism, poverty and ignorance that plague our society." He contended that some writers have become accommodating, "tender to a publishing industry that is receptive only to politically inoffensive ideas and stories that square with the conservative mood of the country." (Audio tapes from NBWC '86).

Not everyone agreed with him, of course. There were those who worried that the consequences of such a perspective could be censorship and the limitation of themes and images in ways that precluded universal application. Nevertheless, everyone agreed there was a need to convene a conference to discuss this issue.

From the beginning, we envisioned that such a conference would be organized for the lay reader, not only for the academic, the writer, or the critic. It would be a conference where readers could engage in dialogue with black writers and those who wrote about black writing—the academic, the literary critic, the cultural critic, the journalist. They would have the opportunity to question writers and critics, to comment on their work, and to insist on accountability, if that was their concern. The conference would be focused on a specific theme, and we would ask panelists to present papers on that theme, but we would also insist that their presentations be made in language that was easily accessible to the general public and not in the esoteric format behind which too many panelists often sought protection.

Although the idea was a natural outgrowth of Killens's concern about the black writer's responsibility to the community, the conference was not limited to his perspective. It attracted the attention of the Public Programs Division of the National Endowment for the Humanities. The Senior Program Officer there was Dr. Wilsonia Cherry. She encouraged us to think big, beyond our immediate issues and local geographic locations, and so the idea of a National Black Writers Conference (NBWC), one that would draw on audiences and panelists from across the country, was born.

Faith Childs, the New York–based literary agent and attorney, commenting on the first conference in 1986, and on subsequent National Black Writers Conferences, contends that our NBWC conferences are the only occasions she knows where the playing field is level for black writers and literary critics, regardless of their status. "There is an unwritten sign for writers and critics at the entrance of the conference," Childs says. "Check your egos at the door before you come in."

And what a playing field we have had at Medgar Evers College! From the beginning, with the first National Black Writers Conference in 1986, we attracted a stellar group of writers and critics who were enthusiastic to discuss their views with the public and to listen to their readers' responses. Our keynote speakers over the years have been Maya Angelou, Margaret Walker Alexander, Gwendolyn Brooks, George

Lamming, Alice Walker, Ishmael Reed, Paule Marshall, and Amiri Baraka. The list of our panelists reads like Who's Who in black literature. It includes authors of best-sellers, a Nobel laureate, recipients of prestigious literary awards and emerging writers experimenting with new themes and styles. Their names are arranged alphabetically following these remarks.

In the past ten years, we have organized four conferences for ever-widening and diverse audiences. Five hundred people attended our conference in 1986. By 1996 the conference audience totaled 2,000, with participants coming from almost every state in the nation. The theme of the first conference in 1986 reflected Killens's concern. It was The Responsibility of the Black Writer to the Community. Killens died in 1987, but we built upon his legacy. In 1988, we held a second conference on Images of Black Folk in American Literature and in the Literature of the Other Americas. In 1991, we convened a third conference on New Directions for Black Literature in the 21st Century. The fourth conference in 1996, which is the subject of this book, focused on the question of whether or not black literature in the 1990s was experiencing a renaissance to end all renaissances.

This conference came on the heels of the 1991 conference when we worried about alarming evidence that black literature was gradually disappearing from bookstores and was increasingly being relegated to diminishing pockets in Black Studies departments. In the 1991 conference, our panelists offered several reasons why that was happening. Some said that there existed in black literature a provincialism that rarely transcended issues of race, precluded the explorations of the total humanity of the black character, and negated the diversity of American culture. Others disagreed, placing the blame on the absence of serious, critical study of black literature; on public apathy; on a lack of interest in reading; on the decline of literacy within the black community; and, particularly, on the politics of publishing and distribution which continue to marginalize the black writer.

As we prepared for the NBWC '96, evidence appeared to point toward an opposite trend: the increasing visibility of black literature in America. In 1993, NBWC '91 keynote speaker Alice Walker, NBWC '96 panelist Terry McMillan, and Toni Morrison saw their novels remain on the *New York Times* best-seller list for six weeks. McMillan was on the list for 38 weeks. Her novel was the basis for a major movie hit. So was *Devil in a Blue Dress*, a novel by NBWC '96 panelist Walter Mosley. NBWC '96 panelists Jill Nelson and Bebe Moore

Campbell were both on the best-seller list. Additionally, since NBWC '91, when we bemoaned the absence of black literature, two black writers were awarded the Nobel Prize for Literature: in 1994, Toni Morrison, and in 1993, Derek Walcott, NBWC '88 panelist. Since NBWC '91, also, two of our NBWC '96 panelists have received the prestigious MacArthur Award: Paule Marshall and Stanley Crouch.

A 1992 *Publishers Weekly* survey, remarking on the growing market for black-authored books, claimed the number of bookstores "specializing in African American titles has grown from a scattered dozen to 200 or more." In a *Village Voice* article (July 12, 1994), writer Nelson George put that figure at over 400 and noted, "a spread of independent black publishing and distribution."

It seemed, indeed, we were in the midst of an explosion of interest in black literature, what literary scholars, including Henry Louis Gates Jr., from whose essay the title of the conference was taken (*Time*, October 10, 1994), were calling a literary renaissance, but a renaissance with a major difference. Gates contended that though the black arts in the 1990s are characterized by an awareness of previous black traditions, today's black artists are discarding the anxieties of a bygone era to presume "the universality of the black experience."

That contention was hotly debated at the Fourth National Black Writers Conference at Medgar Evers College, March 21–23, 1996. Over thirty black writers and scholars, representing a wide range of political, cultural, and literary theories, generational and gender perspectives, as well as varying degrees of commercial and critical success in the literary marketplace, engaged audiences totaling close to 2,000 persons in lively discussions on this topic. The perspectives and theories of these writers and scholars ranged from those who advocated the portrayal of American and African-American experiences in non-essentialist ways, in ways which could account for the complexity of the experiences of blacks as Americans and as African Americans or Caribbean Americans, to those essentialists who advocated the portrayal of an Afro-centric framework and perspective for describing and chronicling the black experience. Both essentialists and non-essentialists debated the concepts of the social and political responsibility of the black writer.

These perspectives ranged from the voices of writers such as novelist Arthur Flowers, who presented himself as a cultural custodian as well as a political writer, to feminist and literary critic Barbara Christian who cautioned us to remember that critics and educators have a responsibility to ensure that the works of black writers be kept alive. Christian also noted that the notion of "political correctness" has been used to define the black experience and culture in narrow and limiting ways. Novelist, essayist, and feminist Marita Golden underscored the fact that we are the world, and that our literary community is constructed by a range of voices which crosses genres and which assumes the universality of their experiences. Writer Thulani Davis called the current literary renaissance a "literary motown" and expressed concern for the future of black art. Writer, poet, essayist, and playwright Ishmael Reed reminded us that although black writers are experiencing a renaissance, there are still many who are unknown. In his view, we are experiencing a "literary colonialism" where only those who can appease a white public are chosen to represent and speak for the majority.

The loudest and most persistent voices at the conference, among both the panelists and the audience, came from those who expressed cynicism about a literary establishment that had defined and labeled black literature in the '90s without consulting the writers and readers. Contemporary writer Jill Nelson, bristling at Gates's pronouncement, asked: From whose perspective is black writing in a renaissance? Whose works are included? Paul Coates urged black writers to submit their work to black presses that would protect the integrity of their ideas. (Little did we know at that time that he would publish Walter Mosley's novel *Gone Fishing*.) In response, Terry McMillan offered to publish her next work of fiction with a black press. Bebe Moore Campbell suggested that as mainstream publishers become more aware of the growing number of black book buyers, they would be more responsive to the real views of African American readers. The audience, mainly black readers, demanded that writers be accountable to their readers, and not to the labels that critics have attributed to them.

Another consistent topic debated at the conference was the importance of race in black literature. Again, a range of views was represented: that of Marita Golden, Brent Staples, and Stanley Crouch who more or less agreed, albeit for different reasons, with Gates's position on the universality of the black experience; that of Caribbean novelist Kelvin Christopher James who accused African American writers of having an obsession with race; that of African American writer Hugh

Pearson who explored the ethical consequences of such an obsession; that of contemporary novelist Arthur Flowers who argued that it was impossible for an African American writer to write responsibly about the black experience without writing about race; and that of Afrocentrist scholar Marimba Ani who insisted that no work by an African American writer can have integrity if it is not centered on race.

The site of the conference lent to an honest debate of these issues. Located in predominantly black Central Brooklyn, a place largely ignored by the media, Medgar Evers College offered a safety zone for writers and readers to discuss their views openly and candidly without the posturing that cameras sometimes encourage. Indeed, this book is very much indebted to Medgar Evers College for the opportunity it offers for rare and refreshingly candid assessments of issues affecting the black community. The remarks and papers presented here reflect that integrity and made it appropriate that we title the book, Defining Ourselves: Black Writers in the '90s.

We have divided the book into six sections, each of which correlates to a topic we assigned to a panel at the 1996 conference. Professors Carlyle V. Thompson and Brenda M. Greene have written forewords to each of these sections, which we hope will be useful in guiding your reading. The remarks of Walter Mosley, who delivered the welcome address, and those of Amiri Baraka and Paule Marshall, who were the keynote speakers, appear in the order in which they were presented.

In his address, Walter Mosley credited writers at previous NBWC conferences with inspiring him to write. He praised Amiri Baraka, whom he called one of his first black male heroes, "for speaking the truth and teaching him how to read." Baraka, taking issue with the criteria used by the media to define the 1990s as a renaissance period in black literature, called for a Black Writers Union that would create and publish works "which are educational, inspirational as well as fundamental to the continued dynamic of a revolutionary democratic people struggling for socialism." Paule Marshall was less direct. She left the debate on the conference theme to the panelists but underscored the fact that black literature today owes much to black writing of the past. She singled out one writer, Olaudah Equiano, a runaway slave, whose book *The Interesting Narrative of the Life of Olaudah Equiano or Gustavus Vassa, the African, Written by Himself*, she contended, influenced the themes of her novel *Praisesong for the Widow* and the themes in the work of younger writers who today make up "the New Wave."

Defining Ourselves: Black Writers in the '90s records the views of many of our most significant writers and critics on "the New Wave," a new wave that has ushered in one of the most successful periods in the history of black writing from the points of view of both literary merit and commercial viability. It takes into account shifts in the tastes and concerns of black readers and offers perspectives on black literature in the 1990s, from both those who write the literature and those who write about the literature.

It should be noted that some of the papers included in this book contain additions and/or deletions that were not in the original conference presentations. After we transcribed the audio tapes of the panel presentations, we submitted them to the panelists for their review. Some panelists took advantage of this opportunity to make revisions.

We hope you find the essays in this book as stimulating as we have found them. We invite you to join us at the Fifth National Black Writers Conference, scheduled to take place from March 29 to April 1, 2000.

NBWC Panelists and Keynote Speakers

Keynote Speakers

NBWC '86
• Maya Angelou
• Margaret Walker Alexander

NBWC '88
• Gwendolyn Brooks
• George Lamming

NBWC '91
• Alice Walker
• Ishmael Reed

NBWC '96
• Paule Marshall
• Amiri Baraka

Panelists at NBWC '86, '88, '91, and '96

Malaika Adero
Marimba Ani
Doris Jean Austin
Houston A. Baker, Jr.
Toni Cade Bambara
Beryle Banfield
Toni Banks
Amiri Baraka
Becky Birtha
David Bradley
Claude Brown
Marie Brown
Bebe Moore Campbell
Wilfred Cartey
Barbara Christian
John Henrik Clarke
Pearl Cleage
Paul Coates
William Cook
J. California Cooper
Jayne Cortez
Stanley Crouch
Selwyn Cudjoe
Ossie Davis
Thulani Davis
Abdias Do Nasimento
Audrey Edwards
Lonne Elder III
Trey Ellis
Mari Evans
Arthur Flowers
Cecil Foster
Henry Louis Gates, Jr.
Addison Gayle, Jr.
Paula Giddings
Marita Golden
Lorna Goodison
Trudier Harris
Paul Carter Harrison
Calvin Hernton
Karla FC Holloway
Kelvin Christopher James
Charles Johnson
Joe Johnson
Yelena Khanga
John O. Killens
George Lamming
William Luis
Haki R.Madhubuti
Roberto Marquez
Stephanie Martin
Sharon Bell Mathis
Erroll McDonald
Susan McHenry
Terry McMillan
Nicholasa Mohr
Nancy Morejon
Walter Mosley
Walter Dean Myers
Gil Noble
Lucious Outlaw
Les Payne
Hugh Pearson
Shauneille Perry
Phil Petrie
Marlene Nourbese Philip
Kenneth Ramchand
Arnold Rampersad
Ishmael Reed
Louis Reyes Rivera
Sonia Sanchez
Ntozake Shange
Barbara Smith
Frances-Anne Solomon
Brent Staples
Percy Sutton
Quincy Troupe
Luz Maria Umpierre
Derek Walcott
Michele Wallace
Mary Helen Washington
Mel Watkins
Richard Wesley
John Edgar Wideman
Brenda Wilkinson
John A. Williams
Sherley Anne Williams
Cheryl Woodruff
Samuel Yette

No Renaissance Without Our Editors and Publishers

Walter Mosley

There were a few things I wanted to say first. I mean, in ten minutes you can say one thing and, hopefully, in ten minutes I'll get to say one thing. Most people don't say one thing ever. But you know, you try, you try very hard. I want to thank everyone for inviting me and I'm really, really happy for being here. For a lot of reasons. One, I always love coming to Medgar Evers College because I always remember Medgar Evers. The thing about him is he was a black male hero and what I try to write about when I write, is about black male heroes. The thing that we forget is that, we're writers, and we work and most of us get paid for it, at least something. And we do it and we expect some respect and a kind of fair and easy life.

I always think of Medgar Evers going home at night. I think, God, that's a heroic effort, just to drive to your house everyday and say, "I'm going home, I'm going to walk to my house." And it's the hardest thing in the world, something I would not have been able to do if I were Medgar. And I always remember that when I come here. I always remember that, actually, when I'm writing and working.

I want to talk a little bit about being here, but one thing I have to say is I'm really happy to be here with Amiri Baraka. This is something else. Amiri has always frightened me to death. Always, my whole life. One of the reasons is that he's so powerful and he always tells the truth, something which most of us cannot manage to do. When I was a kid, I was an actor. I used to act in a bookstore called the Aquarium Bookstore in Los Angeles. Oldest black-owned bookstore in America. I was ten years old and they had books! And I used to sit there and Amiri Baraka taught me that I didn't know how to read. When I was a kid I used to say, "I know I can understand this book, I know!" It took me a long time, I mean years, but I learned how to read and I learned how to read from Amiri. I learned how to read from one of my first black male heroes. And I'm very pleased about that, and I'm very pleased to be here with him tonight.

Now, just to give you the background of what I wanted to say. I want to say that the first time I came here was the second conference. I hadn't finish writing *Devil in a Blue Dress* yet. I didn't have any representation. And I was here and it was both an exhilarating and adapting experience. Very exciting. There were all kinds of writers here, ya' know. David Bradley was here with his big Santa Claus beard, getting people mad, which is the thing that he does the best. Michelle Wallace was here. I was sitting in an auditorium and there were these three really beautiful young black women standing there. And I was, ya' know, looking at them, saying, "Wow, here are these beautiful young black women." And then all of a sudden one of them said, "Quincy!" ya know. Like Quincy Troupe walked in, right. And, like, they all went around Quincy, ya know. I knew who he was and I had read his work, but I had never met him, this aura of this incredible man.

Terry McMillan was there. It was wonderful. Only it was also sad because I was listening to Terry talk and she was telling me what she did to sell her book. She said, "Well, you know, you gotta get out on the road and you gotta go to those churches and those women groups and you gotta go to those barbecues and you gotta get in your car and you gotta put. . . ." And I was, like, damn. I don't even know how to drive. This is not gonna happen. I'm never gonna get published. So after Terry was finished, it was wonderful, ya' know, but I said, well, at least I can love writing anyway.

Then I thought, well maybe I can sell a book. And then the agent, Faith Childs, was talking. The first thing she said was, "Well, listen. I am completely overwhelmed. I cannot take another submission. So I am going to talk to you about agents, but I can't take your work." And I said, "Oh, my God." Ya' know, I thought maybe I can meet her but I guess that's not gonna happen. But also, I was standing outside somewhere and a young woman walked up to me. I don't remember what her name was) but she said, "Excuse me, are you a writer?" I said, "Yeah." She said, "I am, too. Have you been published yet?" And I said, "Well, no." She said, "Me neither, but ya' know, we're the future, we're the future of writers." And I remember thinking, "My God this woman's really going to be successful." And I felt very good that she included me in her aura of success.

Like I said, me being here was both like a dream and a nightmare. It really was. I mean, I was in one room where I didn't know what we were talking about. But some guy stood up and he had a big manuscript and a leather brown thing in his hand. And he talked about his whole experience of never getting published and never having anybody pay attention to him and nobody caring about him. We were all silent, we didn't know what to say. And he said, "But I figured it out!" And so there was a little bit of relief. Then he said, "I need a mentor!" He looked around the room. He said, "I think I should have Toni Morrison as my mentor." He looked around waiting for someone to give him Toni's number. I really identified with this guy, if only I was so brave to ask.

So then the next conference came, and I was here. I was here 'cause I loved it. You could just kind of hang around all these wonderful writers, all these people who loved writing. I had a book out and nobody knew it very much. But I liked to be in the company of writers and readers, speakers and listeners. Then, there was a great deal of concern at that time about African American writers, the term that I use sometimes. I like to use *black* more, but I say African American once in a while. There were fewer books being published and black men, nobody was paying attention to them. Nobody was getting published. I said, "I have one book published." But nobody listened to me. They said, "No, black men are not being . . ." I said, "Alright."

So I was there at that conference and I had a lot of fun again, which is why I really wanted to come to this again. Because it's like a regular thing to me. Now I'm here again, and I know things have changed. The one thing I want to talk about is, what's changed? Very often what one person sees and another person sees is not the same. A point is Rodney King. A good, decent, liberal, everyday, nice, passionate white person will watch Rodney King getting beaten and say, "This is terrible, this is awful, this is bad, this is wrong. Those men should go to jail!" And then they think secretly to themselves, "Nobody could fault *me* for that." Of course, now, a black person sees Rodney King, and thinks: Who cares about Rodney King? The fact is this has happened to everybody I've ever known and to all of their ancestors all the way back and to me, and it's going to happen to my children. Right? And so it's a different view. So when we talk about things having changed, I think about it. I say, well, you know, we have

Terry McMillan and Toni Morrison, and Alice Walker. There is myself, E. Lynn Harris, Nathan McCall, A.J. Verdell, Connie Brisco, Bebe Moore Campbell. There are a lot of us. We've gone out into all of the genres and really kind of taken over. Look, for instance, at Octavia Butler who has been given the MacArthur. A wonderful writer. And of course Toni Morrison who has taken home the Nobel. I mean, this is wonderful. And so, after looking at that, and listing the long list I haven't said, you can say it seems as though we have arrived.

You can say it seems as though we're gonna go through another larger renaissance. My question immediately when somebody says, "Now, we're gonna go through another larger renaissance" is: Well, what happened to the last one? What happened? What happened to the writers of the '30s, the '40s, the '60s, and the '70s? Where are their books? And where are they? Most people can't answer those questions. You can, but when you do, it's kind of sad. You meet people who have written wonderful books and they're just sitting around selling them by hand. Like today people say, "Have you ever heard of him?" No, I never heard of him. "Why you didn't hear about him?" Well, the answer is because white people didn't tell me about him. Because white people are the only people who can tell people about writers. That's true in America. I don't like it, but it's true.

The truth is that the cultural backbone of America is not only the literature, but it's also the book publishing industry. Our history, our culture, our cinema, our literacy, our morality, and our truths are based on the decisions of people in that business, who are almost all white men, liberal white men and women who dine with Nelson Mandela. I say, "This is racist, the way the industry is structured." And they say, "How could it be racist? My children have lovers of color. I gave up my daughter, ya' know." And I go, you know, "Well, this is not what it's about."

The publishers, the editors, the designers, the sales force, the publicity, and the foreign rights experts are 98 percent plus white, liberal white, and also apologetic white. A black person with the appropriate skills can get a job anywhere, they tell me. I ask, "Well, what about skilled white people, can't they get jobs anywhere?" And they don't answer me. They smile and say, "Well, ya' know." There is a belief that smart black people have it easier than white people. It's a funny thing. Ya' know, it's an assumption. A black person, he's smart. Well, there's so few of them, that, you know, we have to spread them around.

We have to worry about our representation in mainstream American and international publishing. Without editors and publishers in positions of power, in ten years from now we will be looking for a new renaissance because of the people who forgot those people were white people in publishing. And they didn't care. Because they're not their friends, they're not their constituency, it's not their language, and it's not their history. You can't even blame them, really.

I was at a party once and a guy came up to me and said, "My name is Joe Jones." Like I should know. Like somebody said their name, ya' know, like my name is Marilyn Monroe. And I go, "Joe Jones, uh-huh," and I go away to somebody else and say, "Who's that?" and they say, "Well, don't you know him? In the '70s, he published two million books!" And I say, "Why, I never heard of him." And they say, "Yeah, isn't that too bad." Well, you know, this is what happens to us, all of us, almost all of us, almost everybody. Remember Zora Neale Hurston had a hard time at the end of her life publishing books, writing books? People forget about Zora Neale Hurston. And when they talk about her, they say her last book wasn't very good. I say, "Well, what about all those other books?" But people don't care. What I want to say is, it's not just Random House and Simon and Schuster and Bantam and Doubleday. We can blame them, and it's nice and everything, but really the problem is here, in this room with us.

Many of us, and I have to include myself here, are making the publishing world rich while our publishing professionals are scorned. I was on a panel in Chicago with Max Rodriguez who cares about us and who publishes *QBR: The Black Book Review*, a wonderful publication. There are a lot of publications, black publications in America which will talk about black people once white people say they're famous, once they're put in big films and sell lots and lots of books. They say, "Oh, let's talk to Toni Morrison, Terry McMillan. Oh, we're going to interview them." But if you ask them about somebody who's just written one book, they'll say, "It's very good, but there are only 5,000 copies. We're not ready for that yet. You'd really have to go to a white press for that." So this is a problem.

I was with Max Rodriguez and Max says, "Well, listen, a lot of you writers here, here's what you could do, you know, if you make it in the mainstream. You publish four or five good books, you're making some money. Give one of those books to a black publisher. Just one mainstream best-seller would mean a lot to a publisher committed to preserving our history and ensuring our future." This is what Max said. I think that it's true. I think that it's important that we work together in every way to pressure and change the hierarchy of American and international culture. We have to challenge, persuade and overcome the walls that are built around us, and more importantly, the walls that are built in our minds. 'Cause someone could say, "Listen, why don't you give that book to a black publisher?" But too many of us reply, "Hey man, sh—, that book is worth $200,000 to me. Sh—, I ain't gon' trust no nigger with that." But you see, as long as that's true, as long as we approach it like that, then we're not gonna get anywhere.

We're not in a renaissance now, and we won't be in one unless we open up ourselves and deal with our people. I just want to add at the end here to my fellow writers who are lucky enough to be in this position, I am not suggesting that we give away income. I'm not suggesting that we say, "Here, take this and go away." I think that what we have to do is we have to get involved. We have to work with people; we have to talk to other publishers and publicists that we have and make sure that we can make our books successful in our own community and at the same time in that other larger community.

The Role of the Writer in Establishing a Unified Writers Organization

Amiri Baraka

We artists, calling ourselves revolutionary or people's artists, must strive to be as necessary to the people's intellectual and cultural development as food is to their physical development. We must create works which are educational and inspirational, as well as fundamental, to the continued dynamic of a revolutionary democratic people struggling for socialism. But as one great writer, Mao Tse Tsung, has written, we must create works which are both politically revolutionary as well as artistically powerful. One-sidedness won't do. We must do both. We cannot forsake the political for the artistic. Whose art would that be? What class would that nourish? Who would it serve? No one but our former, though still living and still aspiring to be, masters. No, our works must serve the politics of the continuing democratic revolution and be part of the cultural revolution which must intensify as fuel for the coming of socialism! But our works cannot be absent of artistic depth. We must strive to create a people's art, a revolutionary art, a socialist art, an art that will help create the new socialist society in South Africa, while we here are alive, and yes, throughout the world. But part of our problem, we would-be people's artists, we would-be revolutionary artists, is that most often we place our whole production, our life's work in the hands of our acknowledged enemies or their faithful lackeys and ideological servants.

We revolutionaries must criticize the enemies of the people, both the slave masters and their agents (and they come in all colors, genders and nationalities). But we must not be content merely to criticize the people's enemies. We must increasingly take up our time organizing alternative institutions, organizations, structures, networks, alliances, and collectives which can forward and develop and create ever more productive answers to the question of, How Do We Liberate Ourselves from all Oppression and Oppressors? How Do We Do Away With All Pests? We must answer Lenin's question, "What Is to Be Done?" with answers of organization and systems and concrete social development.

Our art must serve and be inextricably bound to our political and economic development, as well as our cultural development. For certainly, they are different fundamental aspects of the same quest for democracy, self-determination, and, ultimately, socialism.

I have been raising this question of an Afro-American national writers organization or union for some time. Just last year at the 1995 Black Arts Festival in Atlanta (where some 1,000,000 people attended) we raised this question. We asked various assemblies, and those who administrated (black and white), "Shouldn't we set aside some portion of this festival, in which there has been much fun, much inspiration, much human, emotional, and historical unity to consider this question?" There were many great Pan African artists of the world present, and an impressive number of intellectuals and scholars. Together! It was a wonderful, joyous week. My wife Amina and I went to see Maya Angelou one evening, and Cassandra Wilson and the great Abbey Lincoln later on the same evening! And then off to Miguel Algarin's NuYorican Cafe Theater party for the cast and author of *Life in Wartime*, Wesley Brown. Then back to the hotel where we talked to Abbey in the restaurant even further into the evening, and then talked in rapid succession that night and later to David Murray, the great tenor saxophonist, and to Quincy Troupe, Sonia Sanchez, Calvin Hernton, Don Pullen, Hattie Gossett, Linton Kwesi Johnson, Askia Toure, Haki Madhubuti, Ishmael Reed, Toni Cade Bambara, Wesley Brown, Eugene Redmond, Butch Morris, David Henderson, and on and on. We went to see Thornton Dial's new works, heard Ras Baraka, my and Amina's very fine poet son, read with Angela Jackson. We went to see Ruth Brown, and Little Jimmy Scott made us cry with the blues. We even struggled with various conservatives. We were on panels and forums, held formal and informal gatherings. And on one joyous evening we had a beautiful surprise (to Amina) a 27th wedding anniversary party in which all these folks and more laughed and sang and read in a penthouse ballroom overlooking downtown Atlanta. But still I raised the same questions: Shouldn't we put some time aside to discuss seriously, and with concrete suggestions, which could be implemented by us 'till next we met some time, shouldn't we put aside time to discuss self-determination and self-reliance for African American artists and arts? Shouldn't we spend some time trying to organize ourselves, and, indeed, African American art and artists toward self-determination?

If we really believe that the African American people are an oppressed nation in the U.S., then with the right of self-determination, the renaissance is not about to end but to begin. Shouldn't we be using this grand gathering of some of the finest artists in the world to begin to build the theaters and publishing companies, the art galleries and networks of performance venues and cultural centers so that we never have to rely on people who made us chattel slaves, and after the so-called emancipation, betrayed us again into the same thing with a different name? The people who segregated us, discriminated against us, lynched us by the thousands, who destroyed Reconstruction and delivered us into the hands of the southern whip crackers whose ruling class we had just sent to hell in the Civil War?

Read Patterson's *We Charge Genocide* and shudder at the bloody trace of our residency in the U.S. The United States has never been a democracy. To paraphrase Du Bois, we have never been citizens! Why should we continue to play the vicious American game of paper citizen and real slave? Why should, particularly, our artists and intellectuals continue to function as if they were really integral parts of the U.S. social body politic? Why should they continue to hang around in pathetic "double consciousness," seeing, as Du Bois said, ourselves through the eyes of people that hate us.

Du Bois called for "true self-consciousness" and it is exactly this that the revolutionary artists must be sworn to bring into being. But we cannot do this unless we are part and parcel of the people, no different, except for our consciousness, our role. Certainly, it should be impossible by now for us to think we can function as revolutionary artists and intellectuals under the hood of the massa's Cadillac, making it go. The African people are historic masters of the arts. We are the creators of art, music, poetry, indeed, speech itself. Why should we play Charlie McCarthy, a wooden dummy, to the greedy racists who continue to rule the world?

The imperialists control the arts like they control everything else. They decide what is hailed and what is dismissed. They say what is produced and what will never be. They choose the super stars, give out the grants. They are the creators of the Pulitzer and Nobel prizes, and, indeed, they select who we will idolize and follow. They let us know what literature is serious, what is not. In fact, they tell us what is literature. They have a canon in which they have selected white men as the masters of literature. (There is one white woman, but not one person of color.) They are the genius namers and prostitute makers. They give out Academy Awards for pornography and drive the great artists and intellectuals into exile, anonymity, madness, and poverty. But why do we would-be people's artists and intellectuals collaborate with this? Why do we accept the Devil's sick illusion as the actual? We must, I guess, if we are to be generally published or produced. We may criticize, but that is the limit, though there are some of us who wail on these suckers on occasion in our criticism.

It is crucial now that we organize nationally, from the cities to the counties, to the states, to the regions. What we must organize is a Writers' Union in the tradition not only of Mao, but of the great Pan African revolutionary writers of our tradition, like Sembene Ousman, Ngugi wa Thiong'o, Jacques Roumain, Nicolas Guillen, W.E.B Du Bois, Langston Hughes, and Margaret Walker. In struggling for democracy and equal rights, the African American people must begin with self-determination, for we must move first of our own accord even to fight for complete equality as Americans. Relying on the U.S. government and the big imperialists who own it, or the petty bourgeoisie who run it for them, or their various puppets and clowns who claim they have the answer, in somebody else's pocket, is absolutely backward. And nothing but a continuum of misery will ever come from that stance.

The African American people are an oppressed nation whose historic land base is the black Belt, black majority areas of the U.S. south. Throughout the rest of the U.S., we are an oppressed nationality, having arrived as chattel slaves in the bottom of slave ships, fighting and struggling from the first minute we fell into the hands of our traitorous African brothers and sisters who sold us. As an oppressed nation, the African American people have a right to self-determination, like any people. Democracy is the basis of real citizenship, but we have NEVER had that in the U.S. The extent to which we do not take steps (which we can take) to create for ourselves the things we need defines the limits of the political, social, economic, and cultural dimensions of our national oppression. We are denied rights and robbed as a nationality and as a CLASS, identified as slaves by color caste (i.e. "racial") supremacy, i.e., slave master to slave social relations. The U.S. has never been a Democracy! And we have never been citizens. The main history of the African American people in relationship to the U.S. has been chattel slavery, paper equality, real betrayal, and re-enslavement at the hands of the dead slave master's ex-overseers, now "compradors" of the U.S. oppressor nation.

In our own history is found the form and content, the method and meaning/motive for African American political (and by that, I mean social and cultural) development. Basic to this is the reorganization of our consciousness through the reorganization of our social relations and ideological understanding. Therefore, the cultural revolution we describe here is the fundamental work necessary to produce the "true self consciousness" Du Bois explained, that is, the positive negation of the "double consciousness" which has been pointed out as the psycho-social reaction to slavery, colonialism, indeed, the defeat of the Third World by European imperialism.

For the writers and artists and other intellectuals of the oppressed peoples, especially in the Third World, to let themselves be fixed and unproductive (i.e., with a production that is directed and fixed by the bourgeoisie) and merely seek to better the conditions under which we sell our labor to them, is ludicrous.

Part of the ultimate resistance to imperialism is to be able to disconnect ourselves from it, to the extent that we are fully conscious of ourselves, our real historical material presence. And that truer self-consciousness allows us to understand ourselves and our own needs and problems and their solutions. The very contradictory aspects of our oppression should establish one mode of our development. The weakness of any would-be resolve we make for self-determination is how much self-determination, as the most important democratic resistance to imperialism, can we achieve as a sycophantic and captive suppliant to it, contained within its material and philosophical presumptions, and, therefore, objectively defined/confined by it to our detriment. The common psychological development which has given the African American nation its common culture is made through the arts, into the expression of a National Consciousness, which is the True Self Consciousness, the prerequisite for National Liberation and Revolution.

African American culture is Pan African, but it is Pan American too. This is why black music is a continuing expression of America/ North, South or Central, as well as Afro-America. It is just that as an expression of Afro-America it is belittled, covered, dismissed, exploited, etc., while as an expression of America (like minstrelsy) the very Imitation of Life which such "minstrelsy" is, it is a consistent identification of the U.S. itself. It's ersatz "Humanity." And we must, most of us, one day understand the dehumanization that minimally national oppression and racism bring, cannot be eliminated until their material base, monopoly capitalism, is eliminated, and that this is a protracted struggle.

Spontaneous reaction to these problems is no lasting solution. Hence, in each of the three periods of black political upsurge—19th century anti-slavery, 1920s Harlem Renaissance (essentially part of the international anti-colonial movement that arose as the Russian Revolution exploded) and the 1950s–1970s Civil Rights and Black Liberation Movements—there was significant progress made. But without some overarching organizational construction that would carry a definite strategic and tactical focus past the excitement of these spontaneous uprisings, we will, like Sisyphus, see the rock rolling down the hill, again!

Three things that Malcolm X taught we can regard like the great Chinese democrat SunYat Sen's "Three Peoples Principles": *Self Determination, Self Respect*, and *Self Defense*. The first is basic, so basic that the others are impossible without it. The second, self respect, deals with the eradication of the Double Consciousness and the replacement of it with True Self Consciousness. But this eradication cannot merely be "theoretical," or the result of numerous "Feel Good" sessions nationalists especially treasure, where we whoop and declare our supremacy to our enemies (usually with the same ideological base, and bourgeois nationalism) and our "ancestral greatness" and then return like tipsy slaves to the ghetto. The self respect will emerge, as a material aspect of African American life, through the creation of institutions and organizations that teach it and that have also constructed material uplift of the very productive forces of the African American community itself. Part of the lack of self respect that the Double Consciousness presages is the fact that we must go to our enemies for everything. Now it has gotten so bad that we even have to go to other people's neighborhoods to partake in our own high level artistic culture since white Americans have long since stopped their caravans into black communities to dig the sounds, and have now transported the clubs and performers and artists to their land, leaving us with dead end bars, unimaginative organ trios, and youth whose "role models" are big dopers or dopey Negro politicians and "buppie" servants.

It is as if the culture itself appears in its most "rewarding" form only on television or CDs, or in the high rent districts. But the depth of this analysis is that in the culture itself, the arts and intellectual analysis, can be found the root of our new self determination and self reliance and self defense (which, at base, is merely conscious self organization.) When we evoke the RAZOR image, we are saying Revolutionary Art Cultural Revolution (RAZOR), because we hold that at bottom, we must mobilize the masses of the African American people, and the advanced and revolutionaries of all nationalities, through the use of the arts to inform and arouse and educate, so that the entire culture of the oppressed can be made sensitive to their oppression, True Self consciousness, and influenced to self organize, to throw off first, the mental bonds, and, next, to whatever degree, the material dependency (at least around the question of our expressions of self determination, and what is to be done). To accomplish this:

1. The writers must agree to put in $100 a year (minimally), and this entitles them to publish anything they want to (consistent with S.O.P.s) in the organization's publication. They should understand that anything in the journal can be criticized, but that they will have an opportunity to answer it.

2. Members should be asked to set about creating a particular Arts and cultural base, using the organization's publication as an organizing tool. (Even a monthly meeting to discuss and criticize the organization would be good.)

3. Each writer must take a certain number of the publications, but they will receive enough publications so they can sell and therefore get their money back and even have a surplus to reinvest in the publication or organization projects.

4. Each writer must try to recruit other writers and artist intellectuals into the organization. The basic membership requirements will be: agreement with the statement of principles; payment of financial commitments; and active work in the organization.

5. Each writer should purchase the other writers'/artists' works, as another financial commitment, so that each writer can base the printing of his/her works on the collective readership of the organization. Each person in the organization will take as many of those works as possible and sell them.

6. Each writer/artist must make consistent efforts to see that there is a bookstore or other distribution outlets for the works of the organization's artists. This might also include a theater or arts performing space, so that eventually organization-sponsored tours and lecture/performance circuits can be set up; regular lectures/performances can be scheduled at their locations where written; recorded works can be circulated; and concerts, plays, poetry readings, forums can be held regularly (at least once a month).

7. Continuing attempts must be made to create liaisons and working relationships with public education, so that students (and other youth) in the arts, writing, and performance can be enlisted in the RAZOR, and so that the RAZOR group can increasingly go into the schools to perform. One continuing thrust of the organization's literature and organizing efforts must be to influence masses to self-organize around art and culture and education. The use of schools as arts spaces and centers of mass organization coordinated by RAZOR can be economically beneficial.

The same effort must be made around athletics, as an aspect of culture. The indigenous population must be urged to start their own leagues, from little to adult, and to make such leagues self reliant, and able to employ more and more youth and adults. Proven community athletes should be recruited as coaches and coordinators. In all these efforts in public space, attempts must be made to see that the indigenous population receive aid from the community (businesses and churches and other institutions) and are able to set up small businesses and to employ and organize the people. One important project that must be attempted is setting up bookstores in the high schools. This has already been done in wealthy suburbs where bookstores, which have other school merchandise and memorabilia, are run by students.

8. Organizations in all locations should attempt to set up publishing and recording projects. The idea of "Motown" could be a national phenomenon, as collective arts/cultural developments aimed at employing, educating, and organizing target masses.

9. The organization should have one national meeting every two years, a regional meeting once a year and local meetings monthly. The organization should meet as a "body of the whole," i.e., everybody, until such time that it grows large enough to require elections to representative offices from cities, state regions, and the nation.

10. The organization should, as soon as possible, send out a mailing to selected artists calling for them to join the initial body. Those artists who can afford it should be urged to give more than the required $100 a year, and, where possible, even commit a percentage of royalties to their financial commitment, and for special projects (a national tour, a CD of members and their works, anthologies, etc).

11. The organization should make up a list of respected artists who will be asked to join, but we must also create a body of critical evaluations and begin to give out our own awards (annually and in summation of the years that we didn't) in writing, music, drama, painting and sculpture. This is very important. We must, as soon as possible, intervene and interfere with the capacity our enemy has of establishing aesthetic and philosophical guidelines for OUR CREATIVITY (e.g., the vicious absurdity of a ROCK and ROLL HALL OF FAME or Elvis Presley as some "King," etc.).

The art of African America is, by its own confirmation, determined to live by its own will and design. What it says is who it is. Its "blackness," its feeling, experience, emotion, class, what is deepest, are as animated as our lives. The great art of Afro America, the Belt and the urban nationals, is historically glorious, exquisitely self conscious, democratic, revolutionary, and hip! There is no art "outer" than these peepas got in their mind, heart, memory. The Soul is what lives, even if "the you" we knew already blew. What is, is still alive.

But, again, the African American is the great historic artist of the real America, the real Western Hemisphere, the African of the real Africa, and, indeed, the real world. We can be Charlie Parker and Frederick Douglass. We is Zora Neale and Maya. We is Sweet Lorraine with *A Raisin in the Sun*. We is Jimmy and Richard and the great Margaret Walker. Jelly Roll, Bessie, Ma, and Billie are we. And you know we is Louis and Kid Ory and we is, believe it or not, Duke Ellington and John Coltrane. We is Charles White and Langston Hughes, Paul Robeson and Sun Ra and Scott Joplin. We is Nat Turner and Blind Lemon, Art Tatum, and James P. Johnson. Dr. Du Bois is also we self and Thelonius is our name too. Call me Toni Morrison or Claude McKay. I'm John Biggers and Smokey Robinson. Ornette Coleman and Amina Baraka. I'm Max Roach, Miles Davis, Beauford Delaney, Lester Young, Ella Fitzgerald, B.B. King, Lightnin Hopkins, Fats Waller, Edmonia Lewis, Lois Maillou Jones, JJ Johnson, Romare Bearden, Fletcher Henderson, Ira Aldridge.

Okay, I won't beat you all the way to death. Look, we is also these artists, but they are in the internal body of a lie in which they do not exist. What we create is ourselves and needs no measure but our creation as expressions of our real lives, minds, experience, and consciousness. The Africans who were brought here were from cultures that encouraged great artists as an organic part of social and intellectual life. Part of the doom of white America is it suppresses art, censors it with money and political power, distorts and debases it with commerce.

In France, they called the poet, Griot. The town crier. In the South, we said Djali. Like old Negroes on fire with the gospel, in church, and rising, possessed, like Bird, BA, the Charlie Parker wailing his fetish back into the sun. On out. What is created? An Atomic Bomb or the

Blues? Duke Ellington or John Wayne? Bette Midler or Sarah Vaughan? Let it be. But that Art, that being of us carried as us, seen and been, as and was, to be what we create again. The Real is the Royal (King of Everything) and it is connected. Oh, uncivilized things who ignorantly rule as savage wizards of cannibal power, connected as what is one and all and every. And that truth, that is the beauty of what is alive, as reason!

Black Literature in the '90s: The Past as Prologue to "The New Wave"

Paule Marshall

First of all, let me say how pleased I am, how honored I am, to have been invited to address this, the fourth National Black Writers Conference. I'm especially pleased that this year the conference is being jointly sponsored by New York University and Medgar Evers College.

I'm going to begin my talk this evening with a quote from one of my favorite writers, someone whose work has been around for a long, long time. Many of you will probably recognize right away who it is. "We are almost a nation of dancers, musicians and poets," he wrote over two centuries ago. He continued:

> Every great event, such as a triumphant return from battle or some other cause of public rejoicing, is celebrated in public dances, which are accompanied with songs and music suited to the occasion. The assembly is separated into four divisions. The first division contains the married men who in their dances frequently exhibit feats of arms; to these succeed the married women, who dance in the second division. The young men occupy the third and the maidens the fourth. Each represents some interesting scene of real life, such as a great achievement, domestic employment, a pathetic story or some rural sport. And as the subject is generally founded on some recent event, it is therefore, ever new. This gives our dancers a spirit and a variety which I have scarcely seen elsewhere.
>
> And in battle even our women are warriors. Our whole district is a kind of militia: on a certain signal given . . . they all rise in arms and rush upon their enemy. It is perhaps something remarkable that when our people march to the field a red flag or banner is borne before them. I was once a witness to a battle. . . . We had been all at work . . . as usual, when our people were suddenly attacked. I had climbed a tree at some distance, from which I beheld

> the fight. There were many women as well as men on both sides; my mother was there, and armed with a broad sword.
>
> As to religion, we believe that there is one Creator of all things and that he lives in the sun and is girded round with a belt, that he may never eat or drink; but according to some, he smokes a pipe, which is also our favorite luxury. They believe he governs events, especially our deaths or captivity, but as far as the doctrine of eternity, I do not remember to have ever heard of it. . . . We do believe that the spirits of dear friends or relations always attend us, and for this reason before eating, we put some small portion of the meat and pour some of their drink, on the ground for them. . . .
>
> I remember too that we never polluted the name of the object of our adoration. On the contrary, it was always mentioned with the greatest reverence; and we were totally unacquainted with swearing and all those terms of abuse which find their way so readily and copiously into the languages of more civilized people. The only expressions of the kind I remember were 'May you rot' or 'may you swell,' or 'may a beast take you.'

Those excerpts were taken from a book that was a runaway best-seller when it first came out in 1789. It went through sixteen editions, was translated into German and Dutch, and was said to be instrumental in bringing about the end of slavery in England, where it was published. Its title, is *The Interesting Narrative of the Life of Olaudah Equiano or Gustavus Vassa, the African, Written by Himself.*

When I first came across the narrative, years ago at the Schomburg, it was like finding long buried treasure. First, because it was unique among the slave narratives of the time, in that the author actually remembered his boyhood in Africa, remembered the ordeal of the Middle Passage and the long years of enslavement, and had so mastered the English language he could record it all in vivid detail. There was also the sheer power and authority of the writing: his style, his use of literary devices, imagery, metaphors and symbols to enhance his tale. I knew right off that I was in the presence of a gifted story-teller. But perhaps, most importantly, I found that many of the themes that animated Equiano's narrative two centuries ago were also present in my own work and in much of the black fiction being written today, the work of those who might be called "the new generation." I will be referring to a few of them later.

Naturally, the themes are reworked and recast today in a contemporary mode, given, as it were, a 20th century spin. But I contend they're still alive and well in our literature, albeit, in modern dress. Whether the restatement and reworking of the traditional themes is responsible in part or in whole for the new renaissance in black writing, which is a question posed in the conference description, whether there's even a new renaissance, is an issue I don't specifically address here. I'm sure the answer to this or the continuing debate about this will emerge out of the panel discussions tomorrow. For my part, what I intend doing tonight is to simply, first of all, identify what I consider to be some of the principal themes in Equiano's narrative, and then to take a quantum leap of two centuries to a book of mine called *Praisesong for the Widow,* and to show that many of the same themes are at the heart of my novel as well as in the work of some of the younger writers who now make up "the new wave."

But to return to Equiano, to Olaudah, he offers us the bare facts of his life in the narrative. An Ibo, he was kidnapped at age eleven from his village by local raiders, that is, Africans involved in the slave trade, a painful but true historical fact. He was carried west and south, he said, "across a wide river," probably the Niger, brought to the coast, and sold to British merchants sailing to the Americas on a ship called *The African Snow.* That's right, snow. The ironies, the absurd existential nature of our experience, began on a ship named *The African Snow.* There, followed the trauma of the middle passage. "I cried and grieved continuously . . ." he wrote, "and did not eat anything but what they forced into my mouth." At the same time, he says, he lived in terror of being eaten by "those white men with horrible looks, red faces and loose hair." He longed to throw himself overboard with the suicides who preferred death over captivity, with the many who died of disease and despair or who were simply tossed into the Atlantic. "The Atlantic, a wilderness of waves, a desert of water," is the way Langston Hughes described it in a poem. It's a watery death camp in Equiano's narrative. That image of the Atlantic and what transpired there during the years of the slave trade remains a theme in the literature. There's Tom Feelings' recently published book, *The Middle Passage,* with its powerful, searing narrative paintings of the crossing. There's a sculpture of the *Mel Edwards.* The Atlantic is also present in my own second novel, *The Chosen Place, the Timeless People.* Here's how I describe it:

> The Atlantic . . . a wild-eyed marauding sea, the color of slate, deep, full of dangerous currents . . . and with a sound like that of the combined voices of the drowned raised in a loud unceasing lament—all those, the nine million and more . . . who had gone down between the homeland lying out of sight to the east . . . This sea mourned them. Aggrieved, outraged, unappeased, it hurled itself upon each of the reefs in turn and then upon the shingle beach, sending up the spume in an angry froth. . . . (106)

Miraculously, the boy Olaudah survived the crossing and was brought first, he tells us, to the West Indian island of Barbados, which, at the time, served as the principal trans-shipment point for the trade. Barbados, where my parents were born, geographically sits in a direct line across the Atlantic from Dakar and that infamous doorway of no return on Gory Island. You stand in that doorway, as I've done, with nothing but that desert of water in front of you and you just know you'll never see home again. Before Olaudah was shipped out from Barbados—he would be sent to Virginia—he was cleaned up, greased down, force-fed to fatten him, and renamed Gustavus Vassa, after the Swedish king at the time.

The absurdities abound. For years he was called out of his name, forced to answer to Gustavus, although, he tells us, he continued to secretly call himself Olaudah, a name which in his language had two meanings. On one hand, it signified someone highly favored and having a loud voice and well spoken, and this would prove true many years later when he became an outspoken abolitionist in England. But the name Olaudah, he informs us, also meant vicissitudes, changes in one's fortune, hardships, and adversity. In keeping with this second meaning, he experienced long years of enslavement in Virginia, the West Indies, England, and then back in the Americas again. He had forced journeys back and forth across the Atlantic until he was finally able to purchase his freedom from his last owner, a Philadelphia Quaker. Another irony.

Thirty-three years later and more vicissitudes, but this time as a free man, Olaudah Equiano—he had back his rightful name—sat down and wrote his life story.

"The most remarkable 18th century book to be written by a black man and the finest example of the slave autobiography as a literary art form." I'm quoting the late African American writer Arna Bontemps in his introduction to a 1960 edition of the narrative. Bontemps contends that "Equiano's principal intent in the book was to create a self, an identity that would present him as the barrier of the moral principles and values of his lost Ibo community." Identity and community are principal themes in our literature to this day. "In depicting himself as an African man, the warrior," Bontemps wrote, "as Olaudah of the loud voice rather than as a victim, he moves his narrative to the creative and even the fictional level. Along with the other slave autobiographies, Equiano's provided the spirit and vitality and the angular vision responsible for the most effective prose by a Black American."

The impact of the narrative on my own work was profound. Reading it as both history and literature helped me to better understand and to define what I was seeking to express in my own fiction, especially in *Praisesong for the Widow,* and I'd like to turn to that novel now.

For those of you who don't know the book, a brief summary. *Praisesong* tells a story of Avey Johnson, a middle age, middle class, in fact, upper middle class widow, very proper, conservative, one of those black bourgeoisie matrons who wouldn't be caught dead without her gloves, her three strands of pearls and her fashionable hat. Avey Johnson has long banished the blues and gospel music, greens and cornbread from her life. "Done got shame of the things that brought us through," the old folks would say about Avey.

By dint of hardwork and sacrifice and struggle, Avey and her late husband climbed the proverbial ladder. There's Avey's wall-to-wall carpeted house in North White Plains, her patrician car, a Lincoln, her overflowing clothes closets, everything in good taste, but too many mink stoles, too much of everything. There's also the investments left her by her late husband, and for her vacation each year, now that he's gone, there's the cruise she takes to the West Indies with her two friends and her six pieces of matching luggage. Avey's made it. She's what used to be called in my day, a C.T.T.R., a credit to the race, an American success story.

And then on one of those cruises, my proper, conservative heroine does something absolutely radical and revolutionary: she jumps ship. She gets up in the middle of the night, packs her six suitcases, abandons her two friends and flees at the next port of call. Why? What's the reason for this piece of reckless behavior on Avey's part? A dream. Shortly after the cruise got underway, Avey has a dream, a disturbing dream, that confronts her for the first time in years with the culture and community she has disowned.

As a girl growing up in Harlem, she used to be sent down home each summer to spend time with her great-aunt who lived on a sea island off the coast of South Carolina, Gullah country. And every summer, the old woman would repeatedly tell her a story that she insisted was true, about a group of captive Africans long ago who had upped and walked back home the moment they arrived in America. They had taken one look at the place and the people who had brought them here and had turned on their heels and walked back across the Atlantic.

Others in our mythologies flew home, as the characters in Toni Morrison's *The Song of Solomon*. We're still mining the rich motherload of folk material. In the dream, Avey Johnson is once again the little girl hearing the story of the captive Africans. And it suggests that the same way those long ago captives put the distance of the Atlantic between them and enslavement, she needs to do the same: to place a kind of psychic and spiritual distance between herself and the excessive materialism she has allowed to overtake her life and to separate her from both herself and her culture.

When Avey finds she can't shake the dream, that it gives her no peace, she decides to cut short the cruise and return to the safety and sanity of her house in North White Plains. She is certain that she'll be able to get a plane right away. Well, I see that she doesn't get a plane right away. She's stuck, stranded in the islands, and while there, I subject her to a number of experiences, some of them pretty traumatic, that strip away her fraudulent self and begin to restore her. Aiding in the restoration is an old man she meets, an Eleggba kind of figure, who, along with her great-aunt, serves as an ancestral figure in the novel. "The spirits of our dead friends and relatives always attend us," Olaudah says in his narrative. And so do they attend Avey in *my* narrative. The old man becomes her mentor and guide. He opens the gate for Avey. He leads her to what is essentially a journey back to her center, her true self.

The theme of the journey is one that reaches back to the slave narrative and forward in time to today. It assumes many forms in the literature. It was the journey from the Deep South to the big cities in the north during the great migration. Richard Wright's black boy escapes Mississippi for Chicago. It's the continuing exodus, as from Barbados to Brooklyn, all those West Indians picking up and leaving their little islands for parts north. This odyssey is brilliantly captured by Patricia Powell in her novel, *Me Dying Trial*. Powell is a young Jamaican writer who lives and teaches in the States. It is also in the work of Cecil Foster from Canada, whom I just met and who will be speaking tomorrow at the conference. Then there's Angela Verdelle, A.J., she calls herself. In her moving and skillfully written first novel, *The Good Negress*, published last year, she traces the journey of her young heroine from Detroit to the deep south, back to the mean streets of Detroit—all places that figure in the young girl's rite of passage to adulthood.

The theme of our dispersal, our Diaspora, persists in the literature. And whether it describes an actual physical move from place to place or a psychological and spiritual one, as with Avey, the journey always involves the self, the question of identity. It's always about either seeking to free, to define, to realize, to reclaim, to heal, or to create the self.

Equiano's principal intent throughout his life, Bontemps tells us, was to fashion for himself an identity that would depict him as Olaudah, the loud voice and well spoken, someone highly favored, rather than victim. With Avey, as a result of her Caribbean odyssey, she's able to reclaim what the Trinidadian novelist and political activist Merle Hodge calls, "one's true-true name," her rightful self. And with that, she's once again centered, rooted and thus personally empowered.

But personal power as I treat it in *Praisesong* and in my other books as well, isn't solely about the self; it always involves the larger self, meaning community. The personal is inseparable from the political. One's responsibility also is to work to empower that larger world that is part of your definition of self. This was a central theme, as I see it, in Equiano's narrative. He considered it his responsibility to be the bearer, to uphold the moral principles and values of his lost Ibo community, to remain loyal to it, emotionally connected to it, and to always represent that world in the person of Olaudah, of the loud voice and well spoken. The best of our literature today is also concerned with our relationship and responsibility to community.

I think of the late Toni Cade Bambara in this regard and this talk tonight is dedicated to her memory. Both in her work and in her life, Toni was absolutely committed to rescuing and empowering our community. Her character Velma in *The Salt Eaters* struggles, if you remember, to be healed and empowered again so that she can once more be an effective community worker. This theme of responsibility, of each one help one, forms a centerpiece of *Linda Raymond's* wonderful first novel. She's another gifted new writer on the scene. Her book, which came out, I think, in '94, is called *Rocking the Babies.* It's the story of two older women, two Aveys who work as volunteers in the preemie ward of their hospital. Most of the little preemies are abandoned, crack babies. The two women come and sit and hold and rock them, love them. They're women who live by the principle that two centuries ago informed Equiano's life as an abolitionist. That is, to be human, truly human, is to be of use to more than just the self.

Avey Johnson is also restored to a sense of community once she reclaims her true-true name. She is then able once again to embrace the world she had come to reject. In the novel, I have her re-enter the cultural fold, the circle of the community, by way of the dance. "We are almost a nation of dancers, musicians and poets," is the way Equiano described the culturally rich world of his boyhood. Dance is also an important motif in my own work. Dance is ritual, ceremony, celebration, but also a symbolic means of healing and renewing the self and transcending one's condition. Moreover, dance, as used in my work, is the most profound expression of the confraternity of black people throughout the Diaspora, from Brazil to Birmingham to Brooklyn. *All of we is one,* Trinidadians declare at carnival, and they really seem to mean it, at least for the two days of carnival, as they dance, middle class and poor and every shade of black and brown, through the streets of Port of Spain.

Dance was also once important in Avey Johnson's life. As a young married woman, in the years before "she done got shamed of the things that brought us through," she was known to do a mean lindyhop; she and her young husband had never missed a Saturday night at the Renny or the Savoy. And as the little girl sent to spend summers down home, she had loved watching the Ring Shout dance, performed in the churches there. And it is this, the Ring Shout, which Avey dances at the end of the novel to celebrate her deliverance.

A word about the Ring Shout, if I may. The Ring Shout is a sacred dance that was once popular throughout the south. For the Ring Shout, the entire congregation would form a circle inside the church, and one behind the other, they would do a slow, trudging dance that could go on for hours. They were free to move their bodies as they wished, but the soles of their feet were not permitted to leave the floor. They sang as they journeyed around the church. "Who's that riding the chariot? Well, well, well." They used their clapping hands as tambourines, slapped their knees, thighs and chests in a dazzling syncopated pattycake. The shouters worked their shoulders, rolled their hips and carried on. Their arms shot up, and their hands arched back like wings, as they sang, "Got your life in my hands. Well, well, well." But if the sole of the foot happened to lift so much as a fraction of an inch from the floor that was considered juke joint dancing and the offender would be expelled from the circle. Only the dancers' heels were allowed to rise and fall as they trudged forward, and it is said that sometimes at night the sounds of those heels rhythmically and powerfully striking the floor in unison could be heard miles away.

James Weldon Johnson, that giant of our first renaissance, describes in his autobiography, *Along This Way,* how as a boy growing up in Jacksonville, Florida, he used to be kept awake at night by the powerful sound of those heels in the Ring Shout. The drum. Those heels pounding the floor were substitutes for the drum. They took away our drum, the complex, polyrhythmic, systolic and diastole of our collective heart, and we improvised—or what Albert Murray in stomping the blues calls, extemporized—with the Ring Shout.

There's a scene in the play, *Bring in Da Noise, Bring in Da Funk*, which, by the way, is reopening on Broadway next month. In the play, there's a scene where two young men have what looks like every pot and pan in the kitchen strapped on to their bodies. They're using them as drums and reminding us that we're a people skilled at the art of making something out of nothing. In fact the scene in the play is called just that, "*Making Something Out of Nothing*" and it reminds us that improvisation and extemporizing are essential to the black aesthetic, guiding principles in our creative expressions. And so my heroine dances. She is taken by her aged mentor and guide to an island feast the night before she's finally able to get a plane back to North White Plains, and there, healed and restored, Avey Johnson dances the Ring Shout. And I will close with this brief scene from the novel.

> Avey began to dance then . . . her feet of their own accord had discovered the old steps, her hips under the linen shirtdress slowly began to weave from side to side on their own, stiffly at first and then in a smooth wide arc as her body responded more deeply to the music. And the movement in her hips flowed upward, so that her entire torso was soon swaying. Arms bent, she began working her shoulders in the way the shouters long ago used to do, thrusting them forward and back in a strong casting off motion. Her weaving head was arched high. All of her was moving suddenly with a vigor and passion she hadn't felt in years, and with something of the stylishness and sass she had once been known for. "Girl, you can out-jangle Bojangles." Jay saying it with amazement at the Saturday night pretend dances when he would turn the floor over to her.
>
> Yet for all the sudden unleashing of her body, she was being careful to observe the old rule: Not once did the soles of her feet leave the ground. Even when the Big Drum reached its height in a tumult of voices, drums and ringing iron, and her arms rose as though hailing the night, the darkness that is light, her feet held to the restrained glide-and-stamp, the rhythmic trudge, the Carriacou Tramp, the shuffle designed to stay the course of history.

Avey had come on home.

Panel A1

CHOOSING EXILE: BLACK WRITERS FROM THE HARLEM RENAISSANCE TO THE BLACK ARTS MOVEMENT

Foreword

Carlyle V. Thompson

The theme of self-imposed exile spanning the forty-year plus period from the Harlem Renaissance to the Black Arts Movement exemplifies the continuous struggle of black people in their attempt to find a true sense of "home" in America, despite their vicious, involuntary migration and their genocidal enslavement. In a general sense, "home" can be defined as a place where one's domestic affections are centered, and a place where self-empowerment can occur. However, for many black people, the issues of "home" and America as a "homeland" have always represented a profound paradox: a nation founded by wealthy white racist slave owners who sought religious and political freedom for themselves. Paradoxically, the freedom-loving totalitarian Thomas Jefferson, owner of two hundred black slaves, was the leading philosophical spokesman for black inferiority and white supremacy. What white intellectuals such as Jefferson did was, in effect, to claim America as a white man's country. For example, in *Notes on the State of Virginia* (1787), the duplicitous Jefferson tentatively states:

> I advance it therefore as a suspicion only, that the blacks, whether originally a distinct race, or made distinct by time and circumstances, are inferior to the whites in the endowments both of body and mind. It is not against experience to suppose, that different species of the same genus, or varieties of the same species, may possess different qualifications. (143)

Despite Jefferson's doubts, his racist beliefs stood as the strongest exhortation of black people's inferiority; thus, black people attempting to find a "home" in a country legally and extra legally constituted on the denial of both their humanity and their right to the pursuit of happiness has always been a profound challenge.

Fundamental to black people's challenge to white America is the trope of the "call and response." Frederick Douglass, Harriet Jacobs, Harriet Tubman, Richard Allen, Sojourner Truth, David Walker, and Ida B. Wells are just a few of the individuals who have painstakingly laid the foundation for black people's multifaceted acts of resistance and self-empowerment. While America's white supremacist culture has continually called for the subjugation of black people, blacks have continually responded with the clarion call for America to live up to its democratic dictates of freedom, justice and equality—for all of its citizens. The Harlem Renaissance is particularly critical in black people's challenging response to white America's vehement call for racial hegemony.

With the Silent Protest Parade, July 28, 1917, the "Red Summer" of 1919 (James Weldon Johnson's term for the race riots occurring across America) and with Claude McKay's fiery response "If We Must Die," the Harlem Renaissance reflects a challenge to white society's violent exclusion and exploitation of black people. A few lines from McKay's militant poem read:

> If we must die, O let us nobly die,
> So that our precious blood may not be shed
> In vain; then even the monsters we defy
> Shall be constrained to honor us though dead!

McKay's vitriolic poem establishes the continuous theme of resistance to the enduring strain of white mob violence and the institutional racism that black people faced. Although there is some debate over the long-term impact and success of this Renaissance, we do have significant cultural products from this period that are unprecedented in their variety and scope. In *Modernism and the Harlem Renaissance* (1987), Houston A. Baker Jr. explicates:

> Reflecting on the labors of generations of black men and women in the United States who have been exploited, segregated, physically and verbally abused, denied access to opportunity, and called all manner of untoward names, and who have, nonetheless, forged a mighty identity and forced the white world to stand in awe and, sometimes, to effect powerful imitations of their labors. . . . I suddenly wondered who, precisely, had consigned the Harlem Renaissance to the domain of "failure" and how we, as Afro-American scholars (but more importantly as descendants of a resonant black lineage) could tolerate this consignment. (xiv–xv)

Black people have always struggled against enormous adversity and have always created something out of nothing, and the prolific literary productions of Alain Locke, Countee Cullen, W. E. B. Du Bois, James Weldon Johnson, Langston Hughes, Jessie Redmond Fauset, Nella Larsen, Rudolph Fisher, and Claude McKay give testimony that black people, connecting the past to the present, were "digging up their roots." This "digging up" resulted in the continuous celebration of the self-worth, the self-transformation, and self-actualization of people viciously and violently oppressed by racist dictates. In his essay "The Negro Artist and the Racial Mountain," Langston Hughes, with his echoes of Frantz Fanon's *Black Skin, White Masks* (1967), is particularly critical and celebratory in his deft evaluation of the Harlem Renaissance and the psychological impact of black writers:

> It is the duty of the younger Negro artist . . . to change through the force of his art that old whispering "I want to be white," hidden in the aspirations of his people, to "Why should I want to be white? I am a Negro—and beautiful!" . . .We younger Negro artists who create now intend to express our individual dark-skinned selves without fear or shame. . . . We know we are beautiful. And ugly too. The tom-tom cries and the tom-tom laughs. . . . We build our temples for tomorrow, strong as we know how, and we stand on top of the mountain, free within ourselves. (*The Nation*, June 23, 1926, 694)

Hughes's prose indicates a critical factor about the literature of the Harlem Renaissance: many black writers such as James Weldon Johnson, Nella Larsen, Claude McKay, Jessie Redmon Fauset, Jean Toomer, and George Schuyler along with Langston Hughes were concerned with the phenomenon of black individuals passing for white. In order to permanently pass for white it was necessary to embrace whiteness and reject their black family, their black community, and their black culture. Taken together, these writers were attempting to remove the whiteness burned into the psyches of many black people. Thus, along with black World War I veterans returning "home" from Europe, seeking socioeconomic and political agency after putting their lives on the front lines for democracy, black writers were also in the vanguard in challenging the red, white, and blue of white supremacy. Writers of the Harlem Renaissance laid another foundation for black letters with a complexity, a self-knowledge, and a self-fulfillment that was national and international in scope.

In conjunction with the Civil Rights Movement, the Black Arts Movement, led by the activism and the literary works of Ella Baker, Hoyt Fuller, John O. Killens, Kwame Toure (Stokely Carmicheal), Angela Davis, Muhammad Ali, Haki R. Madhubuti (Don L. Lee), Nikki Giovanni, Sonia Sanchez, Amiri Baraka, and Jayne Cortez brought a heightened sense of black power, black pride, and black self-determination. These elements were especially evident in the poetry—new in style, content, and emphasis. In *Black Writers of America* (1972), Haki R. Madhubuti defines the new attitude and the new language:

> I ain't seen no poems stop a .38,
> I ain't seen no stanzas brake a honkie's head,
> I ain't seen no metaphors stop a tank,
> I ain't seen no words kill
> & if the word was mightier than the sword
> Pushkin wouldn't be fertilizing russian soil
> & until my similes can protect me from a night stick
> i guess i'll keep my razor
> & buy me some more bullets. (809)

Like bullets in flight, these black writers, led by the fiery poetry, prose, and plays of Amiri Baraka, were young and gifted with a revolutionary spirit that connected the black liberation movement to liberation movements around the world and especially in African nations such as Nigeria and Kenya. These liberation movements made African Americans more aware of the connections between imperialism, colonialism, and white supremacy.

Back in America, Medgar Wiley Evers, a liberator, aged thirty-seven, died in the early hours of June 12, 1963. Evers was shot in his driveway while returning "home" to his wife and his three children; his life of activism with the NAACP in Jackson, Mississippi, and his brutal death at the hands of Byron de la Beckwith, a member of the White Citizen's Council in Greenwood, Mississippi, reveal the struggles and sacrifices of black people in their passionate attempt to establish a "home" in America. The brutal murder of black people can be extended by linking them to Patricia J. Williams's analysis of what she names "the spirit murder" of twentieth-century white supremacy. In *The Alchemy of Race and Rights* (1991), Williams, contemplating the murder of a black activist stabbed thirty-nine times, states: "what it was that would not die, what could not be killed by the fourth, fifth, or even tenth knife blow; what sort of thing would not die with the body but lived in the mind of the murderer?" (72). Like the black male bodies lynched, burned, castrated, and hanging from Southern trees like "strange fruit," we can imagine the enduring psychological trauma that Medgar Evers's wife, Myrlie Evers, and their three children experienced around the notion of "home." Discussing her use of the racial house/home paradigm in her work, Toni Morrison in her essay "Home" (1997), argues that many black writers use home as

> an intellectual home; a spiritual home; family and community as home; forced and displaced labor in the destruction of home; dislocation of and alienation within the ancestral home; creative responses to exile, the devastations, pleasures, and imperatives of homelessness as it manifested in discussions on feminism, globalism, the diaspora, migrations, hygridity, contingency, interventions, assimilations, exclusions. The estranged body, the legislated body, the violated, rejected, deprived body—the body as consummate home. In virtually all of these formations, whatever the terrain, race magnifies the matter that matters. (*The House That Race Built*, 5)

Accordingly, how do black people create and sustain a "home" in a society where racist whites are committed to make them homeless? More generally, how can black people be so needed and at the same time so despised, degraded, and denounced?

These central questions were fundamental to and fueled much of the discourse at the Fourth National Black Writers Conference at Medgar Evers College of the City University of New York. In a world dominated by the malignant dogma of white supremacy, black people in the diaspora are continually creating a "home" despite the more malevolent mode of forces that seeks to deny them the peace, power, and productivity that a home can provide. Further, there is a basic premise of humanity that in *The Language of the Night* (1979), Ursula K. Le Guin addresses:

> If you deny any affinity with another person of any kind, if you declare it to be wholly different from yourself—as men have done to women, and class has done to class, and nation has done to nation—you may hate it, or deify it; but in either case you have denied its spiritual equality, and its human reality. You have made it into a thing, to which the only possible relationship is a power relationship. And thus you have fatally impoverished your own reality. You have, in fact, alienated yourself. (99)

Taken together, the black writers and scholars at the March 1996 NBWC celebrated and critiqued the unique achievements of black people during the Harlem Renaissance and the Black Arts Movement: two significant periods in the history of black letters.

In this first panel, the scholars and writers Houston A. Baker Jr., John A. Williams, Yelena Khanga, and Eugene Redmond—moving from autobiographical reflections and deft historical literary analysis to the international impact of black writers—these scholars and writers explore the complexity of the "exile paradigm." This "exile paradigm" is most evident in the lives and literary works of Richard Wright, James Baldwin, and Chester Himes—all of these writers chose exile in Europe in order to escape America's racial hegemony. Like many black jazz artists in Europe, these three writers found a more peaceful and productive sense of "home."

Exile: Taking Apart and Finding the Word

Houston A. Baker, Jr.

During my formative days in the Southland of the United States, I was, I rather now suspect, like a Negro feather wafted by winds of American ideology. As Lorraine Hansberry's strong Big Momma figure emphasizes in *A Raisin in the Sun*, there was during my childhood, indeed, an unctuously Christian and ceremoniously demanding God in our household. Of course, even as a very young man reading Sunday School literature, I knew that God was white, Christian, and male. And like James Baldwin's "native Africans" in the face of "alabaster missionaries," I believed that if the Son of God washed me in scarlet, I would become whiter, yea, whiter than snow! It was this sense of disciplined, color-coded, Christian ethics teleologically directed toward one brand of whiteness that was the core of our household morality. It was the bedrock of our goals, aspirations, manners, and ideals. I like now to think of my childhood as a perverse Beardenesque collage of postwar American triumphalism, integrationist black hopefulness, Ramar of the Jungle Fever, and Cold War xenophobia. With such a mad congeries of ideological winds, how could I help being a feather at the mercy of the breath of grand narratives of American scientific and industrial progress? And with that great humanistic annihilation of hundreds of thousands of "evil" people of color in the "Orient" that marked Hiroshima and Nagasaki, how could any loyal American doubt that "progress," like the Christian "modernity" and futurism preached in my own household, was indisputably white and undeniably American. We Bakers, as American Negroes, were epiphenomenal to this more general and powerful progress. But after President Harry Truman declared an end to segregation in the military and the GI Bill put many American blacks in college and into our first homes, we were sure that some washing in the blood of the lamb had taken place and that we were well on our way toward being more American than America itself. When word reached us of African nations securing their independence in the 1950s, we said: "Thank God! For he hath delivered the heathen out of pre-modernity and given good earnest to white America that being black or African does not mean you can't make progress."

I remember my father animatedly describing to my incredulous mother (who had prepared a perfectly decent American meal of pork chops, corn bread, and cabbage) his fantasies of a liberated Africa where, as he put it, "these black guys are in charge." My father's vision was a combination of Harriet Beecher Stowe, Elmer Gantry, Albert Schweitzer, and the British East India Company. "Voilà," he said to my Mom, "If I could just get my hands on fifty or sixty Coca Cola machines and get them installed in Ghana, do you know what kind of money that would mean for us?" I think my mother turned her eyes toward the ceiling and uttered one of her cherished phrases for such occasions: "Heaven Forfend!" And that was the end of my Dad's export imperialism.

I use this autobiographical lead-in as a metaphor for my own middle-class generation. We were post-war children of college and university educated "Negroes" who had survived the Great Depression, made their way out of the working class, and determined that the United States—slavery, poverty, segregation, and racism notwithstanding—was indisputably their home. Our parents, at least the Jack-and-Jill branch of them, were, first and foremost, Americans on the move. Surely, the 1954 *Brown v. Topeka Board of Education* decision of the Supreme Court reinforced their sense of progress, "American domesticity," and "Negro Hominess" in the United States. So our folks were prepared to fight communism, champion American protectionism, and seal the borders of their children's imagination against the Godless impulses of foreign agitators in any guise whatsoever. They counseled us to avoid the non-cosmopolitan roughness of the Spanish language as a possible high school curriculum choice, and discouraged our listening to radio blues as even a late-night solace from ancestral spirits. We were "at home" with America, even if we could not always feel comfortably Negro and American. There simply was no other Great Good Place like America, "at least," as my capitalistic Dad used to say, "for the Negro." So with his Coke machine scheme heartily disparaged by my Mom, my father and the rest of us settled in to watch *Ramar of the Jungle*, collect money for Presbyterian "missions abroad," and slowly evolve through God's grace, into the educational discipline and Federal protectionism of non-racially-identifiable real Americans. No one chose exile.

Perhaps my story and my parents' generation's story and the stories of their parents are anomalies now under Postmodernist, Post-black-Atlantic, Post-Colonial, and impressively theoretical academic formulations on exile. For what I have described is what seemed a normative course of "Negro" childrearing and family aspirations in the United States—a norm parochially uninterrupted by world-systems analysis, black emigrationist prolegomena, or a willed introduction of world historical forces into family matters. More contemporary theorizations, however, have attempted to uncover a historical lineage of, shall we say, "African American" exilic longings.

Now, what I mean by this can be elided with the *Oxford English Dictionary's* definition of exile which emphasizes the sign *home*, as in: "To banish or separate from one's home [conceived as] a pleasant or endeared place or association." Here, at least for American blacks, exile receives the ambivalently coded psychological effect of an obsessive-compulsive Afrocentricity. As banished tribes forced to sit by New World Rivers of Babylon, African exiles look in the mirror and recognize the uncanniness of themselves. Read as "Negroes," they are "unhoused." And psychological obsession, combined with a certain mythopoeic historiography, turns their dark exilic glass into Prospero's Book of Revelation. They conjure virtual formations of the Nile Valley rising from steamy bathroom mirrors. They drape themselves in Kente and the glories of black Athena. And it is here that a second definition of exile comes—by choice—into effect. That definition, though somewhat obsolete, reads: "diminutive, attenuated, thin. Of theories: Fine-spun." Indeed, fine-spun theories of Afrocentricity enable some American blacks to become, through their own psycho-mythical choice, "diminutive" or "attenuated" Americans. The bumper sticker for such chosen exiles might read: "I'm making a resolutely American salary, but I walk like an Egyptian." It is my belief that it is a very good thing that the majority of black writers in the United States have not chosen this Afrocentric exile.

On the other hand, I understand the romantic appeal of Afrocentric psycho-mythology. For definitions of exile that have been the real trial by fire for Africans in America are far less solacing than Afrocentric obsession. Exile as a verb signals: "waste or devastation of property; ruin, utter impoverishment." And in the Old French to *mètre à essil* is: "to ravage a country, or ruin a person."

It is here that we come face-to-face with the black Atlantic in harrowing exiles that have nothing of the cast of humble white pilgrims in search of religious freedom on a watery errand, as it were, that ends at a fertile wilderness where white men construct a Godly City on the Hill as a beacon to the Old World. No, the black Atlantic exile was a holocaust claiming tens of millions of "ruined persons" and vast tracts of ravaged and appropriated land. The end of the watery journey of blacks across the actual place of the Atlantic was, in the simplest of psychological terms, abjection in labor. This, then, was exile as "enforced residence in some foreign land." This was exile as a pure political function of power and knowledge. It was the horror of exile not as the romance of *Paris Blues* or "April in Paris" of classical black jazz musicians in Montparnasse. It was exile as "expatriation, prolonged absence from one's native land, endured by compulsion of circumstances."

Simply stated, the black Atlantic exile of African enslavement was power and knowledge at work in the service of profit for whites in the Mainland Colonies of that landfall called the New World. I rather like to think of writers of African ancestry in the United States as those who have chosen to regard at least part of their primary identity in America under the aegis of this rather more formidable, and certainly non-romantic, version of exile. It is a very heavy intellectual burden, of course, to endorse such an exilic paradigm because it leaves one in the always already wrenching position of the floating signifier, the uncanny bereft-of-origins positionality that constitutes anything legitimately called an Americas, as opposed to an American expressive cultural authorship, or writerly mastery. What do I mean by this? At the risk of burdening you with one of the most oft-quoted passages from Afro-American intellectual lore, let me cite the following:

> *After the Egyptian and Indian, the Greek and Roman, the Teuton and Mongolian, the Negro is a sort of seventh son, born with a veil, and gifted with second-sight in this American world, a world which yields him no true self-consciousness, but only lets him see himself through the revelation of the other world . . . One ever feels his twoness,—an American, a Negro; two souls, two thoughts, two unreconciled strivings, two warring ideals in one dark body, whose dogged strength alone keeps it from being torn asunder.*

Traditionally, of course, this quotation from Du Bois's *The Souls of Black Folk* is used to demarcate a peculiar form of Negro schizophrenia resulting from American racism. However, in consideration of a version of exile as the uncanniness of deportation, expatriation, "homelessness" as a function of motion from one set of domestic arrangements to an uprooted, ever-shifting quest for stable identity, Du Bois's exilic "seventh son" is far more than an untidy black schizophrenic. Rather, the exiled double-consciousness of transatlantic journeyings, journeyings of bodies, compulsions, nostalgias, orthodoxies, ideas, ideals, and, most importantly, an efficacious New World modernity is the very definition of the Americas.

Let me say that what I am suggesting as the Du Boisian writerly ideal of exile is precisely that which makes Richard Wright's famous phrase on the relationship of Africa to America so precisely accurate. You will remember with me that it was, in fact, Wright who said: *The Negro is America's metaphor.* I would modify this to say that the, per force, exilic cast of the Negro's second-sightedness as thinker and intellectual—as well as survivor of an extraordinarily complicated everyday life in the United States—is what makes the black writer a metaphor or metonym for a kind of borderland writing, degree zero.

I have in mind narratives such as those of Olaudah Equiano or Mary Prince. I think of Langston Hughes's *The Big Sea* and *I Wonder as I Wander.* The poetry of Phillis Wheatley, Robert Hayden, Rita Dove. The novels of William Wells Brown, John A. Williams, Toni Morrison, Toni Cade Bambara. Of course Wilmot Blyden, Du Bois, and other "grand masters" have eternally gestured toward the pleasures and perils of exile. Like exile, considered in its sense of modernity's uncanniness and anxieties of expatriation and imprisonment in the dreams of the "other," multiculturalism in the Americas is compelled, at its most exactingly practical and theoretical levels, to wear a black writerly face.

In conclusion, let me say that writers of the Harlem Renaissance and the Black Arts Movement of the 1960s chose exile in the interest of modernity. And in their choice, they realized that the doubleness of Negro and American is neither more nor less a problem for expressive cultural wrestling than the doubleness and exilic fluencies of the Americas in general. Rather than schizophrenia, inescapable, will-less imprisonment, or romantic and fantasized "hibernation" in preparation for an African "return" to origins, the best of Afro-American choices of writerly exile are texts without which the New World could not even begin to understand itself. Finally, then, I believe that exile in the guise of Harlem Renaissance writers tying their efforts to "new nationalisms" around the globe, or the pro-Africa self-stylings of the Black Arts 1960s—exile in such form is always a sign of a productive intellectual borderland identity where the world is made anew. Exile, at its most astutely problematic moments, always lies beyond a narrow nationalism. It signals a willed intellectual second-sightedness that none have more profoundly brought to the office of defining "American" and the Americas than black writers of our own century. In time, there will be more to say of Du Bois, Wright, Senghor, Césaire, Wright, Baldwin, Julian Mayfield, Ollie Harrington, and classical black entertainers in Paris and elsewhere. But for the moment, let us assume that such transatlantic journeymen, like the writers already mentioned, have been borderland intellectuals, playing across quite intriguing cultural boundaries.

Of course, I had to leave, as all exiles must, my own home and hometown of Louisville, Kentucky, before I could either understand or begin to refashion myself beyond those Cold War, xenophobic, Christian provincialities that took such good care of me as a child. Had I not chosen such exile, I doubt seriously that I would have been so generously invited to speak on such a momentous occasion as this Fourth National Black Writers Conference.

The Dubious Ecstasy of Exile

John A. Williams

For the first moments the very air may seem different. The language can resemble music set in marvelous tonalities. Although the people are curious, their manners at first observation seem uncommonly courteous; "the look," with which we were so familiar in the States, seems to be absent.

At first glance the vistas are like paintings that have leaped off the walls of the museums back home. The streets seem cleaner, the avenues majestically broader. (We haven't seen the neighborhoods yet.) It is Europe, of course, the "Old World," for comparatively few African Americans have chosen exile on the continent of Africa.

(Marcus Garvey's seed did not flower. Instead, we find today that many black folk, from the African continent particularly, have exiled themselves from their homelands to the U.S. for political reasons, mainly, and for economic reasons as well. But the politics are not of race as was very much the case in Rhodesia and South Africa; rather, they are the politics one can still find in Europe and the U.S.—greed, corruption, favoritism and one-party rule. [Here we are late arriving at the conclusion that very little separates the Democrats and the Republicans.] Europeans and European Americans are merely more adept and subtle at doing the same thing; Africans haven't yet mastered those skills.)

Why shouldn't African Americans seek relief from pain? In this country we grow to maturity within the parameters of the family, which nestles within the community, which struggles to maintain values not unlike those the national society professes to live by. But it is always that larger, overarching, restricting shell of government, and its tolerance for negative racial manners and mores, of laws ignored, and of extra-and-illegal laws enforced, that shape attitudes which determine what we do and how we should do it on every level of existence. There is only one politic in the United States and it is race; all else stems from it; it is where the philosophical politic of democracy clashes most fiercely with the economic doctrine of *laissez-faire*, or capitalism or, these days, free-market economy.

In 1924, however, Paris was a place where "it was lovely just to be by oneself and not bothering with color prejudice," wrote Jessie Fauset. But African Americans in earlier times had always regarded France with great warmth and written lovingly about it more frequently than not, despite its contradictory history of republicanism and racism. In Fauset's time, six years after the Great War, the French were still grateful to the Africans and African Americans who had helped repel the German Army. Monuments to the Senegalese can still be found around the city of Lille, and the 93rd Division of the U.S. Army can boast of several decorations presented by the French.

Locke's contention that the black writers of his day exiled themselves to Europe because their works were "inherently political" and politics failed to raise their writing to "maturity," overlooks a simple but crucial fact: all art, in my opinion, in particular writing, is political. For example, the writings of Luther unleashed a war that was to determine if the center of religion and its attendant politics would always remain in Rome. The works of Shakespeare, Milton and Swift, and others in England are not political? Shelley's "Song to the Men of England" is so overtly political that even today it is only infrequently taught in this country; we prefer his "Ozymandias," which is far more political, but couched in an allegory we refuse to decipher. The works of Strindberg and Ibsen are not political? Of Dostoyevski, Hugo, Pirandello and the generations of other writers in Europe were not political?

"We wish," lamented Locke in 1925, "our race pride to be a healthier, more positive achievement than a feeling based upon the realization of the shortcomings of others." The young Locke, of course, experienced prejudice, as it was then called, but found it a less than noble literary topic. So what was his "New Negro" to write about? Were the oppression, submission and behavioral control of black people an unfit topic for those whose forebears could have been killed for knowing how to read and write? Though he long sought to keep his head above the fray, by the beginnings of the Great Depression he concluded that a "racial art was not set apart from universal art. . . .

The more deeply representative it is racially, the broader and more universal it is in appeal and scope, there being for no truly great art, no essential conflict between racial or national traits and universal human values."

Furthermore, the writers he chastised for exiling or expatriating were more visitors to Europe than people determined to set down roots there. Locke himself was an annual visitor. He had studied three years at Oxford and one in Berlin from 1907 to 1911. Those he criticized in the twenties were only doing what he had done. That they were visiting or studying implies that they had the hope that America would or could be changed—or that a visit to the Continent would provide some psychological relief against racial onslaught at home as well as widen their view of the world.

We do need a definition of expatriate here. The expatriate leaves his land and renounces allegiance to it. This did not apply to most African American artists of the fifties and sixties. Ron Fair, last heard of in Finland, Sam Middleton in Holland, James Emmanuel and Barbara Chase-Riboud in Paris, Herb Gentry, Cliff Jackson and Walter Williams are exceptions to the rule; they have lived years away from the States. (Painters on the whole seem to fare better than writers.) But I don't believe any of them has formally renounced allegiance to the U.S.

Many of the visitors and short-term residents in Europe are listed in *The Street Guide to African Americans in Paris.* We do not find among them the 200 African Americans who were living in Berlin in 1903; nor do we find those black workers from Detroit or those black teachers from Tuskegee who exiled themselves in Europe where, like Wright, LeRoy Haynes, Ollie Harrington, Chester Himes, LeRoy Hart Bibbs and the painter, Edward Webster, they remained until their deaths.

Is Europe really escape after all? The cost of living there may once have been far less than now, and avoiding miss-meal cramps may have been bearable. But, unless one has a pretty large bankroll, or a job, pension, or some kind of income, living in exile soon becomes psychologically strenuous. Where can one work? There was a time when European governments provided stipends for foreigners on several levels, usually artistic; these were not overly generous sums of money and may no longer be available. In the private sector, few jobs were obtainable. Europeans looked after their own first and that attitude by now has been carved in stone. A new breed of "expatriate" in today's Europe is the black businessman at work for the corporation back home. And undoubtedly there are those who, like Ernest Just, found the scientific community of Europe more supportive of their work, but, this, a pleasant situation, was only possible if there was support from the States. Just had difficulty securing and maintaining such support.

For the exiled, usually young, African American writer, there is removal from and entrance to a different kind of space in which one scrambles to maintain body, while the soul dreams of plots and characters. Employment as we know it here (or used to) is not easily come by even in the most gracious of host nations, unless one is a star in a clearly viewed heaven, such as opera, concert performance, popular entertainment and a few other lesser constellations, such as restaurateur or night club owner. Writers only occasionally ascend to the European heaven. Since foreigners generally come last in terms of securing local support, one is forced to write; "writers' block" becomes a fatal ailment. The exiled may soon discover that he or she has only stumbled into poverty with another language.

Few black writers probe deeply into the European scene itself; their minds are still at home, and it is this they most often write about because they know it best. This is no less true for the writers of the nineties than it was for the writers of earlier times. It is not that they are incapable of writing well about Europeans; it is that Europeans, like European Americans, do not wish to see themselves as African American writers may have come to see them. Black expatriate writers come to understand this impediment, sometimes more quickly than they care to.

Then what about publishing in Europe?

From the publication of Réné Maran's *Batouala* in 1922, until today, European publishers have insistently sought "exotic" (Chester Himes called it "titillating") writing from the black authors they might publish. If published widely in Europe, it was only after they had first been published in the United States, where a book's potential success in Europe could easily be measured by its track record at home. And if published in the U.S., and if "political," no matter. It was all at a distance for the Europeans. The black writers were not talking about *them* anyway.

A French editor told me thirty years ago that the French like to pretend great interest in the social and political unrest in the U.S., but deep down they didn't give a damn about what was going on racially. My Spanish agent said essentially the same thing. My agent in Milan—

a transplanted American—merely smiled. Writers of the nineties will find that not only does this view remain unchanged, but that the number of publishers in Europe, as here, is dwindling if not already out of business. And this is at a time when the politics of race in Europe is once more at the boiling point. Governments, undoubtedly more so than in the past, if that is possible, are determined not to allow platforms for opposition to their racial policies. This is most specifically true for foreigners. We witness the British reaction to Wright's *Black Power* (1954) and the French reaction to *The Color Curtain* (1955). Then there was *Pagan Spain* (1956). Writing of colonial policies without the expected exoticism was risky business; that's why the Algerian War became absolutely forbidden fruit. We also note that the one book Himes set in France was not published until he had moved to Spain, though the novella, *A Case of Rape*, had little to do with French policies.

Still, one cannot overlook the value of a visit to Europe as a learning experience. Michael Harper once said he was curious to see the people who did what they did to his fathers. A reader can digest that one-sentence opening paragraph of Wright's *White Man Listen!* to understand the European legacy of violence against itself and against the non-white world. A visit may provide insight as to why European scholars can hold conferences on William Faulkner without ever mentioning race. It may also enlighten us on why the Serbs in Bosnia, in mid 1995, demanded that the UN send only white soldiers to police them. It will surely widen the curtain on Britain's current, racially motivated immigration policies, and those sliding out of cover elsewhere all over the European Union.

Those earlier critics who may have been alienated by the racial-political writings of African American writers . . . were they themselves African Americans? I think not, so, of course, there was alienation. But what were the writers to do—quit writing and let racism quietly, at its own maddening pace continue to plague the lives of black people? Racism has never quit. It never will without demand. It is what we battle with the pen. Every concession on matters of race has been gained through struggle alone.

Therefore, irony abounds when we heard lines from Claude McKay's aggressive declaration in "If We Must Die," the lyrical anthem of the black anti-racists, issuing from the lips of Prime Minister Winston Churchill before the Parliament in rolling, resonant tones in 1941 during the Battle of Britain. He did not name, perhaps did not know or care to know, the author, who had spent time in England and Europe. No matter. *We* know the political message, which had meaning for *all* people, went through and that the words of a writer—a *black* writer—helped to straighten the backbone of a nation that has not yet recalled their source.

To return to Locke when he renounced his early criticism of some writings by black authors, ". . . . the more deeply representative racially it is, the broader and more universal it is in appeal and scope, there being for no truly great art no essential conflict between racial and national traits and universal human values." That is, *no essential conflict* between the freedom McKay sought for his people and what Churchill sought for his.

Black writers of the nineties will continue to do what African American writers have always done: Go where they wish, write, and, hopefully, publish their contributions to the struggle. Keeping the faith will not be easy or greatly remunerative. But it will be exciting.

Choosing Exile: African Americans in Russia

Yelena Khanga

(She starts speaking in Russian.)

Usually I start speaking in Russian just to prove that I do know how to speak in Russian, and to prove that a black Russian is not only a drink (a mixture of vodka and Kaluha), and to prove that you can't judge Russians by their color or by their cover, but thanks so very much for having me here today. I'm nervous because I've never spoken with such an impressive panel of males. If I make any mistakes, grammar, or any other mistakes, please be very patient with me. A Russian would say that shortness is the sister of talent, so I'll try to be very talented.

I was invited on this panel to speak about the subject of the exile of black intellectuals. I took it very personally because that is basically my roots; that's how I came to this world, thanks to my grandparents. My grandfather was an African American intellectual who was trying to avoid racism in the '30s, he and lots of other African American intellectuals whose stories are still not told. But it's a very common story. My grandfather, with thousands of other African Americans, was fighting in World War I in France, when, for the first time, he realized there was a world where racism was not institutionalized. So he started thinking: Why do only white people have a chance to live in these countries? Why don't black people try to go and find their heavens? So he made up a group of all African American specialists in agriculture, some of them, like himself, graduates of Tuskegee Institute and they all went to the Soviet Union.

It is amazing how many African American intellectuals tried to find their Utopia, not only in Europe, but in particular the Soviet Union.

You mentioned some of them, but I just want to go through some of the names again, like Anderson and Paul Robeson. Langston Hughes, Claude McKay, Richard Wright, and lots of others visited and thought about the Soviet Union. Lots of books have been written about these people, but not about their views on socialism. Whether the experiment was right or wrong is another question, but the fact is that these people just kept coming to the Soviet Union and they raised much interest in African American culture and they personally were happy there. Definitely, we people from the Soviet Union were also blessed to have them.

We went through the names of prominent people, but how about the names of people you've heard of but didn't realize that they were trying to escape racism? For example, when I was writing my book I knew that one of the people who went to Russia with my grandfather was Mr. Sutton. I didn't know who he was, so when I came to New York, I dialed 411 and I got somebody by the name of Sutton. I asked him if he had heard from anybody who went to Russia in the early '30s and '40s and he said, "Yeah, my brother." So, I went to meet him. He was Percy Sutton, and we talked a lot. He's a very nice person, and he spoke about his brother and while we were talking, it was interesting that the telephone rang and he picked up the phone and he said, "Yes, no," and then he hung up. He said, "Well, it was Mayor Dinkins calling."

Again we were talking, and again the telephone rings, and he picks up the phone and says, "Okay, okay, okay." He hangs up and he says to me, "Oh, this is Ray Charles calling." Then he goes, "By the way, here are some tickets to the Apollo theater, would you like to go?" Soon it became clear to me that this man I came to see, who was the brother of my grandfather's friend, was one of the richest black lawyers in America and the owner of the Apollo theater. So I called him back and I said, "Percy, how come you, one of the capitalist sharks, let your brother go with my grandfather to the Soviet Union?" And he said his brother was among thousands of very talented intellectuals who thought that exile was the only way for them to develop intellectually, to work, not as a janitor maybe, but as persons in their professions. So when his brother said the Soviet Union was the place where there was no racism, he just gave his blessing to him to go to the Soviet Union.

Not many people know that Langston Hughes wanted to make a movie in Russia. He got a big group of African American actors to go there, but the movie was never made though the top producer and movie director invited him personally to go there. So, the movie didn't work out, but lots of people from the group stayed in Russia. The book of Richard Wright, *Native Son,* as a matter of fact, is one of the few books that is translated into the Russian language, and Dr. Du Bois came to Russia a couple of times. As a matter of fact, thanks to him, they started an institute about Africa. Dr. Du Bois went to the head of the country and said that they needed an institute where they could develop issues and discuss and learn the history and cultures of people of color, and that's how they started this huge institute about Africa that is located in the Academy of Science right now. As a matter of fact, my mom was the first employee in this institute.

Paul Robeson, as you all know, he was a very important person in American history, and in my country he was a hero. Everybody in my country knows his name. He used to sing in front of thousands and thousands of people on this huge stage in front of millions of people, and he used to take my mom in his arms and he rocked her and he sang this beautiful lullaby, *Sleep My Baby,* in front of everybody. That's how my mom got her nickname Baby, and from my mom I got the nickname Baby, and if somebody called me Baby in Russia, I knew that was the friend of the friend of our family.

I can't go into detail, because the stories are very diverse. Like, for example, Paul Robeson. I don't know how much he knew about perhaps being used in the hands of the Communists, because, you know, in my country anti-Semitism is a very big issue. Jews are the blacks of the Soviet Union and my country decided, I guess Soviet officials, to use African American people as an antidote. In other words, they said that if people are accusing us of being racist against Jews, then we will talk about Americans being racist to African Americans.

I don't think that our government was particularly sincere in their feelings toward African Americans, but the bottom line was there were a lot of people who were given grants. Health care was free and education was free, and there were lots of things that African Americans benefited from in our society, and, on the other side, people generally became interested in Africa and in African American culture. Thanks to people, these people like I mentioned, we know the truth about African Americans, because, obviously, you cannot get the truth from an official source of information, neither a Soviet source of information nor an American official source of information.

In closing, I hope there will be many more African American intellectuals who will choose to go to Russia. To visit it would be very helpful because if you ask most Russians today what do you know about African Americans, the first name that will come to the mind of a Russian kid is Eddie Murphy. Unfortunately, they learn the English language based on his vocabulary. I personally think that African Americans were among the first people to build the bridges between America and my country, and I think that it was a very positive movement that happened in the early '30s, '40s and '50s.

Of Exiles and Renaissances

Eugene Redmond

Item: There's always a celebration going on, alongside a riot. And today I celebrate the tenth birthday of the EBR Writers Club in East St. Louis, Illinois. Two of the women who founded the club and helped keep it going are here. I want to celebrate them because they've been running the club for ten years in a city with sixty-five percent unemployment. I just wanted to acknowledge the president of that club, Darlene Roy, a fine writer by the way, and Evon Udo. We have brought along some material on what we are doing back home; flyers are available in the rear of this auditorium.

Exile is chance, choice, dance, and happenstance. In 1985, I returned to East St. Louis from a fifteen-year exile in California by way of Baton Rouge, Madison, Lagos, New York City, and Amsterdam.

Item: Today, Terry McMillan, the author of *Waiting to Exhale,* is a hot ticket. Yes, she is a departure from what black women have been writing and that's because she writes about contemporary issues in a contemporary voice. If you pay attention to the way she writes and the way she sounds, it's like rap, and it is about the things that black women rappers are saying. Rappers like Salt 'N Pepa, Queen Latifah, TLC, Oaktown, 357. Terry and others represent the most recent permutation of the shift that began in the black literary community in the mid '70s. Since then, the focus of the writing has shifted from men to women, and, at the same time, from poetry to fiction. Changes, permutations, and shifts, though, have been part of the continuum of black writing since the Harlem Awakening and the Black Arts Movement of the '60s and '70s.

Flashing forward to the '90s we encounter Terry McMillan, Toni Morrison, and Alice Walker, three sisters with plenty of roots and "waiting years." Each of them has also experienced their share of embrace and banishment, and in the summer of 1992, all three of them were on the *New York Times* best-seller list.

In a recent article on the historic Million Man March, Margaret Walker referred to herself as someone who had been "thrown out of the black community several times" in her life. However, Walker's well known exile pales in comparison to that of James Baldwin. Listen, for example, to this exchange between Jimmy and *Essence* magazine Editor-in-Chief, Ida Lewis, in 1970:

> **Lewis:** I am curious about why you are in Paris and not in New York. Haven't you been this route before?
> **Baldwin:** It's a difficult question to answer. But for exercise, let's begin back in 1948 when I first left America. Why in the world, I've been asked, would you go to a white country? When I first heard that question, it threw me. But the answer is obvious; there were no black countries in 1948. Whether there are black countries today is another question, which we won't go into now. But you know I didn't *come* to Paris in '48, I simply *left* America. . . . I was getting out of America. Here, I was in danger of death; but in America it was not a danger, it was a certainty. Not just physical death, I mean real death. The death of working in a post office for thirty-seven years, of being a civil servant for a hostile government. The death of going under and watching your family go under.

* * * *

For me, at least, two trains are running whenever I hear the words exile and alienation coming from a black writer or artist. Two trains, calling up double consciousness and oxymorons like "healthy paranoia," a favorite morsel of ours, or in the sixties, "awesome." Add to this layers and layers of stereotypes, racial estrangement, life-splintering poverty, Jazz, Gospel, Bee bop, R&B and you have cause to speed black writers, individually or en masse, into another country. A comprehensive look at how these writers scored and re-played their catalogues of anguish and defiance; how they chose their various venues of exile or were forced into them; how they adjusted their lives and literary techniques to the spatial/temporal jackets of exile; and how they responded to and embraced banishment in the Americas, Europe, Africa, and the Third World would require volumes of novels, plays, librettos, discographies, blues, biographies, and essays.

Richard Wright, the most famous of the exiled literati, was already a celebrity when he came to Paris. Like his similarly southern born and raised contemporary Zora Neale Hurston, whose folk writings brought her exile and embrace, Wright did not live to witness the Black Arts Movement of the '60s. Hurston, too, exemplified black survival before she resettled in Eatonville, Florida, to a life and death in anonymity. At the same time, Richard Wright explored the multifarious struggles in Africa, America, and the Third World from Paris. His writings helped us access the complexity of concepts and movements like global racism, pan-Africanism, blackness, Négritude, communism, nationalism, integration vs. assimilation, existentialism, revolution, self-determination, independence, and "soul."

Other writers and activists, like W.E.B. Du Bois, James Weldon Johnson, Claude McKay, and Langston Hughes, also contributed to a literary Pan-Africanism. None of them was the first or the last of African derivation to traverse transcontinental shores. Black men and women explored the New World before the *Mayflower*. The pre-Columbian African presence is highlighted in *They Came Before Columbus*, Ivan Van Sertima's 1976 opus published under Toni Morrison's editorship at Random House. Globe-trotting abolitionists, singers, dancers, musicians, activists, writers, painters, and entrepreneurs flourished between the 17th and mid 20th centuries: to wit, Phyllis Wheatley, Olaudah Equiano, William Wells Brown, Henry O'Tanner, Josephine Baker, Satchmo, Aaron Douglas, Katherine Dunham, Eric Dolphy, Countee Cullen, Marcus Garvey, Paul Robeson, Chester Himes, Frantz Fanon, Frank Yerby, and Malcolm X. They embraced banishment, brilliantly, stylistically, dexterously, and prolifically.

Henry Dumas, who perished in a hail of bullets underneath the streets of Harlem in 1968, was in exile of sorts. Exile in his day and age meant exile from Sweet Home, Arkansas. (Look up Sweet Home men in Morrison's *Beloved*.) Dumas left America physically in the mid '50s for an Air Force–sponsored stay in Saudi Arabia. Returning to Harlem, he helped conceptualize the Black Aesthetic and the Black Arts Movement before again seeking exile in Hiram, Ohio, and finally in East St. Louis, Illinois, where he spent the last year of his life. Known as Hank, Dumas rearranged his nickname to spell Ankh, then spelled his last name backwards to say Samud. Hence: Ankh Samud. Multiple forms of exile and self-imaging occurred with this writer who belonged to the Society of Umbra, the forerunner of the Black Arts Movement, which developed out of the Lower East Side in New York: Manhattan. Ishmael Reed, Tom Feelings, Askia Muhammed Toure, Archie Shepp, Victor Hernandez Cruz, Lennox Raphael, Calvin Hicks,

Barbara Christian, Brenda Walcott, and Lorenzo Thomas were also Umbra artists.

The achievements of the Umbra intellectuals, artists, and activists, who Raymond Patterson refers to as the spiritual sons and daughters of the Harlem Renaissance and Post Renaissance, were staggering. They were heirs to legacies left by Zora Neale Hurston, Richard Wright, Countee Cullen, Robert Hayden, and others. Umbra artists and writers unlike the Wrights, Baldwins, and Himes who sought exile outside America's shores, apparently found tolerable social and cultural conditions in their new spaces. It seemed that respite from predictable persecution, quality, ethnic comraderie, and freedom from restraints against interracial and homosexual cohabitation were part of their "mosaic." Like their predecessors, the Umbra writers participated in the continuum of mentorship. Baldwin and Ellison had Wright, while Wright was aided by Horace Cayton and Margaret Walker in Chicago. Langston Hughes played a direct role in Umbra's development, as did Ellison to a lesser degree.

An exile from a Topeka, Kansas birthplace in Chicago's Southside of the '20s, '30s, '40s, and '50s, Gwendolyn Brooks very frequently appeared in publications like *The Saint, Negro Story*, *Phylon, CLA, Quarterly*, and *Negro Digest*. In 1950, *Phylon* celebrated the middle of the twentieth century with a symposium on the American Negro. Blyden Jackson noted, in an essay on Robert Hayden's *Middle Passage* that appeared in the 1945 issue of *CLA Journal*, that "it is infinitely rich and it deserves some extended comment, but I've never seen reference to it of any consequence." Clearly Hayden also "enjoyed" his share of exile "at home."

In the 1920s, the Promise Land was in the "North." Two million blacks migrated from the south before you could say, "Step 'n Fetch it." Up from Georgia came John Oliver Killens, founder of numerous National Black Writers Conferences, including this one at Medgar Evers College, and founder, with Rosa Guy and John Henrik Clarke, of the Harlem Writers Guild that included Paule Marshall, Maya Angelou, Louise Meriweather, Arthur Flowers, and others. High yield from the waiting years! With springboards like Umbra, Harlem Writers Guild and the EBR Writers Club of East St. Louis, black writing continues to soar across the "Soular System."

* * * *

Don't ever let anybody tell you John Oliver couldn't look death in the face and say, "Straighten up and fly right!"

Panel A2

CHOOSING EXILE: BLACK WRITERS FROM THE BLACK ARTS MOVEMENT TO THE 1990s

Foreword

Carlyle V. Thompson

The period from the Black Arts Movement to the 1990s was sustained and propelled into the future by the enduring revolutionary voices of Mari Evans, Haki R. Madhubuti, Sonia Sanchez, Larry Neal, June Jordan, Nikki Giovanni, Jayne Cortez, and Amiri Baraka. They wrote and worked in the tradition of the African griot: a keeper of the culture's secrets, history, and folklore. In *The Norton Anthology of African American Literature* (1997), Larry Neal states:

> The Black Arts Movement is radically opposed to any concept of the artist that alienates him from his community. Black Art is the aesthetic and spiritual sister of the Black Power concept. As such, it envisions an art that speaks directly to the need and aspiration of Black America. . . . The Black Arts and the Black power concept both relate broadly to the Afro-American's desire for self-determination and nationhood. Both concepts are nationalistic. (1797)

It was also during this nationalistic period that the NAACP, the National Urban League, CORE, SCLC, SNCC, the Nation of Islam, and the Black Panther Party made their impact, and, then to a lesser extent the US Organization, the Institute of Positive Education, the East Organization, The Last Poets, the Women of the Calabash, the Black Women's Health Project, Sweet Honey in the Rock, along with the National Black Wholistic Society, rushed onto the national scene. Yet, it was during this period that many black activists and leaders were imprisoned or killed and many black groups were infiltrated and destabilized by national, state, and local intelligence organizations; also the Attica Prison revolt occurred, the Vietnam war escalated, and heroin use proliferated in black communities. Like the modern-day crack phenomenon, heroin in black communities created warlike casualties. However, black writers were paramount in creating black community organizations, challenging academic institutions and continuing to speak their special truth, providing the connections between black people's economic and social aspirations, and literary expression and protest. Here, the literary expressions and protests found a strong voice in novels, essays, and literary criticism. Additionally, established and new black writers ("The New Black Aesthetic") achieved national and international prominence during this period. Quite simply, there was an explosion of black literature, black art, black music, black dance, and black films.

While much of the literature of the Harlem Renaissance and beyond was aimed at white audiences, the literature of this period was speaking directly to black people while challenging and indicting white supremacist culture. Essentially, there was no longer a need or desire to prove anything to white folks. More importantly, some black writers (mainly women) no longer adhered to the dictum against "airing dirty laundry." For example, we heard the gendered protests in Ntozake Shange's *For Colored Girls Who Have Considered Suicide, When the Rainbow Is Enuf* (1976) and Michelle Wallace's *Black Macho and the Myth of the Superwoman* (1979). Then Alice Walker's *The Color Purple* (1982) exposed class and interracial conflict, and Gloria Naylor's *The Women of Brewster Place* (1982) added its voice to this exposure. All of these writers and their works found national and international exposure; they also experienced the passionate wrath from many in the black community. Along with the tremendous success of Alice Walker, Audre Lorde, Terry McMillan, Ntozake Shange, Octavia Butler, and J. California Cooper, Toni Morrison put the entire world on notice that black literature was a major economic and literary force that would never again take a back seat in the literary canon. This was evident in 1992 when novels by Terry McMillan, Alice Walker, and Toni Morrison appeared simultaneously on the *New York Times* best-seller list. Further, this decade saw Walker receive the Pulitzer Prize for fiction and Morrison receive the Nobel Prize for literature. Also, Morrison exposed the fact that many white writers such as Ernest Hemingway were playing in blackness. In *Playing the Dark: Whiteness and the Literary Imagination* (1992), Morrison reveals:

> There seems to be a more or less tacit agreement among literary scholars that, because American literature has been clearly the preserve of white male views, genius, and power, those views, genius, and power are without relationship to and removed from the overwhelming presence of Black people in the United States.(5)

Morrison's analysis of American literature exposes the fact that some white writers were constantly using racist and pejorative notions of blackness to frame their narratives.

During this second renaissance, black male writers joined their female comrades in the struggle and the celebration of black culture; they were stouthearted, innovative, and quite prolific. August Wilson, Ernest J. Gaines, Charles Johnson, Walter Mosley, Samuel R. Delaney, John Edgar Wideman, Ishmael Reed, Trey Ellis, and E. Lynn Harris are the names that come immediately to mind. The expansive breath of these perspicacious writers reveals the complex themes and complex agendas in a racist society where black males appear to be constantly under a relentless attack. In *Black Men: Obsolete, Single, Dangerous?* (1990), Haki R. Madhubuti presents the morbid details:

> The world has gotten worse for Black men. A young Black man, according to the U.S. Census Bureau, has a 1-in-21 chance of being murdered as compared to a 1-in-333 chance for a white man of the same age. One out of two Black young people lives in poverty. The Black male prison population is over 50%, whereas our population in the country is around 13%. Of the six leading causes of death among the adult population, Black men lead the list in each category: homicide, heart attacks, cancer, suicide, strokes and accidents. The status of Black men in America is beyond the endangered species category. (v)

Despite the tremendous political, financial, and social success of some black men in music, sports, entertainment, business, politics, and academia such as Michael Jackson, Michael Jordan, Berry Gordy, Bill Cosby, Reginald Lewis, John Johnson, Jesse Jackson, Ron Brown, Cornel West, Derrick Bell, and Henry Louis Gates Jr.—there are large numbers of black men extremely at risk.

Sensitive to the plight of black men, Henry Louis Gates Jr., Houston A. Baker Jr., Julie Dash, Cornel West, Haki R. Madhubuti, Spike Lee, Stanley Crouch, Derrick Bell, Patricia Williams, Haile Gerima, Gil Scott-Heron, and bell hooks were some of the most articulate voices inside and outside of academia who gave added deft analysis and protest to the threatening ocean of white supremacy that constantly confronted black people. Using prose, films, music, critical race theory, critical legal theory, and black literary theory, these scholars, activists, and artists caused the white literary canon and white supremacist culture to disintegrate and they questioned the fragments that remained.

This exhilarating thirty-year-plus period of black letters can be defined with the title of Terry McMillan's anthology—*Breaking Ice: An Anthology of Contemporary African-American Fiction* (1990). Here, McMillan articulates the passions and the responses of this period:

> Without a doubt, writing fiction requires passion and compassion. A sense of urgency. Excitement. Intensity. Stillness. For many of us, writing is our reaction to injustices, absurdities, beauty. It's our way of registering our complaints or affirmations. The best are not didactic. They do not scream out "message," nor are they abstraction. Our stories are our personal response. What we want to specify. What we see. What we feel. Our wide angle lens—our close-up look. And even if the story doesn't quite pinpoint the solution or the answer, it is the exploration itself that is often worth the trip. (xxii)

In the tradition, black writers have returned to the source and given back to the black community and to the world their unique perspectives on black life and culture. Among the many black writers, Paule Marshall in *Praisesong for the Widow* (1983), reminds us that African American culture is directly connected to the cultures in Africa and the Caribbean. Hence, to truly understand blackness, it is necessary to go beyond America's borders. Finally, it has been often said, "Without vision, the people perish." With their intertextual nuances and the insights of other cultural traditions, black writers have always supplied a vision that speaks to the fundamental desire of all people—the desire to live up to one's potential and speak their special truth.

In this panel, Stephanie Martin, Selwyn Cudjoe, Cecil Foster, and Lorna Goodison explicate the tensions of exile and "making a life." Central to their discourse are the issues of humanity and the need for black people to heal the psychological scars caused by the internalization, or to use Frantz Fanon's term, the "epidermilization" of hegemonic dictates of class, color, and gender.

Choosing Exile: The Publisher Situated in the Place of Exile

Stephanie Martin

I am a publisher of black women's writing and I live in Canada. Over the past twenty-seven years, I have hammered out an uneasy truce with the country I refer to as "where I live," but seldom as home. I'm a Jamaican-born painter and I got into publishing over ten years ago because I was vexed. I was vexed because I love literature and I could not find books that spoke to me of experiences that I was familiar with. As a woman of color living in the north of Metropole, anything that I did dig up I really had to scrunt for. I was vexed because no one, not even the so-called feminist or progressive publishers, were interested in publishing women of color. We did not speak right, we didn't write good, and some of us dared to write in the Creole dialect we spoke, or a fusion of standard English and Creole. And so our language did not conform to literary standards. Also, at that time, issues around race and class were being sidestepped by white folks. It was a non issue.

In Canada, we talk about ourselves as a multicultural society. This all started in the 1970s when an Act was introduced to make Canada officially bilingual, reflecting its French and English population. But many Canadians started to recognize that other cultures had to be validated, and so there was established a Federal multicultural policy to enable communities around Canada whose heritage was neither French or English to be recognized. True, multiculturalism would have meant that doors would have had to be opened. Like, for example, the doors to publishing companies. True, multiculturalism would have meant folks like us getting jobs in certain sectors. Like, for example, in the publishing industry. True, multiculturalism would have meant change and the relinquishing of white privilege. But that did not happen, and it is not surprising that in Canada today multiculturalism has come down to song, dance, and food. So it is not surprising that multiculturalism opened no doors for black women's voices to be published.

One of the first individuals to deal with the reality of black women's lives and experiences in Canada was a man, a Barbadian born writer, Austin Clark, who in the '60s and '70s wrote such novels as *The Meeting Place*. He wrote stories about working class black women and their lives in Canada. In some of his stories, he took the reader from Barbados to Canada to the United States as he explored the repercussions of colliding cultures. Since that time the field of black writers and writing in Canada has broadened, as can be attested by the presence of the fine Canadian writer Cecil Foster on this panel and many others who are not present today.

Back in the '60s and '70s, the actual voices of contemporary black women writers were missing. In 1984, there were four black women who had authored books published in Canada, and a token scattering in a few collections. Back in the '60s and '70s, there was a silent resistance on the part of publishers to take any chances with the work of black women. Black women did not have a place in Canadian literature.

In 1985 in Canada, I co-founded, with Makeda Silvera, Sister Vision: Black Women and Women of Colour Press, flying in the face of the apparent universe with a mandate to publish women of colour. It was the first and still is the only publishing house dedicated to publishing the work of women of colour.

Jamaican born ahdri zhina mandiela, the first woman we published, says in her introduction to *dark diaspora in . . . dub:*

> then the '80s and a different ilk of speaking out—the black woman's voice, heard only before in spaces "for colored girls" . . . .shange's "mistresspiece" had set the tone, newly opened ears were forced to hear black women's voices decrying our shameless struggles and celebrating our near triumphs.

Choosing Exile . . . who are these women we publish? Where are they from? Where do they live? Again I quote ahdri zhina from *dark diaspora in . . . dub:*

> My/aunt vida: lithe
> Bird of youth

Took off to Canada/surfaced
On a river called don, circled
Under dundas bridge: docked
On an edge, lived on a ledge
Like the pigeons

In my opinion, Choose and Exile seem to be words in conflict—much like the conflict of many of us who have chosen to live in a place other than our Native land. Not an easy marriage. Sister Vision Press publishes black women, and many of the women we publish locate their work in Canada—they write about the society they live in. They also situate themselves "back home" . . . constructing the diasporic chain-link—as they write about leaving, choosing the north, choosing exile.

This is an excerpt from *Tales from the Gardens and Beyond* by Hazelle Palmer, whose parents are from the Caribbean, and who came to Canada via Britain:

> . . . the ship was bigger than anything I had ever seen in my life. I would always watch them from a distance when they would bring tourists and goods to Bridgetown. Those times I wished I could grab Luke and stow anywhere, it didn't matter, so long as I was far from Henry.
> . . . one of the other women going up on the same domestic scheme as me introduced herself and stood by my side, looking back at the shore. "Thank the Lord, pray he take us safe to our new home."

It is significant that the writers we've published do not necessarily play into the "Caribbean conundrum," as critique Bruce King says, "and develop older themes concerning [their] colonial heritage and resulting injustices." The writers we publish deal with the immediacy of their lives in their chosen metropole. And the place they have chosen is rife with discrimination and racism. When they write about "home," the stories are not so much about nostalgia as they are about recording, the recording of a period in different times, relationships, personal, familial, community based and those that deal with the society. This excerpt is from Jamaican-born Makeda Silvera who came to Canada as a child:

> "Miss Thorne, yuh don't know what ah just hear not too long, dat Miss Morris and her husband adopt Deanne, dat Deanne not dem own."
> We crept from around the dining table and moved closer to the window to get a good view of our grandmother and Miss Grant. Miss Grant's eyes were wide open, waiting for a shocked response from our grandmother.

"Where yuh hear dat from?" Our grandmother asked.
"From across de street dis morning."
"Well, ah guess Deanne belong to dem now. If dem adopt her, dat mean dem is her rightful mother and father," our grandmother said, putting an end to the conversation.
She turned around unexpectedly and her eyes made six with ours as we rushed back to the porridge.
"Hold it right dere!" she said.
She came close to the window, her face hard, and between closed teeth she said, "If ah ever hear one word out of you two bout dis, de police will have to come and tek me out of dis yard."

I chose this is because it says a lot about the different relationships we leave behind, "the yard" culture, our grandmothers and certain values. Stories like this are absolutely necessary for the exiled. In the tradition of oral history, many of these societies are rich in anecdote and lore. They deal with issues of race, class, gender and sexuality in non-didactic terms. They reassure us of our place in the world. They console and reaffirm us of our human-ness, of our wholeness, when the society we have "chosen" to live in bombards us constantly with our 'Otherness," our un-human-ness, our blackness, our badness. They make us laugh, they make us cry. They validate us, and hopefully, they can help us in the struggle to validate our daughters and sons as they bob and weave through the school systems and around the cops. They warn us of Babylon.

In a recent collection of writing, published by Sister Vision by young black women, many of whom are born in the Caribbean, some in Africa coming to Canada when very young, we read of alienation, exile, and discrimination.

He was old and white
The man who called me nigger.
He was short and fat
The man who called me nigger
He was stinky and dirty
The man who called me nigger.
Who is the man that called me nigger?
He speaks incoherently
Maybe he's a highschool dropout;
or perhaps a bum
or maybe he's a son
A husband
A father
A grandfather

He is old
I should respect my elders
he's a person
I should love all people
But tell me how I should feel about
The man who called me nigger
by sherie outtan from *Black Girl Talk.*, by the Black girls.

Choosing exile. There are those who choose to leave their "home" for the large and more anonymous shores of the metropole for political reasons or for reasons of intolerance around sexual choices. We published *Piece Of My Heart*, the first lesbian of color anthology on the North American continent. Half of the fifty contributors were from the U.S. I can say unequivocally that the book could not have been published, for example, in Jamaica, and the contributors safely use their names. Interestingly enough, for the same reason that certain black writers left the United States in the fifties and sixties for Europe, writers today leave their homes in the so-called "third" world and seek an apparently more "tolerant" home in the U.S. and Canada. An American distributor mentioned to me the other day that Sister Vision Press was ahead of its time when we published *Piece Of My Heart* in 1991, and I think he was right. In fact, *Afrekete: A Black Lesbian Anthology*, published by Bantam Books last year, here in America, would not have been published if ground had not been broken by small alternative presses like Sister Vision Press.

At the same time, however, well known or successful writers do not always stay with a small press, although that is often where they get their start. I can't dis the writer who goes to a Random or a Bantam, because a woman and a man haffi mek a living, but can you imagine what would happen to a likkle black press if a successful writer remains committed to it and continues to publish their work there? We gon clear. We just gon clear!

You may have noticed that I have second thoughts about the concept of exile. So, I would like to redefine exile somewhat. "Exile" is a place occupied by our writers. Exile is located in real people's lives. All writers are in exile in their own lives. They live in a society that is racist, sexist and homophobic. It is not surprising that the recurring theme is one of alienation. They're in a society which tells them they are not artists, they are not writers, simply because of who they are. A small press like Sister Vision provides a space for the writer, the artist, to be liberated from the fear of making art. The small publisher provides a bridge between the exiled artist and the mainstream culture milieu so that they can walk across this bridge and claim their space.

For the exiled in exile, a small press is a political force. A small press like Sister Vision is often connected to the community. It has a political life. We are committed to bringing out the artist; we are committed to liberating that voice. So while publishing is a business, it is that political force, that connectedness, that liberating art that makes us different from the corporate publisher.

I know, you know how black writers can become commodities in the hands of the corporate publisher. Published as "crossover" literature, published as exotica, published when the climate is ripe, when the Other, the different, the exile, is in.

In closing, I can only affirm the integrity of the small press. We work with the writer to break silences, to develop the voices, and to make sense out of our reality in Babylon. To write about it, to share it with others and to build an international community of our work. Sister Vision Press, situated in the place of exile, lives and breathes the lives of our writers.

Choosing Exile: Black Women Writers from the Caribbean

Selwyn R. Cudjoe

> Land: In a dream. I walked through my inheritance, an island of villages and rivers and mountains and people who began and ended with murder and theft and not very much love. I claimed it in a dream. Exhausted from the agony of expelling from my body a child I could not love and so did not want, I dreamed of all things that were mine. (Jamaica Kincaid, *The Autobiography of My Mother)*

> She hated the old woman who had twisted her so in the name of love. Most humans didn't love one another no how, and this mislove was so strong that even common blood couldn't overcome it all the time. She had found a jewel down inside herself and she had wanted to walk where people could see her and gleam it around. But she had been set in the market-place to sell. Been set for still-bait. When God had made the Man, he made him out of stuff that sung all the time and glittered all over. Then after that some angels got jealous and chopped him into millions of pieces, but still he glittered and hummed. So they beat him down to nothing but sparks but each little spark had a shine and a song. So they covered each one over with mud. And the lonesomeness in the sparks makes them hunt for one another, but the mud is deaf and dumb. Like all the other tumbling mud-balls, Janie had tried to show her shine. (Zora Neale Hurston, *Their Eyes Were Watching God*)

In talking about the present renaissance of Caribbean women writers over the past few years in the United States and elsewhere, I am reminded of the story of an Amerindian woman who was kidnapped on the banks of the Amacura River, Venezuela, South America, around 1660, taken to Barbados and subsequently to Massachusetts in 1680. Later, this Amerindian woman named Tituba became the central subject in a witchcraft trial in Salem, Massachusetts, in February 1692. As time went on Tituba became the subject of many narratives (in

Arthur Miller's play *The Crucible*, Ann Petry's *Tituba of Salem Village,* Nathaniel Hawthorne's *The Scarlet Letter* and a 1982 film called *Three Sovereigns for Sarah).* Of more recent vintage, Maryse Condé used Tituba to create a moving story in her novel, *I, Tituba, Black Witch of Salem.* Recounting the impetus that led her to write this moving story, Condé noted:

> I just felt interested by the story and curious to see what happened to Tituba. It is only when I started asking people and historians around me, and did not discover anything factual about her, that I decided I was going to write her story out of my own dreams. I felt that this eclipse of Tituba's life was completely unjust. I felt a strong solidarity with her, and I wanted to offer her revenge by inventing a life such as she might perhaps have wished it to be told.[1]

Later in that interview, Condé noted that she wanted "to turn Tituba into a sort of female hero, an epic heroine, like the legendary 'Nanny of the maroons.' Tituba," she noted, "was an opportunity to express my feelings about present-day America."[2]

In this remarkable story, the winner of the literary Women's Grand Prix in 1987, Maryse Condé confessed that her impetus/desire to examine Tituba's life could not be ignored. As she said: "I can look for my story among those of the witches of Salem, but it isn't there. . . . Not a word about me." And so it was in that quest for a name—an identity—that led Condé to construct her remarkable story. In her introduction to *I, Tituba*, Angela Davis amplified Condé's sentiments when she observed:

> Tituba looked for her story in the history of the Salem witch trails and could not find it. I have looked for my history in the story of the colonization of this continent and I have found silences, omissions, distortions, and fleeting, enigmatic insinuations. Tituba's quest for recorded evidence of her existence as a living, feeling, loving, active individual, who was as much a part of Salem witch trails as her codefendants of European descent, leads her to a belittling, cursory allusion: "Tituba, a slave originating from the West Indies and probably practicing 'hoodoo.'" She counters this footnote that condemns her to insignificance with a strong, self-affirming "I, Tituba . . . Witch." Maryse Condé lends her the words that assist her to tell you and me her story, speaking her life in her own voice—from the womb to the realm of the dead.[3]

In examining *I, Tituba,* Elisabeth Mudimbe-Boyi recasts the questions raised by the text in a way that allows us to understand the ontological importance of Tituba, her sisters and the problematic they present in contemporary works of fiction and non-fiction. She notes that "Tituba is a statement against effacement, exclusion, and reduction to invisibility."[4] In light of this statement, one can conclude that scribed within this proposition is the larger quest of what it means to be a woman and person in a New World society that has been shaped by slavery, colonialism, racism and gender abuse.

In an important biography, *Tituba: Reluctant Witch of Salem*, Elaine Breslaw examines the origins of Tituba's existence, her involvement in the New England witch-hunt and witch-burning, and goes on to make an important point about the unique status of Tituba in New England. Taking care to note Tituba's outsider status—that is, as a slave, a woman, an American Indian—in a Puritanical society, Breslaw concludes that:

> Tituba the story teller prolonged her life in 1692 through an imaginative ability to weave and embellish plausible tales. In the process of confessing to fantastic experiences, she created a new idiom of resistance against abusive treatment and inadvertently led the way for other innocents accused of the terrible crime of witchcraft. Her resistance, a calculated manipulation of the Puritan fears, was intimately related to her ethnic heritage. Puritans were predisposed to believe that Indians willingly participated in Devil worship. That perception of Indians as supporters of the Devil encouraged Tituba to fuel their fantasies of a diabolical plot. As she hesitantly capitalized on Puritan assumptions regarding Satanism, Tituba drew on the memories of her past life for the wondrous details of a story so frightening in its implications that she had to be kept alive as a witness.[5]

And what a wondrous irony? Tituba, slave, witch, and Caribbean woman, had to be kept alive to witness the perverse doings of a strange people and to weave a tale of resistance to remain alive. It is this irony that ought to be interrogated. Moreover, I believe that the source of much of what we find so compelling in contemporary Caribbean writers today—and even our early writers—revolves around questions about this existentialist question: who or what am I in a world that seeks to efface identity, especially in this case, women's identity. In her biographical study of Tituba, Breslaw notes that Tituba brought to America "her memories of life in an Arawak village as well as the image of an emergent Creole society in the Barbados of the 1670s." Tituba also took to New England aspects of the slave's religion: that is, the Ashanti religio-magical practices of obeah and shango that were common to the entire Caribbean.[6] In other words, into a staid Puritan town in New England, Tituba carried another conception of life—perhaps a conception of a life that was more varied, more sensuous, more ready to accept those unknowable aspects of life and possessing a greater tolerance for difference—into a society that was full of suspicion, more rigid in its understanding of morality, more reluctant to give or accept love freely, a society which Nara Araujo, a Cuban critic characterized as following:

> A character of extraordinary power, Tituba possesses a superlative degree of self-awareness. Depository of the wisdom of her ancestors, she has the gift of beneficence. In the search for herself, she lives her experiences of gender, class, and race. Her journey to the White's world of superstition and hypocrisy involves racial confrontation but, above all, the opposition of two conceptions of the supernatural world. What in the vitiated atmosphere of Salem becomes obsession with the devil—a cover for material interests—is for Tituba the world of blessedness and spirituality.

Those accused in Salem, young women caught in the asphyxia of Puritanism, find a way to satisfy frustration and discover sensation through hysteria. The only one who does not need this compensatory mechanism is the subordinate. Her gifts are attributed to demoniacal abilities, according to the scheme of white Anglo-Protestant culture. But Tituba does not comprehend the code in which Lucifer is a dreaded power. Her beliefs are sound compared to the poisoned satanic imaginariness of the Puritans.[7]

Such a statement, however, leads immediately and inescapably into parallel, though opposed themes, advanced by Jamaica Kincaid in her most recently acclaimed work, *The Autobiography of My Mother,* which, among other things, suggests that in the world she has created, the world of contemporary Antigua, little love is possible. Speaking about her father's wife, the major protagonist of the novel notes:

> She was of the African people and the people from France. It was nighttime and she was in her own house, so her hair was exposed; it was smooth and yet tightly curled, and she wore it parted in the middle and plaited in two braids that were pinned up in the back. Her lips were shaped like those of people from a cold climate: thin and ungenerous. Her eyes were black, not with beauty but with deceit. Her nose was long and sharp. She did not like me. She did not love me. I could see it in her face. My spirit rose to meet this challenge. No love: I could live in a place like this. I knew this atmosphere all too well. Love would have defeated me. Love would always defeat me. In atmosphere of no love I could live well; in this atmosphere of no love I could make a life for myself.

Later on in the text, the protagonist asks: . . . "in a life like hers [her mother's], as in mine, what is a real name?"[8] In this novel, the major protagonist remains motherless and unloved (the very first line of the text announces the death of her mother) but in this elegiac work, this dirge-like bit of prose, all is irrevocably loss and irredeemably sadness. Moreover, it tells of a past that cannot be regained; a past that locates itself in the struggle of the Carib Indians of the Lesser Antilles who gave their lives in glorious battle against the English in 1795.

Here, then, is a sketch of two different perceptions of the Caribbean world, depicted by two of her more insightful daughters as they construct their tales in the United States. In scenes that tend to repel and/or encourage, negate and/or affirm, celebrate and/or declaim, condemn and/or redeem, are outlined the parameters of an existence that have been interrogated by our women writers from the very first moment they began to put pen to paper; from the very first moment they found it necessary to ask the existentialist question: how do I create a space for myself in a world in which the savage winds of racism, colonialism, neocolonialism, and advanced capitalist exploitation continue to toss about an angry and restless sea of indifference. As Condé notes in her interview with Ann Armstrong Scarboro: "Writing *Tituba* was an opportunity to express my feelings about present-day America. I wanted to imply that in terms of narrow-mindedness, hypocrisy, and racism, little has changed since the days of the Puritans."[9]

In the short time that is left, I want to examine the proposition outlined above. Moreover, I wish to demonstrate that the impetus for the contemporary renaissance of women's writing derives its importance from the ready echo it finds in these United States because it resonates so well with the concerns that are known at the heart of each black person whether she lives on the continent or in the islands. It is almost as though at the heart of the matter lies that unresolved problematic of race that W.E.B. Du Bois voiced so cogently at the beginning of this century. Were he alive today, Du Bois would certainly have added the question of gender inequality and the way it plays itself out within the context of race, class, and a full-blown capitalist system.

It is not an exaggeration to say that from the inception of women's writing (and BLACK writing in general) in the Caribbean—that is, from the publication of "The Sorrows of Yamba" (1795), one of the earliest pieces of Caribbean verse—that many of the sentiments echoed by Yamba found a ready resonance and response in the verse of another black woman, Phillis Wheatley, who would pen the very first book of poems, *Poems on Various Subjects, Religious and Moral* (1773), by an African American.[10] In their work, each poet reflected a sense of abandon and loss in their New World exiledom. As Hurston may have observed, each tried to find the jewel deep down inside her that the mud of the condition tried to obscure. In the field of drama, there existed a reciprocal cross-over of sentiments and sensibility as it were. The first black drama of the American theater, *The Drama of King Shotaway*, was premiered by the African Grove Theatre, the first black theatre company in the United States, on June 20, 1823. Its playbill described it as drama whose subject was as "founded on the facts taken from the insurrection of the Caribs on the island of St Vincent [of 1795]" Indeed, this uprising against the British was used as a metaphor to describe how African Americans felt about their condition and as a symbol of what awaited the society if they continued to treat them so unfairly. As Jonathan Dewberry notes, "The idea of presenting a play in the early nineteenth century about a black revolution would have been quite courageous, especially with a black cast and a black theatre management."[11] It only needs to be noted that James Hewlett, a leading actor in the African Grove Theatre, also hailed from the Caribbean. Most recently, in an extraordinarily intelligent book entitled *Scars of Conquest: Masks of Memory* (1995) Tejumola Olaniyan, drawing on the works of Biodun Jeyifous, makes an illuminating comparison between the evolution of black face minstrelsy in the United States and the Trinidad Carnival of the nineteenth century.[12]

In the works of the male writers of prose we find a reciprocal sense of solidarity. In the preface to *Emmanuel Appadocca* (1854), perhaps the first novel of the Anglophone Caribbean, Michel Maxwell Philip dedicates his book to his fellow African Americans as he records his disgust at the passage of the Fugitive Slave Law and his disdain at the manner in which Afro-Americans were treated. "This book," he says, "has been written at a moment when the feelings of the Author are roused up to a high pitch of indignant excitement, by a statement of the cruel manner in which the slave holders of America deal with their slave-children."[13] In a reciprocal gesture, William Wells Brown, author of *Clotel*, the first African American novel, demonstrates a similar sense of outage and revulsion when, in 1850, he found himself traveling on the same omnibus with Thomas Carlyle, author of the infamous "Discourse on the Nigger Question" (1858). Brown notes:

> I had read his *Hero Worship* and *Past and Present*, and had formed a high opinion of his literary abilities. But his recent attack upon emancipated people of the West Indies, and his laborious article ["Occasional Discourse on the

> Negro Question"] in favor of the re-establishment of the lash and slavery, had created in my mind a dislike for the man, and I almost regretted that we were in the same omnibus.[14]

One can make similar connections between the writers of the Harlem Renaissance, and, what in another context Hazel Carby called the Trinidad Renaissance.[15] Undoubtedly, writers such as Claude McKay, Nella Larsen, Walter White, and a host of other Caribbean writers participated in the Harlem Renaissance.[16] Zora Neale Hurston's *Their Eyes Were Watching God,* the product of a love affair with a West Indian man, was written in Haiti. Richard Wright was very welcoming of George Lamming's *In the Castle of My Skin* and wrote a very illuminating introduction to the first American edition of the novel in 1953. For Wright, Lamming's novel demonstrated common proletarian strivings to be found both among African Americans and Caribbean people. More recently, in a very important piece, Daryl Cumber Dance noted the tremendous similarities, of what she calls the "black and female" sensibilities, in Erna Brodber's, *Jane and Louisa Will Soon Come Home* and Toni Cade Bambara's *The Salt Eaters.*[17] To be sure, the special cases that seem to transcend both these movements are the now classic work of Paule Marshall's *Brown Girl, Brownstones, The Chosen Place, the Timeless People,* and other similar works.

Against this background, it is easy to conclude that there has always been a sense in which *your* (African American) concerns have been *our* (Caribbean) concerns; a sense in which the capacity to weave and embellish plausible tales about our mutual condition has always found its echo within common sensibility, the product of a common black Atlantic experience that transcends (perhaps inculcates) common geographic boundaries. It is no wonder then that at the same moment that the writings of black women began to explode in this United States in 1970—I refer to works such as Toni Morrison's *The Bluest Eye* and Maya Angelou's *I Know Why the Caged Bird Sings*—women's writings were beginning to take off in the Caribbean when Merle Hodge offered her path-breaking novel, *Crick, Crack Monkey* in that same year. Other works followed and culminated in the first International Conference of Caribbean Women Writers in 1988 at Wellesley College. Similar conferences were held in Trinidad (1990), Curaçoa (1992), Wellesley (1995), and Miami (1996). Yet, it is difficult to talk about exile, voluntary or otherwise, during this period because one observes a very fluid movement of peoples between the two poles, a transmission of ideas and energies across the Atlantic that has become an enabling condition of existence.

Today, Brooklyn looks and feels very much like any part of Jamaica or Trinidad. In terms of sensibility and feeling there was always that common condition—that reciprocal gesture—that made the condition of exile a *physical* rather than a *mental* condition. To be sure, if one stayed away long enough—perhaps unto the third and fourth generations—it became difficult to go back home again. Yet, the popularity of the works of Caribbean writers that one finds in the United States has everything to do with a consonance of feeling, a twinning of sensibility, and a mutuality of response to a common existential condition. I believe that one can draw a graph to demonstrate that it is /was out of common sensibility that the writers of the Caribbean began to engage topics that resonate in a common black Atlantic sensibility. One only has to engage works such as Jamaica Kincaid's *Annie John,* Merle Hodge's, *For the Life of Laetitia,* Pat Powell's *Me Dying Trial*, Erna Brodber, *Myal,* Glaseta Honeyghan's *Father Sleeps with the Mudpie*, Lorna Goodison's *I'm Becoming My Mother*, Marlene Nourbese Philip's *Looking For Livingston,* Elizabeth Nunez Harrell's *When Rocks Dance*, Edwidge Danticat's *Breath, Eyes, Memory*, and Zee Edgell's *Beeka Lamb* to understand the continuity of feelings and sensibility that exists between these two peoples. And then there are two anthologies that sought to fill the gap, explain texts, and set a stage for reading these new works: I refer to *Caribbean Women Writers* by yours truly, and Carol Boyce Davies and Elaine Savory Fido's *Out of the Kumbla.* Each sought to establish the presence of this important body of writing.

Yet, the question remains: what makes these writings so powerful? Is it the state of their being conceived in a state of exile—domestic or foreign—or is there some additional ingredient that gives these writings a sense of power, beauty, and a haunting quality of rememberedness. I want to argue that at the center of some of these texts is the question of culture—religious practices, folklore, growing up—an attempt to recuperate a dimension of spirituality that was given as much emphasis as in other fictions; an inward capacity that gives us the ability to withstand in the evil day and to grant us the courage to move forward again. In this context, I want to argue that the concern for culture—the central contribution to subaltern intellectual thought that was made by Amilcar Cabral—suggests a possibility that many of our women writers inscribed into their work and thereby gave it power and remembrance that was curative as well as life-saving at this moment of our development. Inherent, then, in the sense of literary continuity was the maintenance of our culture[18]—what in other contexts I have called cultural resistance—that provided an important element in the evolution and articulation of our literature from the Black Arts Movement to the present time.

One only has to examine Danticat's *Breath, Eyes, Memory* and Brodber's *Myal* to see how each writer reaches back into a reservoir of cultural heritage of the Caribbean to structure her novels. Each is concerned to show that in spite of the sense of abandonness and loss, some spiritual condition remains a myth. That, indeed, religio-cultural practices such as vodun and myalism that condemned us to oblivion in the past must now be re-integrated into our being to make us whole again. In other words, one cannot abandon the very soul of one's being and expect to live a fully conscious and integrated life. In these examples, Dandicat and Brodber do what Wilson Harris has been advocating for the past thirty years or so. What both Dandicat and Brodber suggest is that one needs to tap that deep reservoir of cultural sensibilities if we are to be made whole again, that is, if we are to construct the kind of narrative that is essential for our survival in a world that seeks constantly to negate our being.

In the New World, our writers have always woven stories of slavery, colonialism (in the sixties in the United States we called it internal colonialism), racism, and varied forms of internal color consciousness. They have also added into the mix, the question of culture—be it religion as in vodun, santeria, or shango—that has defined the specificity of our condition and that has made us distinct. So that when we write in the Caribbean it is not so much that we speak about a different form of humanity; it is only that we come to our humanity from a different angle of vision and that, to be sure, is what makes our re-presentation of our world so specific, so hauntingly dangerous, and yes, so very similar with those experiences of our African American sisters and brothers.

Notes

1 Maryse Condé, *I, Tituba, Black Witch of* Salem (New York: Ballantine Books, 1992) 199.

2 Condé 203.

3 Condé ix.

4 Elisabeth Mudimbé-Boyi, "Giving Voice to Tituba: The Death of the Author," *World Literature Today*, 67:4 (Autumn 1993) 751.

5 Elaine Breslaw, *Tituba: Reluctant Witch* (New York: New York UP, 1966).

6 Breslaw 35, 45.

7 Nara Araújo, "The Contribution of Women's Writing to the Literature and Intellectual Achievements of the Caribbean: *Moi, Tituba Sorcière* and *Amour, Colère et Folie*" *Journal of Black Studies* 25: 2 (1994): 221–2.

8 Jamaica Kincaid, *The Autobiography of My Mother* (New York: Farrar Strauss Giroux, 1966) 29, 79.

9 *Condé* 203.

10 There is evidence of earlier writings by Afro-Caribbean writers prior to "The Sorrows of Yamba"; records of letters of women from the Danish West Indies (St. Croix and St. Johns) written to their religious leaders in Amsterdam about their conversion to Christianity. The first of these letters was written in 1737.

11 Jonathan Dewberry, "The African Grove Theatre and Company," *Black American Literature* 16: 4 (Winter 1982) 131.

12 See Tejumola Olaniyan, *Scars of Conquest: Mask of Resistance* (New York: Oxford UP), 1995, and Brodun Jeyifous, "Theatre and Drama and the Black Physical and Cultural Presence in America," Ph.D., dissertation, New York University, 1975.

13 Maxwell Philip, preface, *Emmanuel Appadoca or Blighted Life* (Trinidad: Mole Brothers, 1893).

14 William Wells Brown, *Sketches, Places and People Abroad* (Boston: John P. Jewett, 1855) 199–200.

15 Hazel Carby, "Proletarian or Revolutionary Literature? C.L.R. James and the Politics of the Trinidad Renaissance." *The South Atlantic Quarterly*, 18:1 (Winter 1988) 39–52.

16 See, for example, Tony Martin, ed., *African Fundamentalism* (Dover: The Majority Press, 1991).

17 Daryl Cumber Dance, "Go Eena Kumbla: A Comparison of Erna Brodber's *Jane and Louisa Will Soon Come Home* and Toni Cade Bambara, *The Salt Eaters*," in Selwyn Cudjoe, ed. *Caribbean Women Writers* (Wellesley: Calaloux Publications, 1990).

18 See Selwyn Cudjoe, *Resistance and Caribbean Literature* (Athens: Ohio UP, 1980).

19 See, for example, Wilson Harris, *History, Fable and Myth in the Caribbean and the Guianas* (1970, Wellesley: Calaloux Publications, 1995).

All Icons Are Mine, Too

Cecil Foster

I would like to pick up on a couple of thoughts that first, Stephanie dealt with, and then Cudjoe dealt with. I would like to talk about some of the things that I discuss in my two novels. My first novel *No Man in the House* in essence tells the story of women, how women in fact run the Caribbean society, but, ultimately, the story is about a little boy growing up and moving on to self-fulfillment, to understanding, and to somehow recognizing that there's something out there for him in this world. I wanted to couple those ideas with the notion of what was happening in the region at the time when many of us were talking about independence, and the corollary that flowed out of that in terms of whether or not we should reexamine the notion of why so many of us go into exile, go into the Metropole, into England, into the United States and into, in my case, Canada.

In my second book *Sleep on Beloved*, what I wanted to do was to look at what life is like once you have made that decision to go into exile. To some degree, I argue, many of us must have been real crazy when we woke up a couple of mornings back in the Caribbean and decided that, yes, I can go to New York, Los Angeles or whatever, and that almost immediately I can fit into that society, not realizing what it was that we were in fact selling ourselves into. Today, part of our feeling is that we have exchanged one form of colonialism for another form of colonialism.

When I thought of that, flowing out of those concerns was a very real one for me as a black writer in Canada. There, I am also a journalist and I work in the mainstream media houses. I also recognize that very often many of the black youth that I see around Toronto and similar areas are alienated. They don't have a sense of connection. And in *No Man in the House*, what I wanted to do was, in fact, to write a simple story, intended to say to my kids, and to other kids of Caribbean and African ancestry, that there are societies elsewhere that have done well. Certainly, the case of Toronto was that if we were to get on a plane and fly forward South, we would end up in societies where, in fact, there would be that sense of connection. There would be that sense of being loved, despite the fact that other writers might say that there isn't the sense of love there. That there, in the Caribbean, you can feel a sense of who you are, and you can have a sense of identification, and you can bring that with you.

In *Sleep on Beloved*, what I tried to do is to argue that we have to somehow nourish the dream that is going to allow us to feel that we belong in these societies, and that we can break out of the colonial set-up that we find ourselves in, and that no matter how much we are beaten down, we must maintain the dream and we must move on. Now, I think that those are themes that are universal, and those are things that I am trying to deal with in my writing. Walter Mosley, on the very first night, talked about when he was telling a story that he often thought of talking to his aunt, and of the listener. [Mosley's response in the Q & A]. Well, I know for many of you, you talk about the double consciousness of being African and American, but for me, based in Toronto, I probably have a triple or a quadruple consciousness because I am writing primarily for black people in Canada, and I'm hoping that the story I'm going to tell is of relevance to people in the United States, has relevance to people back home in the Caribbean, and also has relevance to those of us who didn't choose Canada or the United States, but might have chosen London.

At this point, I want to deal with this question of exile. For me, I am not even sure if I had a choice of exile. I grew up in a society, which, from the time I became conscious, I was being prepared to exile myself. I was being prepared to be sent out of the Caribbean. First, it was the notion of going to England, and when that dream died, it was the notion of maybe joining my grandfather and others in New York. Then it was in Canada, and then it could've been easily just about any city outside of the Caribbean. And, indeed, there was even a time when it might have even been a city in the Caribbean. When I went to a university in Jamaica, there was a time when I actively thought of staying on in Jamaica and living in Jamaica and pursuing other academic studies there. But there was always that notion, that push to achieve self-actualization. You had to achieve it outside. You had to be out of where you were born. The educational system I went through taught me to be a good immigrant. I can remember the stories the headmaster told about someone from the school who succeeded simply by going to New York. He went to New York or Toronto or London. It didn't really matter where. As long as he got out of the island, that was a sign of success.

This brings me to the notion of the universality of what we're writing about, because, as I said, I probably have a quadruple consciousness. The experiences that I want to draw on in my writing are not going to be experiences that are going to be limited to Toronto. They're going to be experiences that are going to be in New York; they're going to be in London; they're going to be in Brazil; they're going to be wherever black people have been or wherever there is a black center. I believe that even though I am proudly Barbadian, that the black and Caribbean experience belongs as much to me, as to the Mighty Sparrow in Trinidad, a Bob Marley of Jamaica as to any artist that you can mention who has the same background and experience. I believe that I can draw on, and I have a right to draw on, those icons and experiences in my writing.

I make this point because it becomes very easy for us to start breaking down into insular sections where we ignored a shared black experience despite the location of our birth. That's why you'll find in *Sleep on Beloved* that I write about a Jamaican family going to Toronto, because I feel that as a Caribbean person, and particularly now that I share fully the black and Caribbean experience of living in that city, Toronto is as much mine as anyone else; the black and Jamaican experience in that city is as much mine even though I am Barbados born. And I feel I have a right to do these stories. For the experience of that Jamaican woman is no different from the experiences of women from Barbados or Haiti. At the same time, I also know that the stories that I'm writing about, even though I might set them in Toronto—the story of an illegal immigrant, the story of a domestic worker, the story of Caribbean people searching for a new life in a new setting—are stories about similar things happening here in New York.

So I do not think that we are doing anything that is extremely exotic to make our writing more appealing, and therefore more publishable. For I think, by extension, the Caribbean and black experience I write about in Toronto is part of the overall black and even western hemispheric experience for people like us. In my case, what I'm simply trying to do is to take what I see as a universal reality and to tell a good story.

The final thing that I'd like to talk about—and this came out of the speech that Paule Marshall gave last night in which she talked about the healing that goes on in these communities—is that very often when I look around in the African and black community in Toronto, Montreal, and elsewhere, I see that there's a great need for healing. When we exchange one form of colonialism for another, we also lose part of our spirituality and there is a need for us to hold on to that spirituality. In *Sleep on Beloved*, you'll see that I argue that maybe one of the ways we can heal ourselves, and one of the ways we can hold on to our spirituality, is by first of all identifying who we are, and becoming very clear in our minds who we are. And second, that we fall back on all of those things that traditionally have always healed us.

In *Sleep on Beloved,* I used the motif of Carnival, perhaps one of the most universal of events in the Caribbean, one of the things you can find in just about every Caribbean island. The notion of Carnival is one of those healing aspects of our culture. In those two or three days we go out and we let it all hang out, and we know who we are; we are unapologetic for who we are, and we have a sense of healing, and then we can go on and come back, and we can continue with the fight, and we can continue to dream.

Not Exile, but Making a Life

Lorna Goodison

I come to represent the case
of one Annie Pengelly,
maidservant, late of the San Fleming Estate
situated in the westerly parish of Hanover.

Hanover, where that mastif
mountain range
assumes the shape of a Dolphin's head
rearing up the blue expanse overhead
restless white clouds round it foaming.

Those at sea would look up
and behold, mirrored, a seascape in the sky.

It is this need to recreate,
to run gainst things, that cause
all this confusion.

The same need that made men
leave one side of the world
to journey in long, mawed ships,
to drogue millions of souls
to a world
that they call the new one
in competition with the original act
the creation of the old one.

So now you are telling me to proceed
and proceed swiftly.
Why have I come here representing Annie?

Well this is the first thing she asked me to say,
that Annie is not even her real name.

A name is the first thing we own in this world.
We lay claim to a group of sounds
which rise up and down and mark out our space
in the air around us.
We become owners of a harmony of vowels and consonants
singing a specific meaning.

Her real name was given to her
at the pastoral ceremony of her outdooring.
Its outer meaning was, "she who is precious to us."

It had too a hidden part, a kept secret.
A meaning known only to those within
the circle of her family.

For sale Bidderman, one small girl,
one small African girl answering now
to the name of Annie.

Oh Missus my dear, when you write Lady Nugent
to tell her of your splendid birthday
of the ivory moire gown you wore
that you send clear to London for.

You can tell her too how you had built for you
a pair of soft, supple leather riding boots
fashioned from your own last
by George O'Brian Wilson
late of Aberdeen
now Shoemaker and Sadler of Lucea, Hanover
late occupation,
bruk Sailor.

One pair of tortoiseshell combs,
one scrolled silver backed mirror,
one dinner party where they killed
one whole cow
with oaken casks of Madeira wine
to wash it down.
And don't forget, one small African girl,
answering now to the name of Annie.

With all that birthday show of affection
Massa never sleep with missus
But I am not here to talk about that,
that is backra business.

I am really here just representing Annie Pengelly.

For Missus began to make Annie
sleep across her feet
come December when northers began to blow.

Northers being the chill wheeling tail end
of the winter breezes
dropping off their cold what lef' in Jamaica
to confuse the transplanted Planter.

Causing them to remember words like "hoarfrost" and "moors"
from a frozen vocabulary they no longer
had use for.

When this false winter breeze would
careen across canefields
missus would make Annie lie draped,
heaped across her feet
a human blanket
nothing covering her as she gave
her warmth to Missus.

So I come to say that History owes Annie
the brightest woolen blanket.
She is owed too, at least twelve years of sleep
stretched out,
free to assume the stages of sleep
flat on her back,
or profiled like the characters
in an Egyptian frieze.

Most nights though, Missus don't sleep.
And as Annie was subject to Missus will,
Annie was not to sleep as long
as Missus kept her open-eyed vigil.

Sometimes Missus sit up
sipping wine from a cut glass goblet.
Talking, talking.

Sometimes Missus dance and sing
like she was on a stage,
sad cantatrice solo
on a stage performing.

At the end of her performance
she would demand that Annie clap
clap loud and shout "encore."

Encouraged by this she would sing
and dance on,
her half-crazed torch song of rejection.

Sometimes Annie nod off,
Missus jook her with a pearl-tipped pin.
Sometimes Annie tumble off the chair
felled by sleep.
Missus slap her awake again.
Then in order to keep her alert, awake
she devised the paper torture.

One pile of newspapers
a sharp pair of scissors later,
Annie leaned about
the cruel make-work task
that is the *cut-up*
to throw-away of old newspaper.

For if Missus could not sleep
Annie gal you don't sleep that night,
and poor Missus enslaved by love
fighting her servitude with spite.

So I say history owes Annie
thousands of nights
of sleep upon a feather bed.
Soft feathers from the breast of
a free, soaring bird,
one bright blanket,
and her name returned,
she who is precious to us.

Annie Pengelly O.
I say, History owe you.

I have come to represent Annie Pengelly and Miss Mirray. My mother, Dorice, and her sisters, Albertha, Rose, and Anne. All of whom were never categorized as exiles, but who were forced by the circumstances of their lives to travel, live, and work in foreign countries.

My mother and her sisters were seamstresses and griots, poets and child minders. They were cooks, practical nurses, teachers, and healers, who told their stories and chanted their poems to the children and old people that they cared for. They also told their stories to their fellow workers, to help keep their spirits alive during long, cold, dark, winters.

Nobody ever said that they had chosen exile. Jamaican people said that they had gone abroad to "Make Life." And that is exactly what I am doing here; something that the people of the Americas have always done: traveled to foreign places in order to earn a living and make a life. I, therefore, have difficulties with the topic of this panel. Like my ancestors, I am here trying to make life, and I am reluctant to bestow any great specialness upon myself and my condition. I am just here doing what they did in the early part of this century.

There is also another reason why I'm reluctant to use the word "Exile," and this has to do with the current status of the Nobel Prize–winning writer Wole Soyinka, who has had to choose exile from his native Nigeria because of the corrupt and violent actions of the present Nigerian Government.

I have a fear of poisoning the wells. Can I too claim to have chosen exile, when I can go home to Jamaica any time that I want to? I prefer to yield up the right to use that term to people like Mr. Soyinka.

The topic, too, would want to suggest that there is only a finite amount of opportunity that is available to writers of color in the United States, and that West Indian writers are being given more than their fair share. That they are, as Jamaicans would say, "Boxing bread" out of the mouths of other writers. I am not convinced that significant numbers of West Indian writers are enjoying great success in this country. It is, in fact, my experience that West Indian literature is today still more appreciated in countries in Europe than it is in the United States of America.

Finally, I have a problem with the suggestion that those West Indian writers who do enjoy a measure of success in this country, do so through practicing the literary equivalent of minstrelsy, or through cultivating some peculiar inverted form of Orientalism. I am not sure that I want to address these particular issues. So, I have decided to come here and to do what I do best.

I also want to follow the advice of my mother who always had the same words of wisdom for me whenever I would go to tell her that I was off to read my poems in some foreign country. "Go" she would say, "and be yourself." I have come to represent my mother, Dorice, and therefore I will be myself and read some poems. And I thank Dr. Elizabeth Nunez and Dr. Brenda Greene for making it possible for me to come here and Make Life. (Lorna Goodison then read more poems from her collection, *To Us, All Flowers Are Roses*, 1995).

Panel B1

PRESUMING THE UNIVERSALITY OF THE BLACK EXPERIENCE

Foreword

Carlyle V. Thompson

Without a doubt the black experience is both universal and unique; this paradox too often defines the reality of black life in America. Blackness has been white America's greatest commercial dividend and greatest national divide. America's horrific legacy of black people's enslavement is that of black children chained to their mother's misery and black children chained to their father's shame. The blood, bones, and broken hopes of many black people have been the fuel to jumpstart white America's tremendous wealth. With white supremacy as their foundation, white people (mainly men) structured a government and a society to their sole advantage. Simply put, America has been built on the bloody whipscarred backs of black people and black labor has created white wealth. Discussing the origins of white wealth, Claud Anderson in *Black Labor, White Wealth: The Search for Power and Economic Justice* (1994), relates:

> Slaves lived in dilapidated, damp, dark cabins, and their worldly possessions consisted of a few rags. A small board and a stick of wood, served as their beds and pillows. There were no physical, financial, nor psychological comforts for them, and worst of all, slaves were intentionally kept without hope. A slave's life was committed to producing wealth and comfort for white masters. (11)

This historical phenomenon suggests the universality of the black experience; yet the Spirituals, the Cakewalk, the Blues, Ragtime music, Gospel music, Black Classical music (Jazz), Rap music, and Black vernacular—among many other unique black cultural productions—give telling evidence of black people making something out of nothing. Black literature operates out of a similar paradigm, a prolific paradigm of transition and transformation. Moving from Negro to colored to black to Afro-American to African American has been a sojourn laden with resistance to problematic definitions dictated by racist whites. Like Native American, Latino, Irish, and African literatures which address histories of brutal oppression, black literature and culture operate out of a totality of definitions, a self-portrait of that culture. From the slaves, narratives to the present voices of black writers, the themes of self-determination and self-definitions articulate the vision of a people seeking democracy in a land founded on racial and class totalitarianism. It is this aspect which makes black literature relevant to a broad audience and suggests that universality can be a desirable objective for all literature.

Black literature started at the point of controversy and racial contemptuousness. Phillis Wheatley was the first black person to publish a book of poetry in English; it was the racist Thomas Jefferson, in his *Notes on the State of Virginia* (1787) who made disparaging remarks about Phillis Wheatley's poetry:

> Misery is often the parent of the most affecting touches in poetry. Among the blacks is misery enough, God knows, but not poetry. Love is the peculiar estrum of the poet. Their love is ardent, but it kindles the senses only, not the imagination. Religion, indeed, has produced a Phillis Wheatley; but it could not produce a poet. The compositions published under her name are below the dignity of criticism. (140)

Like the "high-tech lynching" of Anita Hill, Phillis Wheatley was put on trial to ascertain if she, in fact, wrote the poetry in her book. In a Boston courthouse in the spring of 1772, Wheatley had to undergo an arduous oral examination of her writing. Eighteen of Boston's most distinguished and wealthy white males, including the governor of the colony, Thomas Hutchinson, the Reverend Charles Chauncey, the pastor of the Tenth Congregational Church, and John Hancock, who would later join Thomas Jefferson in signing the *Declaration of Independence*, stood in judgment of this African girl. The preface to Wheatley's book, *Poems on Various Subjects, Religious and Moral* (1985), reveals the outcome of the trial:

> We whose Names are underwritten, do assure the World, that the poems specified in the following Page, were (as we verily believe) written by Phillis, a young Negro Girl, who was but a few Years since, brought an uncultivated Barbarian from Africa, and has ever since been, and now is, under the Disadvantage of serving as a Slave in a Family in this Town. She has been examined by some of the best judges, and is thought qualified to write them. (vii)

Unlike Anita Hill, Phillis Wheatley was believed and her poetry did clandestinely and openly challenge the enslavement of black people and America's racism. More importantly, Wheatley's life and writings reveal the utterly remarkable story of a young girl kidnapped from Africa and sold into slavery; yet she was the first African American to publish a book and the first to achieve international acclaim. Discussing the significance of these two sensational public narratives in *Codes of Conduct: Race, Ethics, and the Color of Our Character* (1995), Karla FC Holloway argues:

> In both cases, words seem to center the conduct of credibility, scripting a rhetorical parallelism that ensnares both events. Anita Hill's claim of sexual harassment was certainly different in kind, but not in degree, from Phillis Wheatley's claim to authorship. Both women's testimonies were labeled incredible and both attempted a negotiation of racial and gender politics within which neither had a stable or legitimized presence. (26–27)

If we can presume the universality of the black experience, clearly the struggle for a stable and "legitimized presence" is fundamental in the work of many black writers. Further, the quest for a "legitimized presence" has been and continues to be very different for black women faced with the "double jeopardy" of America's inherent racism and sexism.

Finally, one of the most universal elements that crosses boundaries of "race," class, gender, culture, and language is music; to contemplate the black experience in America it is important to make the connection between black literature and black music. The literary themes giving protest to violence, racism, sexism, and class hegemony are also found in the music of Marvin Gaye, John Coltrane, Nina Simone, Stevie Wonder, Aretha Franklin, Odetta, Gil Scott-Heron, Tracy Chapman, Sweet Honey in the Rock, Queen Latifah, and Public Enemy. In *So Far, So Good* (1990), Gil Scott-Heron, a musician and a master weaver of words, connects the black experience to black music in his poem "Lady Day and John Coltrane." A few lines from the poem read:

> Plastic people with plastic minds on their way to
> plastic homes
> There's no beginning, there ain't no ending
> just on and on and on and on and . . .
> It's all because we're so afraid to say that we're
> alone

until our hero rides in, rides in on his saxophone.
You could call on Lady Day!
You could call on John Coltrane!
They'll wash your troubles, your troubles away. (28)

Gil Scott-Heron and other musical artists here in America joined the voices of Bob Marley and the Wailers, Peter Tosh, Third World, Miriam Makeba, and Black Uhuru in the clarion call for freedom and justice to all people struggling against all forms of oppression. Within this context, we can better understand Larry Neal, who, quoted in Joyce Ann Joyce's essay "Gil Scott-Heron: Larry Neal's Quintessential Artist," in *So Far, So Good*, views black music as being more significant than literature in the lives of black people. Neal writes:

> . . . the key to where Black people have to go is in the music. Our music has always been the most dominant manifestation of what we are and feel; literature was just an afterthought, the step taken by the Negro bourgeoisie who desired acceptance in the white man's terms. And that is precisely why the literature has failed. It was the case of one elite addressing another elite. But our music is something else. The best of it has always operated at the core of our lives, forcing itself upon us as in a ritual. It has always, somehow, represented the collective psyche. (73–74)

Although Larry Neal's analysis might appear to be too reductive, like Ralph Ellison's *Invisible Man* (1952), he does place black literature and music in a perspective that, perhaps, forces black scholars, writers, and publishers to be even more critical of their work, their audience, and their mission as they get the word "home" to the people. With "high-tech" white supremacy dramatically escalating, a fluid discourse that will empower and uplift black people is extremely necessary.

In a time when white supremacist thinking and behavior are gaining momentum, Kelvin Christopher James, Hugh Pearson, Marita Golden, and Stanley Crouch explore the issue of the universality of the black experience. Through literary analysis, history, and personal life stories, these writers analyze the forces that hold black culture together and those that celebrate the diversity. Included in this section is a quite provocative question and answer session that especially illuminates the rather brief statement given by the cultural critic, Stanley Crouch.

Fractals of a Grander Pattern

Kelvin Christopher James

I am a scientist by profession, by training, by trade and by habit. I write because I have a talent to do it, and I am very happy that people like my fiction. That said, I want to establish that this point of view is the perspective from which I now view the world, from which I speak. I am a guy who identifies with the last active character in my fictional world, the person I have made up. For better or worse, that is with whom I identify.

My last book, *A Fling with a Demon Lover*, was narrated from an African American woman's point of view, that of a thirty-eight-year-old woman who is having a steamy affair with a twenty-year-old Caribbean boy in Greece. That is where the couple meets up with, what in Trinidad we call, Obeah, black magic. Among other things, my novel aims to suggest that nowadays so-called black people are together enough to visit a cradle of Western civilization—Greece, at that—and meet Obeah in the form of a Lamia, a dracula-type critter. Yes, our Caribbean black magic is alive and well among the present day Greeks.

But I was saying that I come from a writer's point of view: a guy whose job is imaginations. And this is pertinent to the matter at hand, because I must admit that my first response to the topic under discussion was: *Forget about it.* I want to make a point that this is a New York expression. It's interesting beyond amusement to me, because I'm a Trinidadian, and my natural response to such a topic's title—if I'm a Trinidadian in Trinidad—would be something like: "They mus' be crazy!" Or some other equivalent local expression, but certainly not, *Forget about it!*

Yet, such was my first linguistic, can I say, natural response to the topic. Now, I don't defend this at all, because what I admire about my immigrant Trinidadian people (we, who leave to stay and come to this wonderful place with the golden mountain of opportunity, and, hopefully, take a good bite out of it), what I admire is our quintessential quality of ingenious adaptability, our fitting in, our ability to blend with the natives and the habitat. Whether they be Trinidadians, or people from every part of the world, that's what immigrants do when they come into this country.

I'll tell you something: there are stories and calypsoes about Trinidadians adventuring to America. They get no further than some American airports, yet when they return home to Piarco Airport in Trinidad they have a heavy Yankee accent. Serious. The accent is heavier than their baggage. Texan drawl. Boston brogue. New York twang. Wherever they had been turned back, they've deported with that accent. They have fellas in Trinidad who didn't even bother to go through with all that. They go to a Western movie and come out two hours later, and they have an accent. I telling you. We's adaptable people.

But back to those Trinis who make it inside, and adapt. I want to suggest that maybe these guys are similar to all the other immigrant souls, adventuring with hopes and prayers into a strange community, and that maybe all such people manage to swim only because they refuse to sink in the foreign waters. This gets me back to the gut reaction I had to the topic: Presuming the Universality of the Black Experience.

Maybe it's only me, but I'm immediately suspicious of fancy language with words fat so, like rich people's steaks. I like to cut down them words into bite sized portions. So, I check out my big word dictionary.

Presuming says, it not down for anyone supposing too much, taking the self for granted. Hmmn!

For me *Universality* is a heavy word. I'm suspicious of it. One dictionary says: a limited range in application and occurrence and comprehensiveness (another big word); another dictionary says: completeness, generality, wholeness.

Well, none of that will change my mind about *universality*. I will only apply that word to the universe, because I don't know how we could tie it up with a notion small as the *black experience*, which gives me a real troublesome definition problem.

Black, as a term for people, is not acceptable. More than that, black experience, as a term describing any set of circumstances, is also unacceptable.

I have weighty problems when we start talking about black. I have heavy questions to wrestle with. Are we talking skin color, or culture or ethnic or racial group? What are we talking about when we say, black?

I have a problem with labels of any stripe. I see a label as an imposition and a limitation. A rude presumption. And I'm always curious about who's making these definitions about *blackness*, and why is this person or group doing so.

Why do they want to define me and put me in a pigeon hole?

I can't support that.

In dealing with the *black experience* as a double-worded concept, should our debates accent the societal history of the *black experience* in the role of behavioral oppressor, or oppressed; as community producer, or consumer; as significantly blessed or damned differently to other defined groups?

And whether compared and contrasted to these other defined groups, can we, thoughtful debaters up here, can we make any realistic assessment or forecast about the *black experience*?

There are a lot of people listening to what we say here today, but does it make a difference?

Bottom line, I think the so-called *black experience* is what individual people do, and how they do it. There are a lot of considerations raised here, with many, new and nuanced responses to them. Yet our job up here is to debate the presumption of universality. I don't know what I have to say. I think it's a tenuous premise that I, me, Kelvin, could fit anything sensible under such a narrow label.

I do believe that in the long run we are the stories we tell of ourselves. If I tell you a good story about me, and I make it that I suffer a lot, then that's how you'll remember me. A sufferer. If I tell you about how I failed my potential, you'll not remember how bright it shone, but only how I wasted it.

I grew up in a country town in Trinidad. That's sort of double country. I didn't go to high school. I went to the library. There, in the bush, I grew up in a place where my potential had no walls, no ceilings. I read anybody or any topic that excited. Shakespeare stuff. Fairy tales. Bible stuff. Frank Yerby. Biology. P.G. Wodehouse. I was not educated as it happens in America. I was never caught into an American cultural thought pattern. During the late '50s and '60s—my indiscriminate reading years—I couldn't care less about civil rights problems and white oppression. Not only was I ignorant about it, I was more interested in cricket, West Indian federation, carnival and calypso. Pertinent Commonwealth matters. I was an able cricketer. And, by the way, Sri Lanka won the World Cup in cricket. Don't ignore this. They beat the colonial masters who taught us the game. I love that sort of irony.

This is stuff I grew up learning: how to defeat the oppressor. I have never seen the oppressor as a real challenge because these people cannot last in my country, in my community. Their very skins spoil; they have to intermix with us to make thriving children. Really! And their children are neither this nor that, black nor white. Mixed is the idea, and I say long live the power of hybridism, which is what I really support.

Might be why I find it a real oppression is that in a country with people as wonderful and varied (I look at the number of colorful faces here, if I can say that, the colored people, here), all the variety gets labeled as *black*.

I en't playing that. Call me brown-skinned. Call me Shabeen, or Red Ibo. Call me Béké Neg, call me Redbone. Call me who I look like. Just don't simplify me with a simple label. I am a complex person.

I believe that in the long run we are the stories that we recount of ourselves. I believe each life experience is an individual, overall circumstance, mystical, undefinable and unique even more than genetic codes. When grouped, these experiences, these stories we tell, suggest that we are more nearly like fractals of a grander pattern in the complex web of life—a pattern that defines our common humanity more than anything else.

Contradictions in the Search for Authenticity

Hugh Pearson

I think a lot of what I'm going to say is going to sound redundant because everybody else kind of said almost what I wanted to say, but, yeah, they jumped me, so bear with me if I bore you a little bit. The key attribute of any healthy group of people is the element in their culture that tells them that they are special in the eyes of a higher creator. However, as people of black African descent, defined by that element which makes us special, our efforts are fraught with contradictions. The racism we face is based on the notion that we are inherently less intelligent than everyone else, that we are a less advanced form of the human being. Too often in our search for authenticity, we inadvertently reinforce that image. We cling to an obsession with traditions. Of course, traditions define all ethnicities, but today the entire world is confronted by an ever escalating push towards modernization.

The American European model of advancement that confronts the world today has plenty of drawbacks. In its present incarnation, it's entirely too individualistic, destructive of the nuclear family and tends to emphasize progress for the sake of progress, even if that progress is of dubious quality. However, in their encounter with this modern ethos, all ethnic groups, including European subgroups conquered by other Europeans, have faced the problems inherent to it. Human history is fraught with the wreckage and triumph of the struggle. Yet, as we engage in this dynamic process, we people of black African descent have been quite hard on ourselves. This tendency causes us to narrow our horizons and ostracize the centers among us who acknowledge their connection to the rest of mankind. In the process, we inadvertently contribute to our oppression, feeding the notion that we are less intelligent than others.

This narrow conception of who we are causes many blacks to question something that should be obvious: Is there a universal element connecting us with the rest of mankind? Of course there is. Convinced that this is true, I researched and wrote the *Shadow of the Panther*. To observe the human connections in the Panther story, I endeavored to assume the perch of a visitor from another planet. In doing so, I noticed the number of parallels between the behavior of people in the Party and the behavior of people in historical movements outside of the Black Diaspora. For example, among the leftists from the 1930s to the 1950s, it was common to extol the virtues of communist Russia. That sort of mentality grew out of the Great Depression when capitalism was in its lowest repute. In the process, Russian leaders, such as Joseph Stalin, were aggrandized by leftist Americans. It wasn't until Alexander Solzhenitsyn was published that large numbers of leftists were finally confronted with Stalin's atrocities.

The lesson we could take from that is, never grant carte blanche to any movement's ideology, no matter how righteous or romantic it paints itself to be. The same lesson is to be learned from what happened in the Black Panther Party. During the late '60s and early '70s, plenty of black Americans were willing to ignore or excuse the problematic behavior emanating from the Party. And today, since nostalgia paints a rosier picture of the past, that is still the case. True, there are many skewed, romantic interpretations of the Black Panthers. There were plenty of well intentioned party members, but there were also plenty of bad apples who contributed to its demise. Party sympathizers told us, and still tell us today, that all of those bad apples were FBI informants. But that wasn't the case. Yes, some were saboteurs collaborating with the FBI, in many cases because the FBI blackmailed them into cooperation. But there were others who helped destroy the Party, who had no connection to the FBI. Too often Party members who witnessed their crimes or who were victims were forced into silence by the tenor of the times.

Radical white leftists from the anti-Vietnam war movement aggrandized the Party as the nation's revolutionary vanguard. A limousine liberal media aided and abetted the process. Thus, with a sympathetic media always ready to construe negative information about the Party as a racist conspiracy, leaders like Huey Newton were granted carte blanche to engage in atrocities, like the atrocities of Joseph Stalin, but on a far, far smaller scale. They beat, tortured, raped and killed many fellow Black Panthers. They robbed the blacks in the Oakland community. They sold drugs and extorted money from drug dealers. Like the romantic white leftists who chose not to believe what was reported of Stalin's Russia, plenty of black people chose not to believe these facts about the Black Panther Party. They preferred to grant Party miscreants "a bye" due to the existence of racism.

Was Party co-founder Huey Newton an intelligent and insightful man? Yes. Did a racist society contribute to his disintegration? Yes. Was all of his negative behavior attributable to racism? Even if we are to assume that ultimately racism was totally responsible, we must ask ourselves, at what point should a black person accept responsibility for her or his actions? Are we to blame racism even when our behavior amounts to genocide? If that's the case then, again, we inadvertently reinforce the assumption of racists that we are so crippled mentally, we can't be treated as full human beings. And I don't think anyone in this room believes that.

The lessons to be learned from the Black Panthers are but one example of the universal connection between black people and the rest of mankind. Another example is the Jewish experience in pre-World War II Germany after Hitler came into power. Nazis portrayed Jews as subhumans. They installed a system of Jim Crow laws, excluding Jews from the most desirable areas and forms of enterprise. They ghettoized Jews. In fact the Nazis' theory places Jews at the lowest rung of the human totem pole. They preached that Jews were lower than blacks because they were lecherous, an attitude which ultimately led to the Holocaust, which, of course, consumed other groups of people as well. Despite what these lessons teach us about how we are mutually connected to other people, plenty of blacks insist on believing that no other group of humans have suffered more than us. Yet what greater demonstration of hatred can there be than to engage in systematic extermination.

The Holocaust teaches us that, historically, like us, Jews have known what it's like to be treated like niggers. Even though today plenty of Jews treat us as inferior to them, we shouldn't allow such racism to cloud our thinking. Do we face the greatest oppression of all God's children? Possibly, but if we deny the universal elements of our experience, we permanently relegate ourselves to second-class status and collaborate in our own oppression.

Troubling Questions About Universality

Marita Golden

Well, if John Killens is twisting in his grave, he's probably twisting no less than I did as I sort of addressed this question because I sort of had the same response: "Oh God are we still talking about this?"

We were sent reams of papers and sort of academic scholarly ways to approach this question and I kind of got a headache just looking at all of that and so I decided to write not as a academic (which I am not) but to write as a writer. So my remarks are really going to come out of my experience as a fiction/non-fiction writer and as a teacher. I'm going to admit upfront, right from the start of my comments that I found the topic title of this panel, Presuming the Universality of the Black Experience somewhat troubling. As a writer of both fiction and non-fiction and one who frequently crosses the real and imagined border separating the two types of writing, I must say that every time I sit down to write, whether it's a letter, a résumé, a novel, an essay or whether I'm scribbling on the sand at the beach, I presume and assert and affirm the universality of my experience, my black woman, African American experience.

I'm going to, in the interest of honesty and fairness to myself and everybody gathered here, acknowledge, however, that I didn't always write with such certainty. The legacy of historical and contemporary racism, the relentless daily diminishment of the black self by the larger society and often by our own community, made my first efforts at writing, strong as they were in my mind, fingers crossed, acts of faith, rather than bold brazen acts that claimed my own literary space. When I sat down over a decade ago to write my first book, *Migrations of the Heart*, one of the most formidable hurdles I had to leap over was not how to write the book, but yes, believing that my story was indeed universal. The autobiography which is a meditation on family, identity, culture, coming of age and coming into self was a kind of love letter I was writing to all my sisters who'd gone through the sixties in some of the same ways I had.

In the years since this publication, however, *Migrations of the Heart* has taught me a valuable, crucial lesson about the necessity and even the duty for black writers to even assume the universality of their experience. This publication, this book which tells, in part, of my marriage to a Nigerian and the life I lived with him in Nigeria has been used by dozens of colleges and is required reading for incoming freshman classes as well as in a variety of academic courses. A young Jewish student at George Washington University came up to me after a talk I gave at her school, in conjunction with the freshmen being assigned to read the book, and told me I had lived enough lives for half a dozen people and that reading the book gave her the courage to imagine a much larger landscape for the lives she would live while in and after college. So I will admit that as an emerging writer, sure I've wondered about the possibility of my work being universal and that wondering, the fact that I doubted for even a moment, says volumes about who I was over a decade ago and how the reality of racism had stunted, to some extent, the reach of my own imagination.

But as someone who has now learned that I write, not by choice, but as a way to live my life, I write not as an occupation but as an avocation, I write because I am doomed and destined to do so, I write because there are books that simply are waiting for me to conjure them into reality and I write because I'm alive, I say again that everytime I write I presume the universality of my experience. I also assume that there are readers who can't get into my work, can't get into it, not because it springs from a black female source, but because they're not interested in the story, or literary fiction, or because non-fiction just ain't their thing.

This question of universality as a topic for discussion troubles me for a variety of other reasons too. I'm troubled by the constraining, corrupting shadow of white critics and historians and exploiters of our culture putting us into boxes that fit into other boxes that fit into others from which we could never seem to escape. Whether it's a box marked the black man has no soul or intelligence, or the black woman has no beauty or intelligence, or the black child has no innocence or intelligence, I keep seeing the boxes when I hear this question. And as for the assertion that our oppression is unique, what older, more ancient, more universal story is there in history than that of a people struggling to be free, autonomous, to control their culture and destiny, to escape the Middle Passage or Wounded Knee or some other massacre, or the Gulag or the Holocaust. I refuse to let anyone (black or white) lock me out of the human story. I think I find this question of universality troubling as well because I hear and see and feel our own literary community constructing boxes as imprisoning and potentially lethal to the spirit of creation as the boxes created for us by others. One of the most amazing and wonderful characteristics of the current black literary renaissance to me is the range of colors, the vibrancy and distinctness of the hues, the mirrored tones of the voices being carved out. Who could ever have predicted Terry McMillan and Toni Morrison and Alice Walker on the national best-seller list simultaneously? Who could predict the voices of August Wilson and John Edgar Wideman and E. Lynn Harris and Trey Ellis ruminating, tall tale telling, storytelling all at the same time? Writers write because they assume the universality of their experience. Believe me, nobody writes for long unless they believe that the story they are weaving and the manner in which it's embedded and rooted in their experience, their fears, their dreams is a conversation with everybody else. Writing is too lonely, too damn hard for anyone to write without the propellant of faith and logical belief in the essentialness of their relationship to everyone else in the globe, as well as in their neighborhood or apartment building.

Several years ago, I visited Turkey as part of a ten-day trip sponsored by the United States Information Agency to promote the international presentation of the *I Dream a World* photo exhibit of African American women. In Istanbul and Isomer, I visited universities and I spoke with students about my own work and contemporary African American literature. At the major university in Istanbul, the students were reading *Their Eyes Were Watching God* and they engaged me in intense conversations about Hurston and her life and legacy. At the university in Isomer I was greeted by a group of faculty members, one of whom was wearing that day a strip of kente cloth around her neck, who had done her Ph.D. on the works of playwright Charles Fuller and had studied under the tutelage of Molefi Asante at Temple University. I met a professor who had been put on trial for teaching *The Bluest Eye* when one of her students protested to the government censorship authorities that the theme of incest in the book was blasphemous to Muslim sensibilities.

We are, indeed, the world; the world is in us, and to say that diminishes nothing in the uniqueness of our triumphs and our journeys and our travails. As I looked over the page of questions that could spring from a general discussion of the topic for this panel, I kept being struck by the implicit assumption that somehow there is no continuum between today's writers and our literary foremothers and forefathers. The assertion that today's black writers have discarded the political and racial concerns that dominated the literary work of our literary ancestors is just plain wrong. Of course our work is a continuum, conscious and unconscious, from Zora Neale Hurston to Alice Walker, from James Baldwin to Randall Keenan, from Chester Himes to Walter Mosley.

While Toni Morrison has been quoted as saying that literature that has no political influence is tainted, I don't know of any literature that lacks political influence. What, for example, is more political than love, the search for the right mate, the desire to create a family. If sex and love weren't political, the state wouldn't regulate it through laws on marriage, divorce and inheritance, and even our relationship with our children. Even the most crass Harlequin romance is a commentary on women's fantasies, their expectations of men and the use of power in the decision to give one's life to someone else or to own it yourself. Even in a novel as political and polemical as *Native Son,* if Bigger Thomas were only a symbol of our oppression, we wouldn't still be enthralled by his story. It is his adolescent confusion, his yearning to be realized as a human being, a man, an adult, a person, that explains why professors I met in Turkey teach the book to their classes.

As someone who teaches writing in African American literature on the campus of an historically white college, I'm informed on a regular and continuing basis of the power, and especially the transformative power of the canon that black writers have created. When I taught a course on black female autobiography in addition to the narratives of Harriet Jacobs and Audrey Lorde and Elaine Browne, we read as well the *Autobiography of Ida B. Wells.* The life of this fiery journalist, this anti-lynching crusader, women's right activist, mother-wife, and communal leader, stirred the imagination of the class. And the class, which was entirely female and 90 percent white, simply fell in love with her. Near the end of one class, one white student asked me, "Why haven't I ever heard of this woman before? How come I had to wait 'till I got to college to hear her story?" This woman asked me this, her voice trembling with a sense of outrage and anger at the manner in which she had been cheated of knowledge of her history as an American because she didn't know who Ida B. Wells was. I told her that she had to wait for the world to change, for a civil rights movement and a women's movement to bring change in universities and make them hospitable places, not only for teachers who look like me, but for the previously buried stories of my ancestors.

This semester I'm teaching a black male autobiography course, and, as in the previous course, the students are reading some of the most eloquent articulations of a people's struggle to be free that have ever been written. We've read Douglass and Washington and Hughes and Wright so far. For their final project, each student will write an autobiographical essay on a living, breathing, live black man. It is a small class, half black and half white, and all the students are totally passionate about black literature. Everyone in the room knows that these men's stories have something essential to do with them. Last week, one of the students, a forty-something white female, told me after class that she had recently sued a mechanic who had irreparably damaged her truck in the process of repairing it. She took the case to small claims court and acted as her own lawyer, a feat that she could never have imagined doing before taking this course. "I don't know how to explain it," she said, struggling to find words to describe the transformative powers of the stories we've been reading all semester. "But it's like reading about how Fredrick Douglass and Richard Wright fought for what they believed in, and all they had to overcome enabled me to get over my fear of not just suing this guy but standing up in a courtroom, the only woman there in a roomful of white guys, and arguing my case." She didn't win any damages, but the judge praised her legal performance and she told me, "I stood up for myself and so in the end I did win. I never would've done something like that before taking this class."

A small victory, perhaps, but it is no small thing to speak for yourself, to defend yourself, especially when you've been raised to believe you couldn't. Our stories are magic, black magic; they are powerful and they are the soul of the planet. Every time I sit down to write, I know I'm universal. I close my eyes and I call on Zora, Audrey and Toni Cade Bambara and Langston and all the rest to lay hands on me, and to help me to unlock the key to my specific song.

We Speak for Everybody

Stanley Crouch

We have had to do what no other great nation in the history of the world has had to do, which is to try and make some sort of sense of this incredible mixture of people and cultures that comes from so many different places. But, do believe me, no matter what you might want to change your name to, what kind of clothes you might want to wear, when you get off a plane in West Africa, within five minutes the Africans will say, "Ah, an American."

Now, the thing is that that means that you carry in you, in your manner, in what you have to say, in your sense of humor, in *everything*, something that is the result of this grand democratic vision that we have all been in the process of trying to purify from as long as it has existed. I do not think it is time for us to give up on that. I think that we have something very, very special to offer the world. I think the fact is that we fought in the French and Indian wars, the Revolutionary War, the War of 1812, the Alamo; that we were central to the winning of the Civil War, the Spanish American War, World Wars I and II; that we did our bloody part in Korea and Vietnam and, of course, that we are somewhere in Bosnia now. And once again we have been involved in the purification, the ongoing purification of our social contract, have been essential to the development of American humor, to the center of American tragedy, to the richest heights of expression in American religious music and to some of the best art in other areas. I think that this is all ours, and when we step out there, we speak for everybody who's interested in anything of human value, if that's what we set out to do. That's my intention, and I hope it's yours. Thank You.

Q–I have a question for Stanley and for Kelvin. For Stanley, you say that since we participated in the cultural development of America and on the battlefield that we should claim the best of America, but I just would like to ask if you agree that, as Jesse Jackson put it, some people look at America from the top and they see a shining apple; some people look at it from the bottom and see a rotten apple? The reason I ask you that is, you mentioned black participation in the battle of the Alamo, but it is my understanding that in the Alamo the whites were fighting to extend slavery into Texas because the Mexicans had already abolished slavery. So for blacks to look at the Alamo as some achievement we should be proud of, I have a problem with you making that statement. I would like you to clarify that. And then for Kelvin, I would just like to say I never hear white people complain about being described as white. The only people I hear complaining about being a color are people who are called black. I just would like for you to respond why you think that is.

A–(Crouch)–Travis, Crocket, and all of them were part of a protest against the Mexican policy to abolish slavery because they wanted to bring what they thought at this point was an all American service industry with them into Texas. But since my family is from Texas, since I am a great fan of Westerns, since I also look at the fact that the history of the United States is both a tragic set of affairs and a victoric set of affairs, I feel that what we have to do is the same thing that people do who claim on the one hand that they want to be free of things that are white, but they use transistors. I used to say this to students. We got to get away from this white man's this, and this white man's that, and the European this and the Western that. Well, the first time I started thinking about that was at a black power conference where the security officers were walking around with dark sunglasses, which I don't think are African, and muttering Swahili in the walkie-talkies. That was a real interesting image to me at that time because they had these walkie-talkies and they were muttering this Swahili, and I thought to myself, Hum? and then they were going on about black this and black that. But anyway, getting back to the transistor, William Shockley, hard core, serious, redneck, racist dog, wanted to teach a course at Stanford—I think it was in genetics—sometime in the '60s to prove the innate intellectual inferiority of black people. He was a forerunner of gangster rap and Charles Murray, but William Shockley was also one of the inventors of the transistor with the three guys who got the Noble Prize award. So I used to say to these kids when they would be ranting and raving about how they wanted to get away from the white this and the white that, I wish they all would reject all of this white stuff because then we wouldn't have to put up with those goddamn boom-boxes.

A–(James)–Regarding the question of white people not complaining about being white, I had a luncheon with my book publisher—a Random House person, I wouldn't say further—a white person, Irish heritage and so on, and she told me that only colored people in America have culture and I think that was a complaint about being white today. She said it in quite a sad way. No, no, no, she was unhappy that only black people, colored people have culture in America. She said that white people don't have any culture that is really important. So I feel that is a sort of complaint. And regarding why I first do not want to be given a label by anybody, a label forced upon this society by white people, listen, when black people came from Africa, they didn't come across here and say, "We are black people." If they said anything they would have said, "We are Africans." And if you think of Africans, you have Africans of all colors who were born in Africa. You have Ibo people in Jamaica. You have red Ibo in Jamaica, right? There we go. We have Jamaicans who are white. No. So, I do not like this idea of assuming that I am complaining. I'm not complaining about who I am or my color. I am complaining about anybody daring to give me a label, because I see a label, any label as a limit of what I do. I write fiction. My first two novels were written from a woman's point of view. A fat country girl in the Caribbean tells the story in the first novel; the second one is told by an African American woman here. If I follow this labeling system, I am a male writer from the Caribbean. I have no right to do that kind of stuff. I, by definition, am unable to write about a woman, or a young, fat girl. The stories as you read them, because I know you people read them, are wonderful stories. You agree, right? Y'all bought the books, right? So, that's my answer to my brother across there. No offense at all, but please don't label me as anything.

(Moderator, Keith Gilyard)–That was a hell of a question about the Alamo. Where is he? I would like to up the intellectual ante, but in a sense I think that I would reserve that for tomorrow's wrap-up, 'cause I don't want to cut into other people's time, but I think that as we get further into this issue of whiteness and blackness, we realize that in fact when Europeans came to America they weren't white either; they turned into white folk over here. So I think you need to look at the whole history of that, and the history of that relative to the construction of blackness. And I understand that one doesn't want to be labeled, but I do know that if you try to catch a cab in Midtown and say you're going to Brooklyn at midnight, they will let you know what color you are in America. But we ain't gonna get into too much of that.

A–(James)–I want to respond to that quickly. I want to know why there are BLACK cab drivers who won't pick up black people?

(Moderator, Gilyard)–What I'm saying is, they will pass "the you." The point I'm making is they will pass "the you." It doesn't matter who is driving.

Q–My question is for Mr. Crouch as well. One of the essays you wrote in your book *The All American Skin Game* deals with the souls of black folk. It concerned William Edward Burkard Du Bois, one of my favorite thinkers, and one of the most profound Africans to ever hold a pen. You talk about telling the truth, and I guess that's the aim to which the humanities, and those of us in liberal arts aim: truth, and in that truth is a dialogue. So I guess my question is, how is it, I mean, so many English professors and so many historians, and even just those of us who read *Souls of Black Folk*, how is it we understand where Du Bois was coming from in terms of the double consciousness; being African and also being in America and the struggle of trying to resolve being African in America? I mean that is a very real struggle. You seem to negate that. I have a problem with that, and I just would like you to clarify that, and also the second part when you made a fallacious assertion that African culture was inferior to European culture, particularly at the time when the Europeans came to Africa. In his documentation, John Hope Franklin, one of our pioneering elder historians, in *From Slavery to Freedom*, documents Ghana, Mali, and Songhai as being supreme African civilizations. They had culture; they had universities. How do you deal with Timbuktu? How do you deal with this?

A–(Crouch)–I said it before, and I'll keep saying it: my fundamental way of engaging the world is based on ideas that fundamentally come out of the proposition of American democracy, or out of the European Enlightenment. My feeling is that those ideas are the ideas that made possible the end of slavery, that made possible, eventually, the emergence of women from different forms of segregation. These are the ideas that are central to what I call the Evangelical humanism, that are at the center of the way in which the world is either addressed now or is not addressed. By that I mean with the Enlightenment comes the idea that we are all connected in some fundamental way that transcends race or place. People over here often do not realize that when they hear a guy, like say, Winston Churchill, use the term, the English race. The Europeans did, in fact, look at it like that, but people from France did not think they were the same as the Germans, or as the British or as anybody else, and then with the Enlightenment comes universal humanism, or the beginning of it. And I would suggest that that is an idea that from a number of African materials that I've read over the years, and from being in Africa itself, that Africans till this day still struggle with, and because of the problem of tribalism, which is a problem, we also see that struggle in places like Bosnia, that is, that the idea that there is not this fundamental connection to other people. So, my vision, so, my fundamental take is that that is what I am particularly interested in. The ideas that come out of American democracy, the ideas that come out of the European Enlightenment, those are the ideas for me as a writer and for me as a thinker, that are the greatest ideas for me. They are not ideas that I think are reflective of anything racial on the part of the people who came up with them, that is, when people talk about great white men and all that business. Isaac Newton doesn't reflect anything about the British. The British wish there was a way you could get an Isaac Newton every week. Isaac Newton represents the same thing that Duke Ellington represents, which is genius, and that's what I meant earlier. That anything great is as much yours as anybody else's, regardless of whether prejudicial people were the ones to come up with it. That's what I meant about Shockley.

Q–(Person with question interrupts)–Sir, will you allow me to maybe clarify. Let me be real plain and simple. My two concerns with your essay in *The All American Skin Game* concerned W.E.B. Du Bois's concept of double consciousness. That is the first question, and the second one is your assertion that African culture was inferior to European culture in the fourteen and fifteen hundreds. In other words, you completely negate Ghana, Mali, Songhai, the . . . (Crouch interrupts and says, "No, no, no, that wasn't it." empires, and say that when you make the comparison to European culture, you say, let's be honest and let's be frank, that it wasn't equivalent when we know that wasn't true. I don't understand what sources you are using.

A–(Crouch)–No, the first thing I was talking about was specifically the village cultures that a number of some of our ancestors came from, because Americans, so-called black Americans, have ancestry that is both European, African as well as American Indian, Hispanic etc. So I don't really accept all of that anyway, the whole idea that you may think that you are an African. But I don't think I'm one. I don't think I'm one at all. A part of my ancestry is African, but a part of my ancestry is also Asian, and a part of my ancestry is Choctaw Indian, a part of my ancestry is Chinese. I'm not out here to go with you and simplify the history of my family in order to fall into a simple-minded political category. That is not a realistic picture of who I am.

Q–Okay, first, I would like to say that I've found it very disparaging that you would say someone was muttering Swahili into a walkie-talkie. I think that it was really a disparaging comment and I just want to put that out there. (Crouch interrupts: "But they *were* muttering into a . . . .") No, no, no, because it is your choice of words and what it connotates that I think harkens back to the point the gentleman right before me was bringing to light. Also, I would caution against a simplistic understanding of the economic oppression of African people throughout the world by saying that you know the people at the black power gathering were talking into walkie-talkies, the implications being Africans didn't make the walkie-talkies or the sunglasses they were wearing. I'm just going to put that out there. The point that I want to make, though, is earlier today Selwyn Cudjoe talked about understanding your identity, understanding that you have multiple identities, that they are relative to where you are. It's the question of positionality. I might say I'm from Crown Heights when I'm in Brooklyn. When I'm in Manhattan, I might say I'm from Brooklyn, and when I'm in Nigeria, I'm going to say I'm from the United States. So it is all relative. Anyway, when we talk about being citizens of the world and just understanding ourselves in this individual self, I think we are really undermining the collective experience of African people throughout the Diaspora. I'm not just a medium brown skin woman, you know. What I'm saying, of whatever age, I'm also of a part a larger continuum.

This is the point, really, that I would like to hear addressed on the panel. I know that Marita Golden in her book *Migrations of the Heart* pragmatized some notions of being African American and what that means and doesn't mean as it relates to being African. That's the kind of struggle we need to have; that's the kind of dialogue we need to be engaged in—trying to understand that kind... I want to put that out there. Mine is not so much a question but a comment, and I wanted to raise it. I would like the conversation to get elevated to a point where we are really struggling with our African identities and are trying to understand our universal struggle, trying to extract away from where we position ourselves in that universal struggle. I would like to hear the conversation sort of revolve around those issues rather than about who's wearing sunglasses and muttering Swahili into their walkie-talkie.

(Moderator)–Does anyone want to make a response to that?

A–(Crouch)–They were muttering. Like I said.

A–(Golden)–I think I understand what you're talking about with the sunglasses business, because the implication seemed to be that Swahili was inconsistent with technology. Simply. Now that may not have been what was intended, but that was what I heard, and I think that's what some of the people in the audience also heard. I think that in terms of the question about identity, certainly when I wrote *Migrations of the Heart*, when I lived in Nigeria for almost four years, that was a real question and I think that the solution you come to depends on the mindset that you take with you. I took a mindset that was very romantic. I was in love with an African. I was integrated into an African family and one of the first things that a tropical sun does is, it wilts romanticism very quickly. It burns it to a crisp. Mine got burnt, but at the same time the experience of living in Africa cleared up that burning process, burnt through a lot of illusions, not only about being an African, but about being an American, and what I found out was that I was an African American citizen of the world. The contradictions were endless. For example, I was living in Nigeria and I was teaching at a university. At the age of twenty-seven, I was sitting on the board of directors of a major newspaper, but if I'd been born in Nigeria as a woman, I would have had a clitorectomy. I would not have been sitting on that board of directors. I was only able to do that because there had been a civil rights movement: there had been a black power movement that had enabled me to have these positions. I could not have done those things as easily if I had been an African woman. So the contradictions are endless, absolutely endless, but after three or four years in Nigeria, I was able to come to terms with the contradictions and to simply state that I was an African American citizen of the world, and I embraced the world. I wanted more of the world. I wanted to feast on the world. Sure, I had my heart broken there, but that only made me stronger, so I think that the solution that you come to, wherever you go, whether it's Nigeria or Kenya, a lot of it depends on what you bring with you. I brought an African Afro-centric perspective that was also contradictory feminist, so I put all the contradictions together, and it added up to African American citizen of the world.

Q–This comment is also for Marita Golden whose books I truly admire. My name is Judith White and I'm a psychotherapist in private practice and I particularly like your book *Migrations of the Heart* because you are one of the few black authors that I'm aware of that wrote about the psychotherapeutic experience and talked about, in effect, using the psychotherapeutic experience as a way of enhancing yourself as a woman and as a black person, and I wondered if you could comment a little more about that.

A–(Golden)–I don't know that psychotherapy exactly describes it. What happened was I was trying to write my book. I was blocked, so I went to a therapist and screamed and hollered for about three sessions; then I was able to write my book. Now psychotherapy is something that's much different from that, but I think you are hitting on a very good point, and, in my case, my therapist was a white woman. She was a white woman who said to me, "Look I'm not black, and if you want, you can go to someone who is black who could understand your stress." And I said, "Look I just need to holler, I need to scream, I need to get this shit off my chest," and she let me holler, scream, and then I was able to go home and write my book. So I think the whole question of therapy and counseling is very important. I think that some people may need a race-specific therapist and I think that in our community we need to get, we need to embrace them more than we currently do. I think there's never been a time when we needed to embrace it more. So, thank you for the question.

Q–I would like to address the whole panel on the question of the universality of the black experience. Someone like John Coltrane . . .

at one point in time he was tortured by music in his head. He couldn't necessarily play in the musical systems. He increased the range of the horns he played in order to express what was within him. I think in terms of language, sometimes writers struggle with the actual ability to say what they have to say in a particular language and form, and there have been new forms that have been created within the African American literary traditions, say the blues, and I think, hip hop. The question is, how can we as writers contribute to that struggle to bring those forms into the academy where they can be expressed freely and studied, instead of doing what Europeans have consistently done, which is to call them ignorant and obnoxious? How can we do that while they're existing now within the mouths of the youth, before the next generation comes around and they finally receive the credit? I would like especially to hear from the brothers in reference to that question.

A–(Golden)–How come you don't want to hear from me on that question?

(Q)–Well sister, sister, because . . .

A–(Pearson)–I would just like to say the first thing that came to my mind when you said that was gangster rap. I find it hard to believe that fifty years down the road anyone is going to see any benefit to records calling women bitches and hoes, or guys holding their crotch, or anything of that nature. I think there are a lot of things African Americans engage in, and black people in general engage in that are honorable, and fifty years down the road will be accepted as honorable, but I don't think that everything we're engaging in right now falls in that category.

A–(Golden)–I actually don't have anything to say about that, but I just wanted to clarify that.

A–(James)–I want to suggest there's a program *The Story of English* that went on public television two years ago. The final episode of that was entitled *The Empire Strikes Back*. I was particularly happy about that because of what the man, I forget his name, was discussing. He was pointing out that what has happened to English is that it has gone down to the West Indies. For example, I'm from there and from India and Africa, and in all these places the language has been flattened and made flexible and more malleable, and maybe docile, even. So English is a better language, a more expressive language of the larger world now, because of who talks English or who tries to talk English. For example, my book *Secrets* (I want to talk about that, which everyone has read) has all sorts of unusual usages of English expressions which is what I got acclaimed for, what the reviewers liked. Whoever they were, whatever color they were, they liked that; they appreciated that you could use languages like that. The Caribbean forms of expression in English are now more legitimate because of Naipaul, my work and the work of many other poets in this house. So, I think there's a lot of good happening, not withstanding "the hoe" and "the bitch" and that kind of thing. That is, not all these guys are doing wrong, by the way. I say these young black fellows, and young black women too, even young white people, they are doing something with their language. This is what language is for. You have to work with it; some of it is going to be bad, but it's like looking for nuggets or looking for diamonds. All kind of things turn up, so I support that sort of action.

A–(Crouch)–I think that most of that stuff that you were talking about, the rap material, it's largely just folk material. There may be some day a Jelly Roll Morton, a Louis Armstrong. A Charles Parker type may come along and do with it what Parker and Ellington and other people did with the big folk music that was surrounding them; that is, it was elevated, made more even more plastic, which means it had a greater range of expression that dealt with more complex, emotional dispositions, and was able to speak to both the world of art at large, and its own specific background. My feeling is that no amount of name changes, robes or anything else is going to change us from being who we are, and what we are. We are Americans. Now those of you who actually think you're Africans, I'll say this: Go to Africa. You will find something out very fast. What you will find out is that the term brother or sister is a vast overstatement. Cousins, perhaps, distant, is more realistic, unless you think that there is something about genetics that makes people connected in terms of the way they feel about the world. I don't think that's very true. What I was trying to get at is that we are the result of this extraordinary mixture, and that mixture is visually obvious. You can look in this audience and see that we're a group of people who are the result of an entire spectrum of humanity on the continent of the United States. What we need is, it seems to me, a broad enough body of material that speaks to the vast, vast complexity of the Afro-American experience. One of the things that has been very disturbing to me is the tendency of Afro-Americans to usually whine about something. You almost always have to have an obligatory experience where somebody black is humiliated. Now, for instance, there are guys who represent what Johnny Cochran represents, the world that he's in, the kind of mastery he represents in the court, the kind of mastery that Bill Grey represented on the Congress floor when he was fighting for sanctions against South Africa. There are black people who are mayors of cities across this country. All of that experience, the people who run entire police departments, who work on Wall Street, who do international deals, all of that is part of the black American experience. Usually when somebody picks up a book and it's supposed to be about somebody black, they say we gonna watch somebody get throttled, humiliated, kicked in the booty, heart broken, etc., almost exclusively. Now I'm not arguing with the person that comes from a culture that produced the blues. That does happen in the world, but that's not *all* that happens. I would suggest that once we accept the true richness of our identity from sea to shining sea, from the Canadian border to the Mexican border, we will have a much broader and richer and more complex literature that will speak to far more facts about Afro-American life than just sinking down in the whining propaganda.

Q–My question is addressed to Mr. Crouch. It's interesting to me that in your discussion you talked about the humanism that came out of the Enlightenment. One of the primary forces in the Enlightenment was John Locke who wrote that black people did not have souls at the same time that his wealth, or a significant amount of his wealth, was derived from investing in slave plantations. You also are speaking, espousing the great benefits of democracy when democracy in both ancient Greek and American cultures legally provided for slavery and also for people like Thomas Jefferson who wrote that all men are created equal when at the same time he owned slaves. My question is how is it that you are consistently able to espouse these ideas while ignoring the contradictions and the realities?

A–(Crouch)–Let's say Adolf Sacks was a super racist. That doesn't change what Charlie Parker and them did with the saxophone. That is the point I keep trying to make to y'all, that y'all don't get. If a guy invents the saxophone, and you can create new things with that saxophone and make a greater music that speaks to the world at large. You think that because Adolf Sacks was a racist, every night that Charlie Parker got ready to get up on that bandstand, he said: "I sure would like to go play this saxophone, but you know Adolf Sacks didn't like my folks?" If he did that, he wouldn't have got right up there and done what he did. That's the point I'm making. These guys gave us an instrument and that's the thing. You don't care that if the guys that refined the kind of glasses you have on were rednecks. You gonna still wear them. You don't care if the people who refined the kind of rubber that's in your tennis shoes are racists. You're gonna wear them. People are gonna use what works. I'm not pretending that George Washington and those guys were a bunch of great guys in terms of their racial opinions. I'm talking about the process, the democratic contract that we have been essential to refining and extending beyond its prejudices. They were put in place by those people. And that's just something that can't be . . .

Q–(Person with question interrupts)–Mr. Crouch, you seem to have this serious difficulty with reality. As I recall, Thomas Jefferson and George Washington created a witch system that specifically oppressed black people, and they were legally allowed to do that. Also, you gave an example of Adolf Sacks, and you said if he was a racist, so what? The saxophone does not work against black people, but democracy did, and it was specifically written into the Constitution and it was allowed to do so, so I don't see how your analogy works.

A–(Crouch)–I'm talking about the structure that we were eventually able to influence and change the direction of the science . . .

Q–(Person with question)–We cease being slaves after a war, not after any type of legislative process. Good evening.

Q–My comments are meant to be constructive and I'm directing this to Mr. Crouch. There are several things that I'd like to bring to your attention, but I'm not going to say but three or four of them to you. One, America never had democracy. Secondly, those African peoples who came over here did not come here as slaves; they became slaves when they got here. Thirdly, you see, when we make comparisons there must be similarities. I can't see how we can compare African culture to European culture. And I'm not making a comparison between Paris and fourteenth century and fifteenth century Yoruba bread cultures, or with Songhai and Mali and Timbuktu. I'm talking about civilizations that preceded those by some 5,000 years, that set the stage for the building of classical civilization.

A–(Crouch)–Where are you from? Are you American? Why are you in the United States?

Q–(Person with question)–That does not matter. I am a part of this universe.

A–(Crouch)–But there is something in the United States you like, too, isn't it? That's why you're here in New York.

Q–(Person with question)–Of course.

(Moderator, Gilyard)–I feel like a referee instead of a moderator.

Q–My comment, I guess is like most of ours, is directed to Mr. Crouch. Just really, briefly . . . First off, I think that you should apologize for patronizing us. I think that you are speaking to us like we don't get it. As if we didn't have the ability to understand what you were saying. We're just simply disagreeing with you. The second issue is, I don't understand how you keep connecting this universal thing to Europe. For instance, you said when you were listening to things, saying these things we claim access to, you mentioned Shakespeare and a litany of other people in the European canon. You never said anything like Gabriel García Márquez, or you never said anything like Reed. I'm just saying that *that* is universal. They exist in the universe, and I'm just wondering why you keep telescoping the universe down to Europe.

A–(Crouch)–First point, Gabriel García Márquez writes under the influences primarily of three people: William Faulkner, James Joyce, and Marcel Proust. Now, if you read those three people, you will find that out. Now, the great giants of twentieth century literature are Europeans by and large, and that's the way it is. Now, you may know somebody that's greater than Joyce who's not a European. If so, I want to read him tonight.

(Person interrupts)–Toni Morrison.

A–(Crouch)–Oh, come on. You have got to be joking. Toni Morrison is greater than Joyce? Oh, you haven't had an education.

Q–My question is to Marita as an educator. My name is Thea Davis, and part of why I chose to teach is because I needed to take an angle from which to defend young people and how they can appreciate literature and things of that nature. As a woman and a black woman at a white institution, at a predominantly white institution, does your strength and your drive to continue there come from the universality of the experience of being black, being female, or where do you derive your strength and support in standing strong within that and all the things you have to deal with being black and female within that situation?

A–(Golden) The kinds of feedback that I get from all my students, in particular white students, affirm that standing before the class, I am not only a role model, but the literature that they're reading does have real power in their lives. It's something that allows them to deal with the racism, the sexism, the oh boyism, the cronyism of the traditional historically white or often black institutions. We don't want to talk about historically black institutions, but the atmosphere there is often very oppressive in other ways. But I think that the power of what you are doing as a teacher is what keeps you going. If you had to focus just on your colleagues and the politics, you would quit very quickly. But it's your students and the value of what you are doing, in particular when you're teaching black studies or any course in black studies. The students who take black studies are usually very serious about it, and very dedicated, and that makes the process of teaching that much more fulfilling.

Panel B2

POLITICALLY CORRECT IN A POLITICALLY INCORRECT WORLD

Foreword

Brenda M. Greene

Currently, the term "politically correct" is a loaded and charged term used primarily by the right to critique those on the left and liberals who support public policies such as affirmative action, nondiscriminatory immigration laws, and multiculturalism and who address what Ishmael Reed calls "legitimate grievances." The term, originally symbolic of leftist, Marxist, and feminist thinking, was initially used by those on the left to critique or satirize those who rigidly adhered to communistic or Stalinistic thinking. It later evolved into a term used to reflect that one had a sensitivity for the historical and sociological concerns of certain individuals and groups. It was a way to demonstrate that one was aware of the inherent biases, assumptions, and stereotypes directed towards certain groups. For example, it became "politically incorrect" to call African Americans "Negro" or Asians "Oriental." We were encouraged to use language which took into account the political factors which had been used to name, oppress, and alienate certain groups and individuals. Over the last decade, the term has been appropriated by the right to label groups and individuals whose behaviors the right perceives as dogmatic, opportunistic, and anti-intellectual.

The dilemma of political correctness, faced by black writers in a society socially constructed by race and gender, contextualizes the theme for the essays in this section. These writers and scholars explore the complicated notions of "political correctness" and politics with respect to the black writer and black literature.

Black writers and scholars who write fictional and nonfictional texts that acknowledge, historicize, critique, and validate their personal and collective experiences in this country, texts that reiterate that "race" is inextricably tied to their identity, and texts that defy the norm by representing complex rather than stereotypical characters are labeled "politically correct." Some of the writers who we could place into this category are Toni Morrison, Alice Walker, Ralph Ellison, James Baldwin, Amiri Baraka, Paule Marshall, Bebe Moore Campbell, Toni Cade Bambara, and Charles Johnson. Within this group of "politically correct" writers are two other groups: those labeled essentialists for engaging in what liberals and conservatives call identity politics, and those identified by the white power establishment as voices representative of the black public intellectual. The scholars Molefi Asante, Houston Baker, Cornel West, and Henry Louis Gates Jr. represent this continuum.

Those black writers who choose to write in genres such as the romance novel, science fiction, and fantasy, rather than address themes related to the black experience, and/or advocate policies such as affirmative action, pluralism, and "political correctness," are sometimes challenged for creating texts that do not conform to the notion of "political correctness" as currently defined. Science fiction writers Octavia Butler and Samuel Delaney, and romance novelists Donna Hill and Gwynne Forster are representative of these categories.

The notion of "political correctness" for black writers, thus, addresses the issues and raises questions such as:

1. What does it mean to be politically correct?
2. Who benefits from politically correct texts?
3. Do black writers have a responsibility to be political?
4. What are the historical, social, and political factors that shape black writing in the nineties?
5. Who decides which voices get heard and what stories get told? and
6. What are the rewards, and expenses of being labeled the black intellectual, the representative of the race?

"Political correctness" aside, politics has always influenced black literature. Given the nature of politics in this country, black writers have no choice but to be political. Black literature was formed out of struggle and out of the need to document the experiences of an oppressed people. Phillis Wheatley, the young former slave, begins this trend. She is followed by orators such as David Walker and Frederick Douglass and by academics such as Booker T. Washington and W.E.B.

Du Bois. Black literature soars to a new height during the Harlem Renaissance, and we witness an explosion of the black arts. Writers, musicians, visual artists, and actors respond to their condition in a society which subjects them to all forms of physical and psychological abuse. After participating in the war, many return to face race riots, lynchings, and continuing discrimination. The arts become a way to critique the experiences of blacks in America and to celebrate and tell the story of black culture. We see a second flowering (a term used by Brent Staples in his essay in this chapter to describe the current trend in black literature) of the Black Arts movement in the 1960s. Writers, scholars, and artists of this movement rename themselves and redefine the arts. Motivated by the Civil Rights struggle, they express their rage and call on the white establishment to be accountable for decades of injustice. They become nationalists and political activists and lay the foundation for the literature of many of our contemporary writers and scholars.

Politics continues to be inextricably linked to black literature in the 1990s. Witness the number and kinds of texts that are currently being published and examine the players and power brokers behind the voices we hear and the texts that we read. The mainstream media promotes writers who have cross-over appeal. Those writers and scholars whose representations of blacks are too "politically correct" invite scorn and are rendered invisible. The politics of a situation may be either subtle or overt; it may pertain to the writer or the text, and it plays a role irrespective of whether one writes directly out of the black experience or whether one writes texts which on the surface appear to be raceless.

The first writer in this section, Barbara Christian, argues that we cannot simplify the debate around the notion of "political correctness" for black writers. She contends that black writers may be "politically correct" or "politically incorrect" and that their tendency to be contrary is often more valuable than not. Arthur Flowers, who views the writer as prophet, encourages writers to master their craft, engage in thoughtful analysis, and accept responsibility for being politically conscious and truthful. Thulani Davis continues Flowers' contention that writers should be politically engaged and notes that writers need to be true to themselves and should define the world in their own terms. Ishmael Reed's essay also pays tribute to the politically engaged writer. Reed comments on the politics concerning the structure of the literary establishment and the marginalization of writers because of their "political correctness." Karla FC Holloway closes this section by arguing that a discussion of "political correctness" is really a discussion about the private and public lives of black people. She reminds us of "codes of conduct" inherent in one's culture and represented in the stories one tells. The essays in this section test assumptions and biases regarding "political correctness" and call for black writers to dare to speak the truth.

Politically Incorrect Struggles/Syndromes

Barbara T. Christian

The term *political correctness* is used in so many contexts today that one wonders sometimes if it has any meaning. In this short essay, I want to focus on two uses of the term which are subtly linked precisely because they proceed from two very different, often opposed constituencies. On one hand, the charge of political correctness has been used by writers like Dinesh D'Souza and Allen Bloom against groups such as African Americans, women, gays, etc. These cultural conservatives charge that "marginalized" groups are using politics, rather than intellectual standards, to dominate discourse especially in matters such as educational curricula. On the other hand, the term political correctness has also been used by members of such groups as African Americans, women, gays, to celebrate, critique, some might even say to police writers, artists, thinkers as to what they should discuss and how? At the core of this use of the term is the question: What is the role of the black writer? It is a consistent question throughout the history of the U.S. I want to distinguish between the relevant uses of the term, discuss some aspects of these uses and possibly interrogate the use of the term itself.

In the last decade, political correctness has been a recurring figure of speech in debates about canonicity and mulitculturalism, especially in the fields of history and literature, both in the American popular media and in intellectual and academic journals. It is fascinating to me that in the 1996 edition of *Webster's New World College Dictionary*, the term *political correctness* is listed, probably for the first time, an indication of how pervasive this concept has become in our national psyche. This is the way the term is defined: "conforming or adhering to what is regarded as orthodox liberal opinion on matters of sexuality, race, etc., usually used disparagingly to connote dogmatism, excessive sensitivity to minority causes etc."[1] Note the words, *orthodox, liberal, dogmatism, excessive sensitivity, disparagingly* and how these are related to *minority causes.*

For many cultural conservatives, art, in order to be art, must transcend temporal matters, must be apart from, rather than a part of everyday existence. In contrast, because many African American writers have tended to see their work as having to have some use in present and future worlds, this literature has often been labeled "political," "propagandistic"—characteristics that have had negative overtones in the last one hundred years of the Western conception of art.

Recently, however, some Western thinkers are beginning to celebrate African American literature precisely, and only because its political character, that is, its oppositional character is considered to be its only quality of worth, as if African American culture is *completely* the result of racism, as if African Americans would not have created anything if racism did not exist.

These two one-dimensional perceptions, on one hand that African American Literature is inferior to that of the West's because it has overtly political dimensions; on the other hand that African American literature is valuable only because it has overtly political dimensions, focus almost exclusively on the term, "political," as in the term political correctness, albeit from opposing perspectives, and have become even more rigid as the battles around the so-called Political Correctness Debate and the Canon have intensified.

The distortions that result when the term *political correctness* is used in this debate and is framed in this way can be seen in books such as D'Souza's widely disseminated *Illiberal Education* (1991). D'Souza asserts that those deemed "other" in this society—blacks, people of color, feminists, gays, the left, poststructuralists—are attempting to take over educational institutions for their own purposes and are not at all interested in education, standards, or ideas. Almost as apocalytic in its rhetoric, another widely commented-on book, *The Disuniting of America* (1992) by the celebrated liberal historian, Arthur Scheslinger, Jr., sounds the alarm that multicultural education will fragment our country for there will not be a unifying narrative that joins us all. Rather, the country will disintegrate into fragmented populations, opposed to each other.

The way in which these books frame the debate assumes that there is no intellectual worth to African Americans or any other American people of color culture; that, in fact, these cultures are a *political* fabrication; that there has been a monolithic culture, a unifying narrative until the cultural heathens of the last decade dared to threaten the body politic. "Political" becomes a narrowly defined concept in this debate, primarily used in the way that *politicians* use it, that is, as a way of acquiring power for the sake of power. In that sense of the word, *political* means something dirty, rather than referring to the power dynamics at work in our society.

But if one knows how educational curricula, *the* literary canon developed in this country, it is clear that it is tied to a particular nation state's sense of that which is considered philosophically and aesthetically important. Curricula and canons change according to changes in perception about the national character. The content of canons, curricula, then, is decidedly affected by the nation state's definition of itself, and, thus, has always been partially determined even by the narrow definition of political as well as by that abstract term, intellectual concerns. In fact, the political realm and the intellectual realm are hardly two discrete realms. When one looks at the debate about the American literary canon in the latter half of the twentieth century in this way, then one can see why there is such furious rhetoric. What is at stake is the meaning of terms like *culture, American* and *Western*. Who is considered an American and who is not, determines standards of the good and the beautiful. Ironically, as Martin Berube points out in his comprehensible, witty essay, "Public Image Limited: Political Correctness and the Media's Big Lie":

> For all the talk about "the West," the debate over canons gets most poisonous when it's conducted about American literature—partially because the canon of American literature has been redrawn substantially every 30 or 40 years since it was solidified in the late 19th century (when it was conceived to be a moral representation of the Puritan national spirit) and partially because Americans have something of a history of debating what "American means."[2]

It is no accident that the charges of "political correctness" coming primarily from the Right have amplified to a deafening level during the last decade when threats of "the browning of America" are being responded to by politicians and conservative intellectuals alike. To use a phrase from the African American legal scholar Patricia Williams, the negative use of the term "political correctness" is "rhetorical robbery" in the struggle for cultural property. As she points out, "it is a calculated evaluation of political property values no less than the 'white flight' organized by the National Association of Realtors a few decades ago, which left us with the legacy of 'the inner city.'"[3] This comes at a time when "hate" language is increasingly boisterous on American campuses, and fraternities can put on a mock lynching as a "supposedly" meaningless prank. That charges of "political correctness" are being fought out in the area of humanities and canon formation, rather than in more overtly recognized political arenas, is, if nothing else, a indication that while it may appear that literature may be a luxury, it is central to the ethos of our society because it is powerful as cultural property, and the struggle over cultural property is as critical as that over economic property.

I have just briefly sketched the first meaning of "political correctness" as it is being used by cultural conservatives on the Right today. That their use of the term connects "minority causes" to words such as "dogmatism," "excessive sensitiveness," and "orthodox" is linked to the second use of the term that I want to discuss. What should be the role of the black writer? I want to focus on two variations on the theme of "political correctness" within African American discourse.

I think about the many times when the black people I've talked with in the streets, at book clubs, and on planes, have literally begged for what they call "positive images." It is practically a refrain. For example, why did Alice Walker in *The Color Purple* hang our dirty laundry for all to see? How will that affect our status as a race in this hostile United States? Why does Toni Morrison write about such painful issues? Why are writers presenting problems; why aren't they presenting solutions? Interestingly, these observations usually occur in Black History Month when black people want to be celebrated.

The other aspect of African American political correctness focuses on the split between what is called "the political" and "the aesthetic." As I was working on this essay, I happened to read Charles Johnson's review of Albert Murray's new collection of essays, *The Blue Devils of Nada: A Contemporary American Approach to Aesthetic Statement*. Johnson begins his review by stating that:

> At this troubling juncture in American literary criticism, when too many discussions of black writing substitute a myopic emphasis on issues of race or sex for a truly sophisticated understanding of the integrative dimensions of the creative process, I hope that the publication of a new novel and a collection of essays by Albert Murray will be cause for widespread celebration.[4]

These two issues—blacks' desire for positive images and the apparent split between the political and the aesthetic—are not just contemporary ones; they have a basis in history. Black literate people have, since the 19th century, desired positive literary images and resisted what they thought were negative ones about their culture. One need only note the black press's response to Richard Wright's *Native Son;* to Claude McKay's picture of "low life" in *Home to Harlem* (the first black best-seller); W. E. B. Du Bois' doubts about Langston Hughes' portrayal of black folk life; Alain Locke's questions about *Their Eyes Were Watching God,* Zora Neale Hurston's folktale about the rural South, which was published at a time when blacks were to be portrayed as moving into the urban modernist narrative; or *Incidents in the Life of a Slave Girl,* Harriet Jacobs' 19th century exposé about black female sexuality in slavery; or more recently, reactions to Audre Lorde's explicitly black lesbian poetry. In each of these cases, black people "worried" about white people's reactions to "negative images" and desired what they considered to be positive representations of cultural expressions.

What was considered to be a "positive image" of black womanhood when Harriet Jacobs wrote her narrative in 1861? William Wells Brown's *Clotel* (1853), the first novel to be published in this country by a black person, is the story of a light skinned, aristocratic, Christian heroine and includes scathing comic representations of dark-skinned bandanna-wearing coon-talking black women. Wells Brown's representation of these two classes of black women, one positive, the other negative, or at least not to be taken seriously, was partially constructed for the sake of a worthy cause, the Abolitionist Movement. These images had little relationship to the majority of slave or free black women of the time. Though Wells Brown had good intentions and was serving a worthy cause, his representations have haunted black people for over a century, circumscribing the ability of dark-skinned, clearly unaristocratic women to get their story told or published. William Wells Brown helped the abolitionist cause by presenting a positive image, a black woman who fit the norms of white womanhood in the 19th century. Or if we were to investigate the literary debates of the 1920s, we would have to confront what we now would consider the conservative attitudes of W. E. B. Du Bois and the magazine *Crisis* towards writers like Langston Hughes. Yet Du Bois' *Crisis* helped to radicalize black Americans returning from World War I even as Langston Hughes' *Manifesto* that younger black artists did not care whether they please white people or black people, resulted in some of the finest writing of this century.

The tendency to reduce black debates into either/or, either against or for the "revolutionary position" of the day, or more precisely U.S. society's, including the literary establishment's tendency to fix blacks as being only one thing, is reflected in the continuing debate in black writing circles as to what is the proper role of the writer. In the review that I mentioned earlier, Charles Johnson refers to that debate when he comments that: "Inevitably, he [Murray] is at odds with black writers whose work is written to illustrate some very special (and often very narrow) political theory, or ideology of blackness, or to promote some special political program."[5] Writers like Murray, Ralph Ellison, and, to a certain extent, Charles Johnson have felt themselves under attack from some who consider these writers to be literary nationalists. Yet Murray's aesthetics refers to the *very important fact* that African Americans have written to express the forms, vitality, and philosophical tradition of their own culture, which has its roots in Africa but which has also been influenced by other cultures—European, Native American, Asian American—in this crucible called American culture.

As is true of all other cultures, African American culture is concerned with self knowledge and group definition and represents modes of knowing/feeling that include opposition to the systems by which people of African descent have been oppressed but *not vanquished* by the racism of the West. Though intersecting with resistance to racism, African American culture, from Murray's point of view, would exist without racism. This, of course, is not the first time that that point had been made. That was one of the central tenets of the radical aesthetics of younger writers of the Harlem Renaissance such as Langston Hughes. The assumption that is often made is that if aesthetics is one of the writer's main concern, then political resistance is not; if overtly political ideology is central to a writer's work, then that work somehow cannot be concerned with aesthetics.

Let me give an example. Central to Murray's aesthetics is the attention an artist gives to "ancestral imperatives," that is, the writer's deliberate choice of mentors. I expect that an author whose writing Murray would see as "illustrat[ing] some very special (often very narrow) political theory, or ideology of blackness or to promote some special political program" might be Alice Walker's works— in this case, her special political program might be called the womanist agenda. Yet, ironically, Walker was throttled in black presses all over the country not for lack of aesthetics, but for her exposure of racism and sexism in the novel *The Color Purple*, a novel which very much focuses on those "predecessors" Murray writes so passionately about. For in using black folk English, by "stylizing . . . the idiomatic particulars of everyday life into aesthetics," to use Murray's words, Walker both recuperated and revised not only her own personal biological ancestors but also her maternal literary ancestor, Zora Neale Hurston, in her novel, *Their Eyes Were Watching God*. And if there is any other contemporary writer who has reached out to literary predecessors from many different cultures, male as well as female, it is Walker, an example being the epigraph of her second collection of short stories, a quotation from the great German poet, Rilke.

A writer like Alice Walker might claim that Albert Murray is not giving sufficient value to one of the central themes, not only of the African American literary tradition, but of most great literary traditions—that is, that writers have always been concerned with the exposure of that which inhibits human potential and through language actively seek to liberate that human possibility. That, in the deeper and richer sense, they do write from a sense of social values. Yet, without question, the concerns that Murray expresses about aesthetics are central to the definition of African American literature.

The point is that writers' tendency to be contrary is valuable to us precisely because they insist on thinking the unthinkable, on speaking the unspeakable and on moving us beyond our familiar construct of thinking/feeling to another level of creativity. Writers, whether they are perceived as "aesthetes" or "political" tend to be "politically incorrect," tend to resist that which is comfortable, that which is the status quo.

What then of standards? As Toni Morrison has so often pointed out, black people have very high standards of art, as exemplified by their relationship to their music. As any music lover knows, what is good about a piece of music has much to do with how well you understand how its style and content are not separable but irrevocably linked, so that standards for that piece are not based on exterior impositions on it but on those that are organic to it. That construct of standards does not mean some kind of relative sloppiness, but that one pays close attention to what that piece of music is trying to do and is doing.

The irony of the term, "politically incorrect," is that it rests on the assumption that attention to and analysis of "political" matters automatically means orthodoxy and restrictiveness in thought and craft. Yet the first use of the term that I discussed, the way in which cultural conservatives have attacked what they call "the dogmatism" of those different in the society is intended to stifle, that is, to restrict the protests coming from these groups. In other words, some people's orthodoxy is other people's protest. Often I think the debate, for example, as to which writers are perceived as being "political" or "aesthetic," has more to do with what is favored by the publishing industry this year as to what is appropriately black literature, than it has to do with any intrinsic argument about the relative worth of the writings themselves. Thus, the debates in African American literary circles as to what is the proper role of the black writer are also influenced by the national concerns about American art and culture and who owns that culture.

In celebrating and critiquing writers in this tradition, I think we need to acknowledge that there are many strands of the tradition, that African American literature does not mean only protest, or style, or folk narrative, or literary density, or overt liberation narratives, or a celebration of grace under pressure that the blues denote, or elegance, etc. It can be each of these and all of these. For me, it is crucial that we locate our biases and where we stand as we relate to the writing. It is crucial that we understand the impact of the writing of our deeply held beliefs as well as the impact of our deeply held beliefs on how we view that writing. We need politically incorrect readers as much as we need politically incorrect writers. And we also need those who think and feel deeply about what they read.

Notes

1 *Webster's New World College Dictionary* (New York: Macmillan Press, 1996) 1045.

2 Martin Berube, "Public Image Limited: Political Correctness and the Media's Big Lie," *The Village Voice*, June 18, 1991: 31–37.

3 Patricia Williams, *The Rooster's Egg: The Persistence of Prejudice* (Cambridge: Harvard UP, 1995) 28.

4 Charles Johnson, "Keeping the Blues at Bay," *The New York Times Book Review* 10 March 1996: 4.

5 Johnson 4.

Big Nommo: The Writer as Prophet

Arthur Flowers

I am Flowers of the Delta clan Flowers and the line of John O. Killens. It is for me a great honor to once again be at the Medgar Evers National Black Writers Conference. I very much enjoy being part of this recurrent gathering of scribes in the House of Life. This is the fourth one, and each one has been evocative and significant and even more so as we approach the millennium. I think history shall one day judge them seminal.

When I realized though, that I had been put on the political panel, I wondered: Is this a compliment or have I been dissed? We political folk tend to be defensive; people accuse us of being unsophisticated, artistically challenged, strident, fascists with pens, and we often feel unappreciated.

Witness the subheading of this panel—"Is there still a role for the politically conscious writer?" I, of course, think so, else I would not be one. I think there will always be space for the politically engaged writer. We are a fundamental component of the human condition. In fact, I like to think we are both the consciousness and the conscience of the human race.

I am political in part because I aspire to be one of the world's great writers. I aspire to historical stature and significance. Many of our great writers have been literary activists. This is, in part, because we are a culture under siege and our really great voices are expected to speak out in our name: folks like Langston and Zora and Douglass and Du Bois. Our culture in return has always valued its committed writers.

There has always been tension in black literature between art for art's sake and those who believe in art as a social force and attempt to wield that force. The committed writer is conscious of the power of the word. The Word. The almighty and sacred word. The primary vehicle of communication. Words are powerful things. We communicate with others through words. We respond to words. We define ourselves and our world through words. Words cause people to act, to do, to be. Here is the core of the writer's power, Nommo, the ability to use the magic of words to forge reality.

The word, like any power, is amoral. Words can be and often are used to enslave, to move people away from a true understanding of their condition, but the word at its best is a tool of human evolution, used to expand the human horizon, enhance the human condition, free the human soul and allow it to soar.

Consciousness is a function of words, knowing and using them. A person in ignorance is truly enslaved, bound. Literacy itself is an act of freedom; it ennobles the mind and makes you a functioning member of an increasingly complex society. That's why tyrants burn books and slavemasters deny slaves the right to read and write. Literature frees the imagination. Without imagination there would be no achievement, no dreams, no vision of what could be, of just how high we can fly as individuals, families, communities, and as a people.

Literature is a primary force in shaping human society and evolution, a time honored means of touching people's lives. Literature opens minds and passes on ideas. For instance, Marcus Garvey was highly influenced by a book by Casley Hayford, *Ethiopia Unbound*, from which he extracted, among others, the phrase, "One God, One People, One Destiny." In turn, Marcus Garvey influenced thousands, if not millions of blackfolk, and the historical dynamics of his times. The ramifications of Garvey's legacy still resonate, so imbedded in the tribal soul that it shall continue to influence our destiny for the foreseeable future.

This happens to some degree every time a reader is touched by your work. Literature allows folks to see themselves and their lives in a new perspective. Literature can blow your mind. It's like that quote that says, "When you open a person's mind, it never goes back to its previous dimensions." It's opened forever to greater understanding of this infinite mystery—life. And the more you understand, the more conscious you are, the freer you are.

Literature (especially sacred literature) is a primary instrument of cultural retention, of a culture selecting what it feels to be pertinent to the survival and prosperity of its generations. Culture is itself a tool by which significant survival information is passed from generation to generation, and it is the writer who observes, chooses, shapes and expresses the ideas that determine a culture's evolution. It is the writer, by definition, who forges the visions that will enable generations to meet the evolutional changes to come, and to shape the contribution of our culture to the worldspirit. We are mythmakers all, consciously evolving old tribal myths and forging new ones as necessary. At best, the committed writer is a prophet, the epitome of the word as power, using the literary vision to peer as far into the future as possible, determining the challenges that the tribe will have to face and preparing the tribal soul to meet them. Trying to impart what is good and useful into it. Trying to extract what is not. The committed writer is shaman, guardian of the tribal soul, guardian of the tribal destiny.

The person who has most influenced my understanding of the writer's responsibility has been John O. Killens. It was John O. who taught me the divine responsibility of the word. In my youth I wanted to be a Machiavellian thinker. Power was my thing. I was running hardgame. People were factors to be manipulated and this was reflected in my work. One day, John O. pulled me aside and said, "Arthur, you are a brilliant writer, but with a little compassion you could be profound."

I didn't get it then; brilliant was cool with me. It was only much later that I realized John was trying to make sure that my contribution, my legacy as a writer, his student, would not be a hard, cold one but one that was warm and loving and nurturing. An old shaman trying to keep the tribal soul healthy.

The committed writer understands the role that writers and literature play in shaping and ameliorating the human condition and feels that it behooves us all to strive always to make it a better world for everybody. Writers are creators, God's assistants on earth. Your works are a legacy for future generations, and you should be very conscious of what you want that legacy to reflect. This legacy is the immortal you, the mythmaker's greatest myth.

John O. not only taught us how to write but how to be writers. To understand both the power and the responsibility. He tried to nurture within us the soul of a writer.

We black writers who feel called upon to be a voice of the people have unique challenges. First, as must any would-be writer, the committed writer must master craft. Folks going to want to diss your work anyway, so you have to be a fierce craftsperson. John O. used to tell us, "The more that what you have to say is important, the more obligated you are to say it well."

As a committed writer, you must strive always to have a sophisticated understanding of the way of things. You should not be shallow in your thinking and your analysis. You should be serious, highminded and bighearted and tolerant of other visions. You should not let yourself become a narrow, parochial thinker. You should be the best that you can be, always willing to grow, to accept responsibility, to be a worthy writer, to have a worthy vision.

And you must be prepared to pay dues, to accept the cost of being politically conscious. You may not get as much play as folks who don't threaten the status quo. Being a committed writer may cost you in the short run but you aspire to legacy. The generations shall call your name with pride.

The committed writer, passionate in position, must also avoid demagoguery, playing to the passions of the mob. This weakens us instead of strengthening us. You must speak to the truesoul of the race, tattered though it may be. The generations can only love the voices who call us to our very best. The voices of our greatest dreams.

More than anything, as a committed writer, you must be willing at all times to speak when called. There will be times when you may have to walk alone. Black, white, yellow, brown or indifferent, it has always been dangerous to be a writer who speaks truth to power, to manifest the prophetic function of the word. Socrates was made to drink hemlock. Galileo recanted when threatened with being burned at the stake. Rushdie got fatwa'd, Martin Luther King Jr. had to say Vietnam was wrong, Ida B. Wells was run out of Memphis, David Walker was found dead in the streets. And what was on Sojourner Truth's mind when she named herself so? Or on the minds of slaves like Frederick Douglass who risked torture and their lives to learn how to read, who somehow knew the word was a magic that would literally free them from bondage? Why did Malcolm X speak out against the Nation's cultic leadership when he knew it could cost him his life? Wole Soyinka had to leave Nigeria in the dead of the night because he dared declare that the generals had no clothes. At least he got away. Saro Wiwa didn't.

Ken Saro Wiwa, your words shall not be in vain.
Ken Saro Wiwa, we shall sing your praise.

At his show trial, Saro Wiwa said if they can treat me like this with my international rep, think of how they treat people who have no voice. Black literature at its best has never been afraid to be the progressive voice of the people. To speak when called. Granted, in the United States if you don't go along with the program, you don't get jailed or executed. You just don't get paid, which is, of course, for some of us an even more terrible punishment.

The committed writer strives to expose the dynamics that affect our lives and our political condition in such a way as to make them handle-able, so that folks better understand the challenges of life, liberty and the pursuit of happiness and are able to develop effective, empowering responses to its trials and tribulations, its challenges and opportunities.

Those of us who feel the obligation to be cultural custodians, who try to keep the culture healthy and growing, evolving and nurturing our generations, and who yes, sometimes rant when raising the alarm, may often fumble, but by the seven powers, we are trying to live up to our responsibilities as writers. We care. We understand that our well-being, both personally and professionally, is intimately bound up with the well-being of the culture we represent and is a part of the culture that has nurtured us and our visions as writers. We see no contradiction in the nationalist and the universal worldview. If your sensibility as a person and a writer is comprehensive and cosmic enough, you become part of the world canon.

Historically, significant writers always operate out of a canon and contribute to it. As an African American writer, I operate out of two cultures, American and African, both components of the world canon, the worldspirit. I distinctly remember the point in my literary development when I consciously made the decision that our culture was a valid member of the worldspirit, with a contribution to the human mosaic worthy of any other, and I have since devoted my life and works to its nurturement and evolution. I chose to contribute my lifework to the strength of that culture and defend it against those who would cripple and destroy it.

As the voices of a culture under siege from both the basic stresses of life and hostile/competitive forces who consider our weakness their strength, we feel a certain pressure to be responsible and effective cultural forces. Because we are skilled cultural custodians, conscious of the relationship between the health of the culture (the tribal soul) and our concrete conditions as a people, we feel obligated to use our skills and cultural resources to nurture the strong, vibrant culture we need to survive and prosper. This function becomes all the more pertinent as we approach the millennium. Black folks, and consequently black writers, 'bout to go through some mighty rough water.

Black literature has always reflected what the culture and the people were going through. Previous renaissances, such as the Harlem Renaissance or the Black Arts Movement, were periods of political ferment and social transformation. In response to the assault of the right wing and our pressing internal challenges, blackfolks are about to experience a period of political mobilization and transformation as never before, and the literature shall reflect it. Gon be some trying times y'all and it is our job to both record and channel it.

What we calling Renaissances are merely highpoints on the continuum. However, there are factors that make this particular one interesting. One, we have a better literary infrastructure this time; we are not as totally dependent on the cultural powers that be. There is a greater degree of sophistication about the process of literary success. There is a black book buying public; black books sell well generically, got a few good people in the halls of power, strong alternative publishing and distribution systems, thinkers struggling with issues pertinent to our times, some strong mature literary voices and some good young talent in training. We in pretty good shape, all things considered.

True, there be true challenges facing African American literature. Some facing literature in general, such as consolidation of the industry and marginalization by new media, and some that are specific to black literature, such as institutionalization, empowerment, forging a vision for the millennia, and refocusing a Movement hijacked by mercenary conservatives and rabid fundamentalists. Still and all, there is a pretty good chance this renaissance will leave us in a good position for when the pendulum swings again, as it always does.

But true success or failure will be determined by the legacy we leave future generations. What will our works say to and for our times? What are the issues that we are wrestling with? What ideological instruments will be forged to finesse them? I say the question of the 21st Century will be one of empowerment, both political and spiritual. You, of course, may see it differently. Whatever it is, it shall be we—the writers, thinkers and cultural orchestrators—who shall be at the forefront of this struggle to once again redefine ourselves, our vision, our destiny as a people, and our contribution to the worldspirit, to the cosmic way.

The millennium y'all, I think we can turn it out. We did all right with the 20th Century, just one generation out of slavery. We did okay. And I'm an incurable optimist. I just don't see us losing. We've never lost. Lord knows it's gon be a struggle now, and though our challenges seem sometimes insurmountable, we must remember they have always been insurmountable—slavery, southern peonage or urban sojourners—our struggle has always been epic and we have always overcome.

As to the future of committed writers, not to worry. Folks will always need us. We are the triumphant voice of the culture. We are shield and spear.

Art versus politics? Nationalist versus universal? Don't see these as real problems. A true writer must speak for all God's creation and I'm comfortable with human contradiction. Room for all kinds of voices even within, all kinds of songs. I remember once remarking to Aishah Rahman that I wanted to be the greatest novelist that ever lived. She said, "No, Art, that's not what you want. You want to sing your song the best you can sing it. That way you can appreciate other folks singing theirs."

What works for me doesn't necessarily work for all writers. No writer should let agendas determine what he or she writes. Writers must write about what really moves them or they have no voice. Writers must speak to what's true to their hearts. And this is what's true to mine: I love being in the game. I love being a skilled ideological orchestrator. What am I supposed to do, go through life without playing when I see the game in play?

I've often thought about how glad I am to be a black writer in these days and times, 'cause I believe writers need a passion, a mission, to really achieve their best. And black writers, we born with a cause.

The power of the word is both a blessing and a curse. It is a burden I carry with pride and I would hope, with some dignity. I honor no one as I honor writers throughout history who have used the word as a tool of freedom, who have striven to free the human soul no matter what, folks like Saro Wiwa, Ida B. Wells, and David Walker, folks like Toni Cade, Doris Jean Austin, John O. Killens and the folks on this panel, my fellow travelers, we who care. I love being a committed writer and I assume that there will always be a place for the likes of me.

You never know when truth comes calling and you must answer. Sometimes society needs to hear the very best truth you can give them.

Why do tyrants quake when writers speak? Because a writer's word means something. Because people trust you to care for them and to speak when they need a voice. Because all the world expects a writer to be a writer, a master of the word in the most grand and glorious sense of the word. Somebody who cares.

Nommo is a Dogon word. It refers to the power of the word to shape reality. It is a magic that we, all of us here, all humanity, possess.

As I define so shall it be
Be I then worthy of I gift
That is all
Ase.

In Our Own Terms

Thulani Davis

There are many questions raised for us to deal with and I was captured by the notion of answering and asking the question again, "Do we have responsibility?" In other words, are we really trying to ask the question of whether political issues and political responsibilities are reflected in the work now, as in times in the past? I'm going to start by reading a list of works that were made from 1959 to 1971. During that period we are said to have been producing an enormous amount of politically conscious work. It's a period, I think, against which all conscious writers are nowadays compared. I have been told to my face that I'm a relic of the '60s and that political engagement is a passion only for my generation. I think this politically conscious work sets a standard to live up to and develop further. So I want to read this list because I do think there is some mythologizing about the past, and I will make a couple of comments, and I will be short.

In 1959, Lorraine Hansberry had a play produced called *Raisin in the Sun*. In 1961 James Baldwin published *Nobody Knows My Name.* In 1962, Baldwin put out *Another Country* and Adrienne Kennedy had a production of *Funny House of a Negro*. In 1963, Baldwin released *The Fire Next Time;* in 1964, Martin Luther King Jr. published "Letter from a Birmingham City Jail." Also in 1964, Amiri Baraka, then Leroi Jones, had a production of *Dutchman,* Lorraine Hansberry produced *A Sign in Sidney Brucestein's Window*, and James Baldwin had a production of *Blues for Mr. Charlie*. In 1965, Claude Brown published *Manchild in a Promised Land; The Autobiography of Malcolm X* followed Malcolm's death, and Baldwin released *Going to Meet the Man*. In 1966, Lorraine Hansberry finished *Les Blancs*. In 1967, John A. Williams published *The Man Who Cried I Am*. In 1968, Amiri Baraka and Larry Neal produced an anthology called *Black Fire*. In 1968, Ed Bullins and Larry Neal produced the summer issue of *The Drama Review* which opened with Bullins's reflections on the death of Martin Luther King, Jr. and Larry Neal's manifesto of the Black Arts Movement. Eldridge Cleaver published *Soul on Ice*. In 1969, Toni Morrison published *The Bluest Eye* followed in 1970 by Maya Angelou's *I Know Why the Caged Bird Sings*.

These are the major works of that period. They are the works of ten writers and three full-time activists. Nine of them are still alive and some of them are in this room. You could ask them if they think that kind of phenomenon is ever going to happen again. It was an extraordinary period. It is the period I came up in; I was a student of this literature. This is the literature that made me who I am. I don't think that's going to happen again, and yet the present is often critiqued by that standard. But there is something we should pay attention to in what was happening there. The commitment of these people had an impact larger than the life's work of most published writers. It is incredible to me that these people were able to do something that people can toil for forty or fifty years and not achieve. And that is not only to get readers, and they have readers, generations of readers now, but to have students. They have followers, believers and people like myself who hope to do a small share of work in this tradition.

During that time, there were hundreds of other writers published whose names I have not mentioned (some of whom are no longer published). They were printed by organizations with the names *Negro Digest, Broadside Press, Culture Press, Da Sein, Jupiter Hammond Publishers, The Journal of Black Poetry, Liberator, Umbra* and many others. And while we do have small presses now, most of the organizations I've named no longer exist. They have all paid a price as black writers joined the mainstream marketplace in such big numbers. So there's always a tension between what we do in the community (where the work is often first heard and printed), and what happens, as with integration, when we step into the mainstream.

Throughout the century, there has always been a tension for black creative minds between whether we were going to try to work in the middle of the great American stream or whether we were going to keep alive those black-run institutions which actually sit on the margins of this society. I now have come to understand that those institutions which sit on the margins need to be maintained and protected. That is what politically engaged writers also do, often out of necessity, to keep the work alive. I'm going to give an example from show business.

Bob Cole and Jay Rosamond Johnson were composers and lyricists. They also danced, acted; they did everything it takes to make a show. They started creating musical shows in the 1890s. They were part of a group of people who attempted to destroy minstrelsy. Everybody in the group was a minstrel; that's how they made their living. But Cole and Johnson had this idea that they could take minstrelsy down. At the beginning of the century, they were kicked out of Broadway theaters and went to Harlem. After the end of World War I, some of these people who had been doing shows in Harlem, at the Lafayette Theater and all, decided that they could take jobs with the Ziegfeld Follies. So while on Broadway they had begun to be popular and enter the mainstream and then they became a separate black theater movement.

And so from about 1907 to 1917 or 18, there were no black people on Broadway. All of that work went to Harlem and continued to thrive. The people from Broadway came to Harlem and bought all the music for those shows, took it back downtown, gave it to white performers and the music went on. Then they joined Ziegfeld. That is part of our legacy. Jay Rosamond Johnson said late in his life in the 1960s, "Seeing what we were doing then, you know, I think we made a big mistake to go straight to the mainstream. We lost our black theaters at that time." So I just want to say that really for our work to survive, both are necessary: the mainstream allows the widest distribution of the work, but it will not demand of us the most difficult and extraordinary work.

The period of the 1960s was extraordinary because so many poets and playwrights, whose names have now faded from view, were published by small presses and journals. It is extraordinary because this baker's dozen of authors had an impact that most writers never have in a lifetime. In general, though, the period also falls into the larger pattern of rises and ebbs that characterizes our history in the arts. When great movements of social change take place, usually most of us are in the midst of dealing with it rather than writing about it. The literature of such a period comes almost as the social movements wind down.

In the periods of great social change, such as during the World Wars, popular culture came to the fore, whether it was Vaudeville and Cakewalk or the Lindyhop and the Nicholas Brothers. This was true in the 1960s too, an era we also remember for the sounds of Motown. The '60s was the decade of a highly produced rhythm and blues, a decade's worth of highly sophisticated, universally appealing, but definitely soulful, sociable music that was itself very slow to become socially engaged. Just to take it a bit further, Stevie Wonder had to leave Motown to make records that mentioned Vietnam and criticized national leadership. Marvin Gaye had to figuratively break arms to make "What's Going On" in 1971. It was really during the '70s that experimentation took place in every black art form, creating the development of avant-garde movements in dance, music, literature, theater and film. In the '80s and '90s, we've seen the publication of some true master works. We have seen the loss of other writers in mid-career and the growth of a market for our work. The market has opened to a wider view of the black experience. The market is always looking for new product. Right now we are the new products for an industry that is anxious to find new buyers.

In every era there has been protest art and politically correct art, and there has always been literature and art that were not explicitly concerned with the issues of the day. Some black art has been slyly subversive, coded and now looks more like protest work than it once did. Some work has been just for the moment, just for the laughs, or just for the books. What was extraordinary in the '60s was the political focus these writers brought to the rest of us. What is extraordinary now is the number of works being published, not necessarily their content or message. This phenomenon is appealing, highly produced, and soulful. The industry has created a kind of literary Motown. I am going to be proud to have been part of that, and I am going to still keep my eye out for those works which step out and try to make the statement: The What's Going On of the '90s and 2000s. Larry Neal wrote in that 1968 issue of *The Drama Review*: "The Black Arts Movement is radically opposed to any concept of the artist that alienates him from his community." That still makes sense to me. Do I think we should tell artists how to express their responsibility to the community? No. Are we going to tell Ishmael Reed what to do? Are we going to tell Toni Morrison what to write? Are we going to tell Terry McMillan what to write? I hold up as models also, some people from other cultures who share our understanding, people like Salman

Rushdie who stands for the importance of writers being contrary, independent thinking and speaking about oppression, about the human condition.

In the words of Larry Neal, "A main tenet of black power is the necessity for black people to define the world in their own terms." Is that still necessary? Absolutely. Particularly, if you're a writer. We have to create the world and the language will sustain us and still one day be appropriated. You continually have to create new language in order to maintain that ability to make definitions. The last line Neal wrote, I will put to you to answer for yourselves: "If art is the harbinger of future possibilities, what does the future of black America portend?"

"Fourth Renaissance" Art Is Muted Art

Ishmael Reed

The hemisphere's first protest literature was played on drums. Africans spoke many different and complex languages, and the drums were able to unite Africans of many different backgrounds by using the tonal part of the African vocabulary to transmit messages. Drums and instruments, like the conch horn, were used to summon revolt in South America and the Caribbean. The Africans in these parts of the hemisphere also successfully maintained their cultures. One reason given is that the Catholic pantheon was consistent with that found in African religion: one god and a bevy of Saints. The Catholic church in Cuba, for example, tolerated African religion as long as its practitioners came to Mass and, as a result, African religion has millions of followers throughout this hemisphere and the younger generation of writers and intellectuals in this country have revived these traditions, a phenomenon that I anticipated with my Neo-hoodoo Manifesto, which, at the time when it was written, in 1969, was ridiculed by missionaries posing as critics. In the recent film *Love Jones*, about the lives of Buppie bohemians living in Manhattan, a young poet invokes Yemoja and Oshun, "saints" of the Yoruba pantheon.

African religion in the United States is also being buttressed by the arrival of immigrants from the Caribbean. Obviously, the older African American modernists, the late Ralph Ellison and the writer the New York Literary Establishment has appointed as his successor, Albert Murray, and their younger followers, who believe that African Americans are an exclusively western people with no memory of their original cultures, are wrong. A similar debate is being waged in the Chinese American community, and Frank Chin, one of the participants, argues that to say that a diaspora community forgets its culture is like saying that when Anglo immigrants arrived in this hemisphere they forgot Shakespeare.

But the Africans in the United States have had much more difficulty in maintaining their cultures under the domination of armed Protestants who have traditionally been anxious about African American art, an anxiety that is sometimes expressed though repeated attempts to suppress African American popular culture, just as drumming was outlawed in previous times. Obviously there's something about potent black culture that gets under the Yankee skin, unless it's watered down by imitators like Elvis Presley or by white writers who've been congratulated for their ability to write in a Jazz style by critics like Michiko Kakutani, who once wrote that black men treated black women the way that the slavemasters treated blacks, but, who, as far as I know, has never commented about Japanese American misogyny.

I think that it's interesting that Henry Louis Gates, Jr., who advocates an African American art that would make its consumers less anxious, is also a critic who recently came under fire from African American scholars for using the term "VooDoo Scholarship," in an obvious attempt to ridicule African religion. This is the same Henry Louis Gates, Jr., who wrote a brilliant work, tracing African American literary styles to their African origin. I believe that his "Fourth Renaissance" essay in the October, 1994 issue of *Time* Magazine was not only an attempt to sell an African American art that would be acceptable to the so-called "mainstream," chiefly white feminists, but it is an essay written by a critic in crisis. Gates is on a roll, as a result of the patronage which resulted from his demagogic attack on African Americans as anti-Semites, and now, with his right-wing speeches, and cliché sermons against black social pathology, he has found a constituency as diverse as the Pacifica Foundation (as a result of his attacks on Louis Farrakhan), *U.S. News and World Report*, *Forbes* and The American Enterprise Institute, an organization so far right that two black conservatives resigned over the organization's support for Dinesh D'Souza's neo-Nazi attack on African-American culture, *The End of Racism*.

The *Gates* renaissance article for *Time* was a blatant example of bottom line criticism in which Gates seemed to be saying that we judge art on the basis of what sells, an example of how the notion of renaissance can be used by the marketplace. When I criticized an issue of the *New Yorker* which, in my opinion, used Gates to promote stereotypes of blacks as criminals, in a manner reminiscent of how the

Nazi media portrayed Eastern European Jews, who were arriving in Germany at the time, Gates referred to the controversial black issue, which was introduced with his tired black pathology lecture, as an edition of the magazine that had the highest sales in its history.

This issue did nothing to educate the affluent white readers of the *New Yorker* and presented them with the stereotypes with which these readers are comfortable: black fathers committing incest, basketball, and an editorial Gates co-authored with Hendrik Hertzberg which blamed the behavior of the black underclass for its problems. Gates and Hertzberg have commented on the moral backwardness of blacks since then. They talk about the "rigorus" separatism of blacks, but I haven't seen any comments about the discussion of the separatism vs assimilation, or identity politics in the Jewish community. Hertzberg, Taub and Klein are among the *New Yorker* writers who discuss the moral turpitude of blacks in a manner that the morality of Jews was discussed in the Nazi press. History makes strange bedfellows, indeed.

An indication that Gates didn't have editorial control over this issue came when Tina Brown, the *New Yorker* editor, justified the rejection of work by thirteen black cartoonists on the grounds that they would make the readership uncomfortable, the same kind of reasoning that Gates used to construct his Renaissance, which omitted many young African American writers and artists who are doing "cutting edge art" in favor of some odd choices. When he chose George Wolfe as a playwright representative of "a Renaissance that will end all Renaissances," was he saying that Mr. Wolfe is superior to playwrights like Ed Bullins, Adrienne Kennedy, Charles Gordone, Oyama, Richard Wesley, Aisha Rahman, and the most original African American playwright of our century, Amiri Baraka?

With all due respect to Mr. Wolfe, who certainly knows what sells, Gates can't be serious when he speaks of Mr. Wolfe as so great that he diminishes all of the work of past African American playwrights. And why does Gates assert that Wolfe's art thrives on uncertainty? "The Colored Museum's" point-of-view is plain. Its protest against the social realist theatre of Lorraine Hansberry is blatant. Clearly, Mr. Wolfe is no Beckett. He mentions Spike Lee, but where's the uncompromising work of Saint Claire Bourne or Charles Burnett or Bill Duke? Why is there no mention of the brilliant film *Chameleon,* or the work of Bill Gunn? And how can he congratulate artists for their refusal to hew a "preordained ideological line" when he is an ideological feminist to such an extent that Michele Wallace criticized him for becoming head black feminist? He is also H.N.C., helped to that position by radical feminist Karen Durbin and Jack Rosenthal whose Magazine section of the *New York Times* is so hateful and vicious toward black people that it has been picketed by black readers. In fact, the coverage of African Americans by his magazine is no different from that by American Nazi magazines like *Torch*.

I found other parts of the essay to be patronizing and hypocritical. Gates knocks the writers of the Harlem Renaissances for having white patrons when some of the people he mentions as members of a "Renaissance to end all Renaissances"—the sort of hyperbole that caused *Time* to call him P.T. Barnum (who said "there's a sucker born every minute")—wouldn't be in the "mainstream" without white patrons, theatrical producers as well as white feminist consumers and studies programs. And what about the white patrons behind Gates? The *New York Observer* reported that Gates and his colleague Appiah recently came away from the Harvard Club with a two million dollar commitment for the *Encyclopedia Africana*, including one from Sy Newhouse, publisher of the *New Yorker* to which Gates is a frequent contributor. He writes semi-tabloid copy that drew the ire of Bill T. Jones and the Lower East Side Puerto Rican community when he gave Bob Holman credit for building an institution, the Nuyorican Poet's Café, when Miguel Algarin founded and nurtured this organization. (Millions are being raised by invoking W.E.B. DuBois' name, but when I visited his home in Ghana, last year, the museum located there was in a dire need of funds).

Gates dismisses the Harlem Renaissance by saying that "in terms of formal literary achievement they mostly failed to raise their art to its adulthood," yet he includes its writers as part of the canon in his *The Norton Anthology of African American Literature*, which, inexplicably, excludes many important African American writers, men and women, just as his *Time* essay does.

His article rejects African American "Essentialism" in favor of a transcendent humanism, the kind of position that African Americans are encouraged to take by ethnocentric and eurocentric publishers, but when I asked him why he didn't criticize the racism of some Jews (including his friend, Marty Peretz, *New Republic* publisher, who said that black women were "culturally deficient") as harshly as he did the regrettable anti-Semitism of Louis Farrakhan, he told me that he wasn't interested in what white people were doing and described himself as some kind of cultural nationalist. For Gates there's one moral standard for the black poor and one standard for the white rich, one standard for Louis Farrakhan's bigotry, and one standard for some of his Jewish right wing friends, who, given the history of their people's struggles, should be ashamed of some of their ugly generalizations about black people. Herbert Hill is right. Some Jews became white in the 1960s.

If crass commercialism has something to do with a Renaissance, then I agree with Gates that we should suspend with the notion of a Renaissance, a notion that is based upon a racist assumption and one that can be used to manipulate trends in African American culture.

Why don't we hear the term Renaissance applied to white writers? It is assumed that white writers steadily produce work. Their writing doesn't come in spurts. Their writing doesn't need a talented tenth that shows up from time to time to sustain it.

Besides, African American writers didn't stop writing in the late twenties when the Harlem Renaissance ended. They didn't stop writing when the so-called Second Renaissance ended (and if one uses a Renaissance as a measurement, why aren't the Chicago writers of the 1930s deemed part of a renaissance?).

Gates also seems to believe that African American literature should be dictated by the tastes of suburban women, many of whom insist upon a literature that holds African American men responsible for all male misogyny. Both Joyce Ann Joyce and bell hooks have commented about how the feminist movement has separate tests for black misogyny and white misogyny. This movement is softer on the latter. Writers Sandra Gunning, Drew Gilpin Faust, Shirley Lee, and Angela Davis have written books about racism in the feminist movement; some of the 19th century feminists even advocated lynching. If Gates believes that this readership is where cash for African American writing is to be had, many African American writers, both men and women, who do not write for this audience, will remain poor.

Time magazine speaks for the establishment, and so the purpose of the *Time* article was to promote an African American literature that would best fit the political environment of the 1990s, to discourage the traditional black populist literature that has irritated and often infuriated the establishment, and to create a Talented Tenth that would implement this plan. What Dorothy Gilliam, president of the Black Journalists Association, said about trends in black journalism can be applied to the African American arts in general. She said that black journalists are under fire, having their columns killed or cut back, and others are forced to play by different rules that decrease their impact as a result of new operations accommodating a conservative tide. Barbara Reynolds, who was fired from *U.S.A. Today*, said that her employers preferred black columnists who were "muted." Similarly, "Fourth Renaissance" art is muted art.

Correctly Colored

Karla FC Holloway

It's clear to me that we are really engaged here in a discussion that's colored. And I only mean part of that in a signifying way, the biggest part to be sure, but still only a part of it because it seems to me that we're not quite sure yet as a community that these matters of color, or that something called literature, has, for whatever reasons I cannot imagine, escaped the issues that the rest of our living in America has not. We deal with these issues of color in both public and in private ways, from shopping at malls and grocery stores, getting cabs, getting an education, keeping our calm, keeping a job, growing up, growing old, growing sick and tired. In our front rooms, back rooms, back parlors, and in the nest of our neighborhoods, in urban towers, ivory towers, and urban centers, colored politics rings. And it occurs to me that the inquiry here may be really about these matters of public and private as much as they are about the matter of writing in a politically correct or an incorrect way. In other words, correctness is about what we choose to tell, to show and to whom, and this is a matter of what's made public and what we hope never is.

Now, there was a time when I could talk quite academically about all of this, when a program title like the one that we were given—"Politically Correct in a Politically Incorrect World"—would lead me down a path completely familiar to any other English professor at any other university. But then something intruded in the midst of trying to figure this out. It was my life and it wouldn't stay private. For what seems now to be a time that stayed with me too long, I have been following a very traditional academic path with my writing. I want to pause here just a moment to read just a short section from *Codes of Conduct* because it will help me explain these matters. This short section illustrates the way in which I could no longer contain my life in the traditional prose of my profession.

In way of preparation, let me state that I believe that we are talking about matters of color that were once held quite intimately in the secure confines of our families. I believe we are talking about matters of conduct that we learned and associated with certain performances. They were how we behaved in church, in school, or on the job, or in the street, and these matters of our behaviors were, whether we like it or not, matters of color. In other words, we were taught quite explicitly how to behave, how to act, how to be "*correctly colored*." When asked for a title for this presentation I gave the title "Correctly Colored" and I chose it as a title because I think politics is a code word for color, at least in this environment and probably in many more. So our behavior, how we look, and, finally, as I argue in *Codes of Conduct*, our character, have more to do with color than we would wish. This is how I begin that in *Codes of Conduct*.

> My grandmother warned me away from red. I thought about this when I watched Anita Hill's appearance before the United States Senate Judiciary Committee. She wore a teal blue suit with a modest row of military-like double buttons down the front. Her family sat supportively arrayed behind her. As she introduced them proudly—pausing to note her parents' upcoming anniversary—naming cousins and other kin, the event seemed like anything but what it was: the beginning moments of her testimony against (then) President George Bush's nominee for the United States Supreme Court.
>
> My grandmother was right; nice girls did not wear red I thought—and Professor Hill had clearly been raised as a nice girl. She was very properly mannered, neatly attired, softly spoken, and in every dimension certainly a "credit to the race." Professor Hill was clearly what my grandmother had in mind when she encouraged me and my sisters to carry ourselves well, to speak with precision and care, and to bring honor to our families. However, although all of the same behavioral codes from my private, family-centered education were being remarkably emulated in Professor Hill's polite demeanor, the occasion was, nonetheless, a serious challenge to the weightier directives I had been urged to follow in public situations. For all the frank talk about sexual harassment, pubic hair, and pornography, Professor Hill may as well have worn red.
>
> Now, my grandmother's admonition was a part of her ongoing lecture series to me and my sisters on morality, values, and proper conduct for young Negro girls. I remember the color lecture (wearing red, having dark skin) and the peach speech the best.
>
> The peach speech happened in the summer. We were in Eastern Market in Detroit—a large open-air market that began our summer Saturday mornings and that my older sister Karen and I called Easter Market. I was trying to pick out free stone instead of cling peaches and Grandmother Celia decided it

> would be a perfect time to give me and Karen the fuzz lecture. So she had us "handle" a peach—passing it back and forth between us, rubbing it smooth and clear of its soft fuzz until the contrast between ours and the one she still held was evident. That, Grandmother said, is the difference between a nice girl and one that has been passed around. If we put the one we had passed between us back with the others, no one would choose the well-handled peach over the fresh ones. Karen and I looked. It was absolutely apparent which peach had been passed around. We shook our heads, agreeing with our grandmother. Then we went home and made cobbler.
>
> Grandmother's other lesson was not to look common. Looking common was the ultimate sin in my grandmother's eyes. One of the reasons we had to polish our already white sneakers and shoe laces with white Kiwi polish until they looked "immaculate," was so that we would not look common. I learned that word, immaculate, long before I should have. I am sure I knew it as a preschooler although, if asked, I would probably have said it had something to do with sneakers. But unpolished shoes, ashy elbows and knees, and red dresses could all lead to the same unalterable state—looking common.
>
> I have carried grandmother's warnings with me for many years. Sometimes when teaching T. S. Eliot's poem, "The Love Song of J. Alfred Prufrock," in an American Literature class, I tell them her peach story when we come to the line," Do I dare to eat a peach?" My class mostly laughs at the old-fashioned idea of virtue my grandmother's story advances. But some of them look reflective, struck by the decided contrast between fuzzy and de-fuzzed peaches. In the same way that her peach story recurs for me at what seem to be incongruous moments, her warning about red, connected as it is to her lessons in comportment, has fixed itself in my memory.

Now, I read this recollection to show how our living is intimately connected to the ways in which we have learned to think about ourselves, our families and our communities. A story that precedes the peach story is about standing in a line at a bank and hearing a mother chastise her son: "Act your age, not your color." Some of you remember hearing that admonition. Some of you sitting here have used it. Well, I reflect there about the force of those words and their ambiguity.

We're talking about this issue this afternoon because it's still ambiguous and it's still forceful. In other words, being black, like Reverend Purlie says in Ossie Davis's play, *Purlie Victorious*, is "a thing of beauty, a joy, a strength, a secret cup of gladness." But then being black is also, despite what Zora Neale Hurston claimed, being tragically colored. It's what collects our children and our youth into a community where the act of growing up is vulnerable. It's what made some of us wear black arm bands in the early 1980s when black youth were found dead in alleyways and roadways and on the banks of rivers in

Atlanta. It's the faces of our men and boys in prison cells. It's the tragedy of Pecola Breedlove in Toni Morrison's *The Bluest Eye*, who knows that she is ugly and believes that her ugliness and her blackness have an intimacy she can only break by the spell of blue eyes. It's hearing a news story about a carjacker or a rapist or a murderer or whatever and saying to ourselves, "Lord, I hope he wasn't. . . ." This is, we all know, both the stuff of our fiction and the fact of our lives. It's why we have a contemporary novel about Emmett Till in the 1990s and why books like *The Good Negress* and *Coffee Will Make You Black* are current today. Writers who care deeply about blackness because being black has been the story of their public and private lives have no choice but to write these stories.

Now it's clear this identity is not without some problems. Ralph Ellison said in *Invisible Man*, "Now black is an' black ain't, black will git you and black will make you and black will un-make you." This ambiguity, this twoness in a way Du Bois probably did not mean it, is our shared concern. As a community of readers, we quite correctly look for stories that are colored like us, but we are not always so happy when these stories tell us about our making and our unmaking. If these stories injure our collectively colored characters, we readers are likely to say, "Uh-uh, that's private blackness; keep it home." After all, we know this is what happened when we dealt with *The Color Purple* and it's happening now with *Waiting to Exhale*. But if writers tell their truths, this private knowing made public can't discriminate. Tell it all. Slant it with whatever biases, or give us our distinctive voices, but colored with whatever biases make a conference like this one, collecting black writers, a completely predictable enterprise, and so unique that it's clear to all why the author of *Bridges of Madison County* can't cut into this colored line.

When we gather like this, it's both an affirmation and a challenge. And we've been here before. We've been in this conflicted space. What troubles me is that we're losing control or maybe giving up control of this debate. For example, I mean if I hear somebody like Larry King or Greta Van Susteren or Roger-what's his name ask if O.J. hasn't betrayed his race one more time, I think I'll scream.

It's critical that we interrogate the interrogation. Who's asking these questions about allegiance, and identity, and visibility? If it's not the same folk who have to stay in the cold while one cab too many goes by, or who have to stand in the line outside a prison to visit a father, son, or a brother, or who have to stand in a line to wait for a job application that you know won't go to anybody who looks like you, then they have no place, I mean no space in their characters, in their experiences or in their psyches to question our intimate involvement with the politics of identities that are made public or kept private.

Our choice to tell or need to keep silent is paid for by the very experiences that keep giving us something to talk about and something to write about. And we're writing in record numbers and proving that visible blackness is powerful. That's why the visual impact of the Million Man March was undeniably rich. It was public-blackness, in-your-face-blackness and it made a public issue of formally private fears. If our writing dares a public blackness, then we must respect the complications. It's no simple thing.

Being correctly colored means that you would know that my being black means that I remember with both pain and fondness my grandmother's warning, and I hesitated, even though it was just briefly, before putting on this red dress that I'm wearing today. Being correctly colored means that I know that the worry which black mothers have about their sons is intimately connected to their gender and their color. If I understand the "Act your age admonition" even a little bit, then that's a story too and it's mine. Being correctly colored means that I understand black identity politics, that I understand race matters and I make it clear in my writing, whether it's academic or artistic, that these matters of race are matters of public record. Then that's a story, it's mine and through whatever act of courage or necessity, it's ours as well. The bitter with the sweet, the public with the private, the color with the character. These are the matters of our times.

Panel C1

BLACK LITERATURE: WHO ARE THE READERS?

Foreword

Brenda M. Greene

Sunday, February 2, 1997, was the anniversary of the Eighth African American Read-In Chain. Its goal was to have at least one million Americans across the nation reading works authored by African American writers. Dr. Jerrie C. Scott, National Coordinator of the African American Read-In, began these Read-Ins eight years ago. Schools, community and professional organizations, businesses, churches, libraries, bookstores, and interested citizens were urged to centralize literacy for Black History Month by hosting and coordinating Read-Ins in their communities. These Read-Ins could involve bringing together family and friends to share a book or book readings and media presentations that featured African American writers, thereby creating a chain of readers across the country that would extend to African diaspora communities across the world.

The success of the African American Read-In Chain is just one indicator that there has been a substantial growth in the number of black readers. Some have called this growth a "renaissance," a "flowering," or a "rebirth" in black literature. Today, black books are being sold in mainstream bookstores and independent bookstores across the nation, and African Americans are reading and buying black literature in record numbers. A survey conducted by Target Market News in 1995 revealed that African Americans spend more than twice as much on books as on video games and hardware combined. There now exist a number of black book clubs across the nation. The Go On Girl Book Club, which was begun by three women in New York City in 1991, currently has eighteen chapters across the nation. Blacks are reading and selling books in beauty shops, churches, community organizations, etc. The *QBR* (The Black Book Review) has a black book best-seller list and magazines such as *Essence* and *Emerge* regularly print excerpts from black books. In 1992, three black writers: Toni Morrison, Alice Walker, and Terry McMillan were simultaneously all on the New York Times best-seller list. Terry McMillan's novel *Waiting to Exhale* later became a successful movie.

Books make the best-seller list because they are read and bought by a cross-range of people. In the literature authored by blacks, one finds autobiography, biography, recovered texts, and historical fiction, as well as extensive books on personal and spiritual healing, "race," identity, marriage, relationships, family, parenting, romance, mystery, science fiction, fantasy, music, film, and popular culture. These texts, which represent all aspects of black identity and culture, cut across class lines and represent black characters in more complex ways. A listing of the top best-sellers from the July 1997 edition of *QBR* is an illustration of the range of texts written and read by blacks. Among the top books for Nonfiction Hardcover were: *Don't Block the Blessing:_Revelations of a Lifetime* by Patti LaBelle and *No Free Ride: From the Mean Streets to the Mainstream* by Kwiesi Mfume; for Nonfiction Softcover: *The Value in the Valley: A Black Woman's Guide through Life's Dilemmas* by Iyanla Vanzant and *Sister to Sister: Devotions to and from African American Women* by Susan D. Cook Johnson; for Fiction Hardcover: *Sister, Sister* by Eric Jerome Dicker and *Good Hair* by Benilde Little; and for Fiction Softcover: *Song of Solomon* by Toni Morrison, and *Just as I Am* by E. Lynn Harris. Commercially successful books such as these, cross genres and appeal to the general reader.

This commercial success in the black publishing industry and the rise in the black readership, however, raise other issues. Have we, in essence, redefined the black literary tradition? Are readers drawn to a particular kind of literature? Is there a difference in the gender of the readership? Data from the publishing industry support the fact that much of the growth in the black readership is due to women. The list of books identified above attests to the fact that there are proportionately more women writing books, and more books which appeal to the female reader.

A corollary to this rise in the black readership is the presence or absence of certain themes. Are certain themes resisted? Is there a tendency to silence certain kinds of readers? We tend to hear only about books published by mainstream presses or books that have crossover appeal. Writers who author texts which address themes not desired by mainstream publishers are rendered invisible by the mainstream press. In illustrating how pervasive this problem is, Brent Staples, one of the panelists in this section of essays, discusses the obstacles faced by black male writers. He recalls that if a writer did not write about a black man who had at one point been part of the prison system, he would not be offered a publishing contract. This apparent silencing of certain themes and the marginalization of certain writers from mainstream presses have been addressed by independent black bookstores and small presses. These bookstores and small presses are the means by which we have traditionally come to know black writers.

The reading habits and range of black readers are complex and some readers have questioned the scarcity of classic fiction. Is this recent explosion in black literature due to a widening of the gap between the literature read by the general public and the literature read by writers, academics, scholars, and critics? Readers want to know where are the Richard Wrights, the James Baldwins, and the Ralph Ellisons; they look for the parallel Zora Neale Hurstons, Paule Marshalls, and Toni Morrisons. While they applaud the commercial success of new and emerging writers, they also critique the absence of classic black fiction, fiction that can be found in our classrooms, universities, and literary anthologies. Are these readers too quickly dismissing emerging writers, or are they perhaps being too critical of the emerging literature? We must remember how long it takes for a text to become a classic and the process by which a text becomes part of literary studies. Writers such as Hughes, Hurston, Ellison, Wright, and Morrison are now part of the American literary canon, but how long did it take for them to achieve this status? We must also remember that publishers are driven by the exigencies of the marketplace and are reluctant to publish serious literary work that may not have much shelftime in large bookstore chains. Thus, we cannot, yet, predict which texts will emerge as classic, nor can we foretell how many readers will yearn for more classical texts.

The issues of readership, themes, and publishing frame the discussion for the essays in this section. Bebe Moore Campbell opens the discussion by noting that part of the reason for the increase in a black readership relates to the fact that blacks are seeing themselves represented in print. In addition, she points out that given the status of black literature today, the myths surrounding the marketability of black books no longer have any validity. William Cook acknowledges the increase in the number of texts written by blacks, but finds it troubling that fiction by African American males does not appear to have been touched by this explosion in literature. Brent Staples supporting Cook's argument, contends that there are still a number of black men who have been marginalized in this current "renaissance." Jill Nelson's essay closes this section. She takes issue with *Time* magazine's October 1994 article on the Black Arts movement and questions the right of the editors of *Time* to declare that there is a renaissance. Her essay ends with an open letter to the editors of *Time* magazine.

Black Books Are Good for Business

Bebe Moore Campbell

In tackling the very multi-layered question of who are the readers and how we increase the readership, I'd like to start by telling you a little story. There's a junior high school, a middle school, in my neighborhood in Los Angeles which is predominately black and Latino, and I do a lot of volunteer work there. I was called by a friend of mine who is a teacher there to come over and do a reading, since it was February. I am so busy in February. When I began reading from *Your Blues Ain't Like Mine*, there was a little Mexican-American boy sitting in the front row. Almost as soon as I started reading, I could see boyfriend's eyes start to glaze over. I mean, he was on black history overdose. This was just one program too many and he started going into a nod. I got to a part in a passage I was reading where there was this character called Hector Bonilla. As soon as I said the name, his eyes opened, his chin went up, and he was with me for the rest of the reading, and I say that to say this: we read because we want to see our images in print and because we want to hear a good story well told. Everybody wants to see his or her image in print.

I think there're some things that have happened around publishing and around black literature particularly that have increased that readership. And I can also say one pivotable event happened following the civil unrest that occurred in Los Angeles. I'm sure you've heard it mentioned before at this conference. I have. In April of 1992, Toni Morrison, Terry McMillan, and Alice Walker all wound up on the *New York Times* best-seller list together. They stayed on that list, together, for weeks and months, and I don't think Terry ever got off. With that occurrence, the three myths that permeate the publishing world began to shatter. And I think you're aware of those three myths.

- Myth #1–Black people don't read;
- Myth #2–Black people do not buy books; and
- Myth #3–White people do not buy books written by or about black people.

Those myths were shattered because it was quite clear that three sisters wound up on the *New York Times* best-seller list together because black people were buying their books. White people were buying them as well and were continuing to buy them for the length of the time that they were on that list. So publishers had to go and close the doors, scratch their heads and come out realizing that they had been leaving money on the table.

Publishing is, despite whatever romantic illusions we have about it, a bottom line business. It is not in business to free us as black people, to make sure that our wonderful stories are told; it is in business to make money. And what publishers saw in those three sisters arriving on that *New York Times* best-seller list was a way for them to make more money. We're reaping the benefits of what that resulted in, that is, more African Americans being published, and not only published, but being promoted. Having lived through the '60s and the '70s and '80s, I can remember a time when we sort of sat around and looked at our watches and said, "You think Alice is going to write something, or when is Toni coming out with something?" There was not that much to choose from, and there was not that much to choose from because publishers thought they could not make money from our work. They were taught differently in 1992 and they have continued to learn differently.

I think that most of us could have disputed those myths a long time ago. Certainly, the first one: that black people don't read. I don't know about you, but I had a grandmother who had a closet full of paperbacks. Mickey Spillane, Harold Robbins. I mean, I can remember sneaking into her room and reading the *Carpetbaggers* when I was in junior high school. Now if there had been a number of works available by black authors at that time, I have no doubt that my grandmother, who bought me black dolls, would have gone out and bought books by black authors. But there wasn't anything available, and so, because she had a need for literature and a need to escape, she chose from what was available.

Now we've got a growing audience for black writers and one that does include white people. I hope we understand that this is not a new phenomenon either; that when we had our mini-renaissance in the

'60s, there were certainly white liberals, particularly Jewish people, who were reading Baldwin, Walker and Morrison and who helped put Richard Wright on the best-seller list in the '40s. So there has always been a myth that white people don't read books written by or about black people. I'm not talking about in huge numbers, but there always have been some white people who read our books.

It's important to understand that the new diversity and hunger for black literature did not occur in a vacuum, and that a number of factors came into play, not the least of which is the changing demographics of black America. Now, readers of black fiction are overwhelmingly female. I've talked to a number of bookstore owners, particularly those who are African American, and what they're saying is brothers tend to like a lot of non-fiction. Thus, the readership for fiction is still predominately female. These are single women, many of them with leisure time.

Books are a relatively inexpensive recreation and they're a wonderful escape. So when we talk about our readership, we have to recognize that women are finding a wonderful way to socialize with books. Everywhere I go, I'm greeted by book clubs. It's a way of bonding and being able to belong to an organization and to have some intellectual discourse. And I think the fact that it's not too expensive has hastened the rise of black book sales and has increased the readership.

It's also important to understand that the readership did not grow overnight and that even though the 1992 *New York Times* best-seller list was important, that wasn't the only thing that contributed to that readership. During the '70s, the appetite was whet for fiction, and black magazines gave us short fiction, more importantly, excerpts of upcoming novels. *Essence,* particularly, has played a big role in that. If you look at the books that are being publicized, that are really getting to the community, the excerpts often started with *Essence.*

I think that we've matured as a people, particularly after the Civil Rights Movement, the aftermath of which opened us up to a wealth of new experiences: the experience of integration, and the experience of getting into the corporation and bumping your head against that glass ceiling. We have become a much more diverse people, and because of that, we need novels that speak to the diversity of our experiences.

I think authors now are beginning to expand on that literary tradition that is black. Although many continue to write about blackness and race as a problem, the overriding factor for whatever we do in life, some black authors are choosing not to write about it in that way. I write about race. That's my emotional terrain. That's what I like to do, but I don't explore it in the same way that Richard Wright did. I don't explore it in the same way that Ann Petry did. *Brothers and Sisters,* which is my latest novel, is very much a book about race, but at the same time the protagonist, Esther, the black woman, and Humphrey Boone had issues that are human issues, that you can always link to race, but which go beyond that.

I would just like to give you an example of that by reading a portion of a chapter that deals with Humphrey Boone. Now he's a brother who has really pulled himself up by his bootstraps and he now finds himself in the enviable or unenviable position of being the most important, highest ranking black in a bank. He is poised to even one day take over that bank, but at the moment when he should be keeping his oats, he is brought back by some other problems, that, while having to do with race, are not race specific.

> Humphrey slipped off his suit coat and hung it on a padded hanger on the back of the door, loosened his Hermes tie just slightly, and sat down at his desk. In another hour, he would convene his first staff meeting, a meeting for which he was totally prepared. He'd come in early because he wanted to enjoy his first hour on the job, to savor it by himself. There was nothing to do for the moment but indulge himself in his own vanity, congratulate himself for paying attention to all the signs on the highway, following the rules, dotting his i's, crossing his t's, and working three times harder than any white man he'd ever competed against. And now he was claiming his reward. He flipped on the small clock radio in front of him to KJLH. He leaned back in his richly upholstered chair and put his feet up on his brand-new desk and tapped them to a familiar beat.
>
> The telephone rang just as Humphrey stretched out. He hesitated for a second, then pressed the button for the speakerphone. He wanted to give the impression that he was already so busy, so important, so powerful, he couldn't even pick up the telephone.
>
> "Humphrey Boone," he answered smoothly.
>
> "Humphrey, that you baby?"
>
> His mother's flat Mississippi drawl—an accent that was still thick though she had lived a half of a century in Los Angeles—blaring into his palatial corporate office seemed the essence of incongruity. A chilly wave of apprehension rolled up under his shoulders. Humphrey reached for the receiver. "What's wrong Mama?" He felt a sense of dread, the same foreboding that was present whenever his mother called him. For as long as he could remember, his mother brought him nothing but bad news. Hearing her voice always made him want to run. Her words sounded the way she looked: heavy and tired. Oh Mama. Sometimes he wanted to take her in his arms. Sometimes he wished he could flee to where he'd never have to hear from her again.

"Chontelle called. The oldest boy done got himself in some more trouble. She scared to call you because she didn't pay you back from the last time, but I was just wondering if you could let her have some money for his bail. She your sister, Humphrey. Everybody ain't had your good fortune."

Good fortune? He bunched his fingers into a tight fist. She made it sound as if his success was something he picked up in the street one day. As if he hadn't worked two jobs through high school and two through college, straining to make good grades and take up the slack that his absent father left. Nothing stopped Chontelle or the others from doing exactly what he'd done. Nobody told Chontelle to have three babies by a high school dropout who couldn't keep a job. Why did he have to be responsible for everybody?

"Mama I work for the bank, I ain't—I'm not the bank." He tried to sound hard and cold, but the attempt fell flat and he ended up merely whining.

"Baby, I know that."

"I take care of you, Mama. Isn't that enough?" He heard his mother sighing. He'd made her feel guilty and he didn't mean to do that. He couldn't stand the thought of his mother feeling bad. Her whole life had been nothing but hard times. He remembered how when he was small his mother would clean offices at night to augment the pittance that the state gave her after his father left. He was in charge of the other children while she was gone. He had to feed them, bathe them and make sure they got to bed. Sometimes, after his sisters and brothers were asleep, he'd wait up for her. He'd hear the bus screech to a halt at the corner, and five minutes later his mother would wobble through the door of the tiny apartment the five of them shared, taking slow steps like an old woman, reeking of ammonia and furniture polish. He would have a plate waiting for her, and sometimes she'd fall asleep at the table before she finished eating.

"I won't ask you no more, Humphrey," his mother said. "It ain't fair, you got a right to enjoy yourself." She was getting ready to cry. He could hear it in her voice.

"How much do you need?"

When he hung up the telephone, he wrote out a check for $525, the $25 being the amount that the store near his sister would charge her to cash his check. He shook his head, an involuntary gesture. She couldn't even afford to open up a checking account.

"What was the difference?" he wondered for the millionth time. He had made it somehow, but why not them? Chontelle was on welfare, and his brother, Louis, was in and out of jail and on and off drugs. Only his younger sister, Latriece, was self-sufficient, working as an administrative assistant in city government but she was too busy partying and having a good time to think about going to college. He'd talked to her about getting a degree, shaping a career, but she wouldn't listen to him.

Sometimes he hated them all. Hated them for not being as smart as he was, for not being as strong. He'd blazed his way through school, earning nearly straight A's. When things were horrible at home, he would open a book and escape. Maybe that was one of the differences between him and his siblings: he always knew that things were bad, that other people didn't live the way

> they did. In the library, flipping through the pages of *Ebony*, he would see pictures of black people, even people as dark as he, living in beautiful homes, wearing gorgeous clothes. The fact that some of the models and subjects of the articles were his particular shade, he took as a kind of redemption. He was the darkest of his mother's children, and he was darker than most of his friends. His mother lovingly called him Black Berry but other people weren't so kind. A few of the kids in the neighborhood teased him, calling him "Ape Man" and "Gorilla," but mostly he could read in their eyes that people thought he was ugly. Not everyone, of course, but enough, especially girls. So when he saw the black-skinned people in *Ebony*, lounging in their luxurious homes, posing behind the desks of their splendid offices, he believed that the photographs were a foreshadowing of things to come. The pictures also convinced him that what he always suspected was true: his family's lives were small and mean and hard. But there were other people, people who looked just like them, who were on a different path. And he trusted his mother and teachers, the coach on his basketball team, the owner of the store where he worked after school, when they assured him that the path he was walking led to success and wealth.

I think what black writers are doing now is giving us more complex characters, characters who are both bad and good, who have a history that you can touch and feel in the book so that you understand why they act the way they act, and realize that their actions don't come out of a vacuum. I think that's attracting the new expanded readership. There is more being written. We all have different experiences. For those who like science fiction, we've got an Octavia Butler and some other people. We've got romances; we've got novels; we've got nonfiction. There's more being offered and it's being promoted so that you know about it. In the past, it was one thing to be published, but then quite another to let people know that you had a book out, because, while the publishing houses were willing to give you the advance (a small one at that), they were not willing to put the money together to give you a tour so that you could show up in cities across the country and read your work and let people know what you had out.

We, as African Americans, really owe a debt particularly to African American independent bookstores. Before we were going into the large chains, before they even wanted us, we were going into the African American bookstores and those brothers and sisters were getting the word out about our work. That's how we got to you. Through them. I think the other things that are expanding are the booklists, the book clubs, the way that we're marketing, and the way the publishing houses are marketing us. Also, something that happened around '92 which was very interesting was the emergence of a black best-seller list. This has really been a way for people to advertise. You see something on a list and it makes your mind go, "Hmm. Maybe I'll check that out," particularly if you see it staying on the list. So now you have lists in *Essence*, in *Emerge*, in *QBR: The Black Book Review* and I think to continue the perpetuation of this readership, writers are going to have to take up the mantle and go into the schools and read to black children, particularly black boys who don't want to be labeled nerds.

When your adolescent gets to twelve and thirteen and you notice that he or she is not reading anymore, don't stop reading aloud to that kid. I had to chain my daughter to the sofa when she was like fourteen and fifteen. We read *The Catcher in the Rye* aloud, and that got her back into it. Slowly she's become a reader again. She's been a reader all her life, but you know adolescents: "Oh, you like me to read? Well, I guess I won't do that." But don't give up on them. You have to continue to do that. If you see some neighbor's child, give that child a book. You all are responsible for creating the readership and keeping it alive.

What Is Reborn in a Renaissance?

William W. Cook

I was surprised on Sunday, March 18, 1996, to find an article on E. Lynn Harris on the front page of the Style section of the *New York Times*. The article continued onto the page on which engagements and weddings were covered. I was surprised because I expected such an article to appear in the Book Review section of the paper. That this gay African American novelist should occupy column one of the first page of the Style section of the nation's paper of record points to a change in the status of African American literature directly related to the question posed to our panel: Who are the readers?

I read the positioning of the article as indicative of a series of changes in African American fiction, changes which point in the direction of greater differentiation. But the foregrounding of an openly gay writer does not only point to an inclusion rarely experienced a few decades ago. (It is worth noting that for some African American critics it is still treason to speak of the many gay writers who dominated the Harlem Renaissance.) The initially strange placement of the article on Harris also signals readers for that author who do not neatly fit into either gay or African American categories. The appearance of his third novel, *And This Too Shall Pass,* on the best-seller list of the *New York Times* indicates the new audience his fiction has reached. As Mr. Harris states: "A lot of people of gay life . . . they just identify with the characters. They identify with the love, the closeness." Mr. Harris states that his readers claim that he "writes as though he has been eavesdropping on their lives" (*New York Times, 43*). The audience for this African American gay man turned out in large numbers at the Barnes and Noble bookstore on Astor Place for Harris's reading and book signing. This differentiation in audience represents one of the new directions which mark the new phase of African American literature.

A second change will be found in sheer numbers; that is, more readers are picking up books by African American writers; more writers appear on best-seller lists; more works by African American writers are finding their way into such mainstream sources as the bookstore chains. That expanded readership, while most notable when we consider books by African American women, is not limited to them, although I would guess that women writers do account for a disproportionate share of the increase. The most recent example of the above would be the history of *Waiting to Exhale,* which seemed to live on the best-seller list both as hardcover and paperback. It moved in record time to become the source of a major motion picture. This same experience of exceptional sales exceeds the usual numbers of black readers, and also points to a wide readership outside that group. Everyone, especially every woman, seemed to be reading McMillan's novel. One could make the same argument using Maya Angelou whose *I Know Why the Caged Bird Sings* spent fifty-two weeks on the *New York Times* nonfiction best-seller list in 1993-94, or her *I Wouldn't Take Nothing for My Journey,* which in February 1994, had been on the *Publishers Weekly* best-seller list for nineteen weeks, or Toni Morrison who had the distinction of occupying the *New York Times* best-seller list in fiction and nonfiction at the same time. The list could be extended to include the explosion of interest and the brisk sales that greeted *The Color Purple* and certainly the sales records of Bebe Moore Campbell's *Your Blues Ain't Like Mine,* which, even in its third year, remains a steady seller.

Even though it cannot be disputed that the writers mentioned above have greatly expanded the African American reading audience, we must not ignore the fact that they have, to steal a term from the record business, great crossover appeal. Morrison, Walker, Campbell, et al. are read by an unusually large number of American women. As the popularity of Morrison as the subject of Ph.D. dissertations and her popularity with African American women outside the academy will attest, this readership crosses boundaries of ethnicity and class; Ph.D. candidates completed as many dissertations on Morrison in the last decade and a half as on Richard Wright, James Baldwin and Ishmael Reed combined. By the same token, writers like Harris speak not only to an African American audience; they have expanded that audience and added to it a gay audience inclusive of a range of ethnic groups.

Another interesting genre of the novel that points to an increasing feminization of the audience for African American novels is the romance. While this has always been a popular genre, it is only recently that romances and historical romances aimed especially at African American women have appeared in great numbers. I mention, as an example, the Indigo Line, published in cooperation with Genesis Press, which lists five new titles.

Science fiction and fantasy, which once existed at the borders of African American literature, are experiencing a major renaissance. Octavia Butler is the author of ten novels and also winner of both the Hugo and the Nebula Award. She describes herself in terms that point to the varied audience which she attracts: "a hermit in the middle of Los Angeles, a pessimist if I'm not careful, a feminist, a black, a former Baptist." Samuel R. Delaney, another science fiction writer who happens also to be gay, is amazingly multi-talented and has attracted a large audience since his first novel *The Jewels of Aptor*.

Responses to the above described explosion have been many. Haki Madhubuti of Third World Press argues, in the December, 1995, issue of *Publishers Weekly* that "the variety that exists now did not exist five or ten years ago . . . It's a rich time. You now have a highly literate black reading public." We can add certainly other genres to the above list. One which seems to dominate the movement I am describing would be the self help/how to/wise sayings category of texts. And here I am concerned only with those authored by African Americans and speaking directly to them. This increase can more confidently be attributed to an increase in African American readers for writers like Susan King Taylor (*Lesson in Living*, 100,000 1st printing, 200,000 2nd printing; *In the Spirit*, 350,000), and Eric Copage (*Black Pearls*, 220,000) who single out such an audience. The increase in numbers and variety can also be recorded for readers of books intended for young readers, books on beauty and health, books on relationships, books on religion and books on business.

One area which seems not to have been touched by the above explosion is fiction by African American men. These texts seem not to have the crossover appeal noted in relationship to the other categories. The absence has been noted. Gerald Howard, W.W. Norton vice president and editor, expresses a wish "that there were more black male literary writers selling more books."(*Publishers Weekly*, 40). He suggests that this lagging behind may be attributable to the "resistance on the part of the culture at large to deal with the realities of black life" and to the social construction of the African American male as either super athlete/hero or "threatening presence." Commercial black male fiction, according to Howard, is obviously the "next frontier."

I find this last situation, the comparative absence of fiction by and about heterosexual African American males, troubling because of my own bias toward the power and importance of narrative. The literary record provides us with innumerable African Americans who speak of the power of reading to redirect and redeem. The record can begin with Frederick Douglass in the first half of the 19th century and his exhaltation, on reading *The Colombian Orator*, to Langston Hughes's retaining of his copy of Walt Whitman, to Richard Wright's gaining a sense of artistic vocation from reading Mencken's *Prejudices;* to Maya Angelou's graduation day salvation by James W. Johnson. They, and a host of other writers, pull an I-remember-the-day-and-hour testifying act when they mention those books that set them flowing. Given the present state of African American men, more, and not fewer real texts are needed.

Toni Morrison's *The Bluest Eye* is a testimony of the mental derangement which is a consequence of encountering an absence of one's self in the texts one reads. The running motif of that novel is a passage from the *Fun with Dick and Jane* basal readers. Juxtaposed to these passages, which become more and more unintelligible as the novel progresses, are contrasting experiences from the life of Pecola and her family. With no available model for self construction but those peculiar to persons and situations radically different from their own, Pecola, her mother and her father disassociate themselves from the life they lead and dream their way into the world of the white texts offered to them as normative. They dream themselves into madness. This observation can be found not only in our fiction, but also in the work of our scholars, scholars like Carol D. Lee. Her *Signifying as a Scaffold for Literary Interpretation* is a must read for anyone interested in literature and African American readers. I point here only to her definition of "dialogic reading," which reading, she argues, is dependent on three factors:

1. The extent to which a reader empathizes with characters;
2. The extent to which a reader recognizes and construes a meaningful function to the literary conventions used in the text (perhaps because they are consistent with the conventions of his or her own oral style); and

3. The extent to which a reader gains insight into the depth of values explored in the literature because the reader has had to grapple with similar or comparable human tensions without benefit of the insights of the author.

Literature can be more than a good read; it can be enlarging and empowering. It may well be a force with which to counter the already alarming statistics about African American men. Of all groups surveyed from 1982 to 1992 in the *Chronicle for Higher Education* (September 1, 1994), no other group showed as wide a disparity between enrollments in college of men and women. The gap is growing each year. While we celebrate what appears to be a renaissance in African American letters, we should not lose sight of the fact that the blessings of that renaissance may not be shared by all segments of our population.

The Importance of Writing for Black Male Readers

Brent Staples

Not long ago, I gave a reading at a bookstore in Atlanta. Before I started, the owner asked me to sign a dozen books for a beauty shop across town. When I asked why, he said that the parlor kept a schedule of visiting authors and requested signed books from those who looked interesting. "They'll take a dozen copies and pass them out to people getting their hair done," the bookstore owner said. We are now learning that books are sold everywhere—in laundromats, beauty shops and on the streets.

Something else has changed as well. Three years ago, the Atlantic Monthly Press published a book called *Monster*, the story of this L.A. gangster whose name was Cody. Cody became famous during the L.A. riot. He had killed a dozen people and hacked some of them with machetes. He'd done rapes and all those kinds of things. When Atlantic Monthly Press put out the book, they put out a press release that said: "The primary voice of the black experience in America."

The primary voice of the black experience in America! Some of us in the media took real umbrage at that. We were raised to go to church, to do the right thing, to eat three square meals a day, to keep our noses clean, not to shoot people or hack them to pieces. It didn't occur to us that murderous violence was the mainstay of the black experience.

So hell was raised. I wrote a column on the editorial page of the *New York Times*, walking up and down the Atlantic Monthly Press. A few other black writers wrote as well. As a result, they changed the press release to say, "A principal voice of the black underclass." That's very important. That's a very important construction when you look at Cody's life. Let me just read from the column.

> Cody photographed in dark glasses, machine-pistol in hand, his mammoth torso bare, presents himself as the inevitable product of the urban inferno.
>
> "To be in a gang in South Central when I joined," he writes, "is the equivalent in growing up in Grosse Pointe, Michigan, and going to college. Everyone does it."
>
> But Cody's life, Cody's criminalization, was less inevitable than he lets on. The singer Ray Charles was his godfather. Cody's mother, though estranged from her husband, was an indigent homemaker and homeowner. Cody's brother Kevin was an actor living in Burbank. His brother Ken joined the Airforce. A third brother Kuron worked at a market near his home. His sister Candice was studying data processing. Certainly the law of the streets was strong, but Cody Scott had choices. He chose to become a monster.

Now, I don't want to get to preaching too heavily on this subject, but I want to say the essential conflict in black letters and in black plight over the last fifty years has been the conflict between this view of black people as monsters (and black people themselves embracing this view), and the contrary view represented by Ralph Ellison and a few others: that black people were in fact mainstream Americans, with a great stake in middle-class values and middle-class ideas. Now, I understand how middle-class values have been used by the Right to demean black people, but don't let them knock your eyes off the prize here. The conflict has been destructive for us, because, overwhelmingly, we have embraced this view of ourselves as monsters. It's been evident in what we have written; it's been evident in what we have chosen to read, and it's been evident in the films we have chosen to act in, up until quite recently.

The cost has been great. And when we talk about the cost, we can talk about the fact that one in every three young black men in this country is involved in the criminal justice system. We'll go to jail, do some time, be on probation at some point. Bebe Moore Campbell talked earlier about reading to her daughter, and she mentioned that it's particularly difficult to get young black men involved with books and with ideas. The view of us propounded in books precludes a literary awareness. It makes involvement with books a feminine activity. It makes involvement with ideas nerdiness. This has been a real struggle for us in this culture, so in our hunger to see our image in books, we have, in fact, run disproportionally to that monstrous image and we've embraced it. The social consequences are readily apparent.

The fact that a lot of writers rose up to say to Atlantic Monthly Press, "That's wrong; this is not representing mainstream black values," is a new development. Ten years earlier, in 1983, twenty years earlier, in 1973, those voices would've been drowned out because we were still in the thrall of the monster, of this non-literate person, of this person who was completely visceral and violent. Look for that image in writing. Mr. Cook was talking about black male writers not crossing over. Let me tell you: when you write a book about your family, as I did in *Parallel Time*, you hear a lot of things from television producers and movie producers about what you write. And if you're a black male, they will tell you: You're not writing if you don't have some jail experience. If you haven't really done some crimes, you are not enunciating the true black experience. Now, my book came out in February, 1994. Although Toni, Bebe, Terry, and the whole crew are racking up sales on the best-seller list, we still have this really strong view, this almost unassailable view, until recently, of a black man as monolithically animalistic. Writers have been compliant in that. I just choose not to be complacent about it.

When you come to publishers and movie people, they will tell you that they want the authentic black experience and it has to be that way. What has to happen is black people have to stop buying those books and writers have to stop writing them. It's as simple as that. It's very simple. In the last three or four years, we've had a flowering, I think. A renaissance is maybe too strong a term, but, in fact, just to reiterate what Bebe said, we have more complex characters; we have a wide range of characters; we have more realistically textured novels; and we have novels that reiterate more of the classic forms.

I went to a classic university. One of my favorite books is a few thousand years old. It's Homer's *Iliad*. And my favorite scene in the *Iliad* is the scene when the Greeks come to get Helen. It's a classic capture story. Helen gets stolen; the Trojans take her; the Greeks come to get her; they bring their whole tribes; it's like a battle outside the walls of Troy. Thirty thousand men, all bloody and crushed in mud, fighting. But, as you know, the gods always like to play in the battles, so the gods would come down dressed as people to participate in the killing in the course of the battle. In one of these cases, the god of war, Ares, is in the ranks chopping up men to pieces, and Aphrodite, a significant sister, throws a spear and wounds him in the side. Ares screams so loudly that thirty thousand people on the battlefield stop. Every clank of a sword and every shield stops and he rises to Mount

Olympus to get his wounds fixed. You're beginning to see work by a few black writers, Ralph Ellison was one already in the fifties, that reiterate classic forms, that tie into the basic endowment of Western Civilization and stake their claim on that and those images and those ideas.

It's a very exciting time, but I want to reiterate just one point Mr. Cook made: black men have been, and are still marginalized in this movement. They are marginalized in the mental landscape of the culture. They are alienated from books and ideas in a dangerous way. There's no accident that one in three black men are in jail or on their way to jail. It's no accident that 60-70% of the people in jail are illiterate. Half of those people could have been saved from crime if they were given the opportunity to reflect on ideas and on themselves. So the battle in the future is to push this frontier of reading in the male direction, to bring young black men into it. I think that's a real imperative, and if we don't succeed in that, we're going to see even more of what we see now in the urban Holocaust.

Who Declared the '90s a Black Literary Renaissance?

Jill Nelson

When her book came out, *1959*, my friend Thulani Davis signed one for me and in it she wrote, "All I know is that it's about the work and that's pretty much all I know." It's about the work for me too, and trying to be as honest as I can in my writing. Sometimes it's just about the work of getting finished, of being able to write to the end.

I'm not too sure who my readers are. When I wrote my first book, I knew that my eight girlfriends, whom I talked to on the phone and sometimes read chapters to at night, would read it. I knew my family would feel obligated to buy a copy and since there are relatively many of them, I figured I'd sell a couple of hundred books. I think once you do the work, though, you get out there and you try to let people know your work exists and hope that they will come to a reading and read a book review and maybe see a quote that will grab them. You hope that they will pursue your work.

I'm a writer of nonfiction. I think it's kind of different from writing fiction. I think the readership is different and that many of our people are hesitant about reading nonfiction. My book is called *Volunteer Slavery*. I've had so many people come to me and say: " You know, I loved your book, but it took me a year to buy it because I just didn't want to read about slavery." This is a profound, a profound problem for us as black people, that we don't want to read about slavery in either 1990, as I wrote about it, or in 1850. I also think that our running away from reading nonfiction is really troublesome, and, as a good friend of mine loves to say, "problematic."

For me, one of the most wonderful things about writing is, as my friend Thulani said, "the work itself." I'm completing my second book now and I'm at that point where I just sit there and write and cackle. I think my jokes are so funny and my insights so deep, and I listen to James Brown and sing along with him: "I've Got Soul and I'm Superbad."

I also think that we have to be real clear about the fact that we have to seek out books ourselves. We have to find them. The books that get the most play and the most reviews get them for various reasons. Sometimes it's luck, sometimes you have a large publishing house that put money behind your book and sometimes it's that you knew someone who knew someone who could get you reviewed. I've read some wonderful books in the past year, a number of them by African American men that deal deeply with the experience of African American men. One of them is *Losing Absalom* by Alex Pate, published by a small press; others are all the work of William Perry and the work of Leon Forrest. So this work is out here, but I think we need to be really clear about what gets pushed in the culture. This is not a meritocracy. The best does not always rise to the top. The cream is usually stolen long before we get to the supermarket, so let's be quite clear about that.

I have a feeling of discomfort with the conference because I always get scared when we declare ourselves free, or say the renaissance is here, or we have made it. When you look at an industry like the publishing industry, which is one of the most segregated in this country where we basically have no power, you can see that, as far as I can tell, most of the black folks the people in the publishing industry know, they know from TV. Of course, black folks on TV, if you're watching the news, are being arrested whether they are the good guys and gals or the bad women and men. So I think that to declare ourselves having reached the renaissance to end all renaissances when we have very little control, if any, in the industries is profoundly disturbing.

I realized that the name of the conference, "A Renaissance to End All Renaissances?" was kind of messing with me. *Time* magazine came out; I bought it. I really don't read *Time* or subscribe to *Time.* I read it at the dentist's office if it's there, that is, if someone else has *Vogue* and my dentist doesn't get *Jet.* So I bought it 'cause the cover line said Free at Last and it had Bill T. Jones and I was, like, "Well, damn!" You know, I felt like it was Juneteenth and no one told me. So I bought this *Time* magazine and I read the article and then I did what I usually do when I read something. I called my friend Thulani Davis and said, "Did you read *Time* magazine?" And she said, "Yeah, that is really disturbing." So we started talking about it and decided we'd write a letter to the editors about the article since we're writers and we know lots of writers.

As we wrote this letter back and forth on our computers and through the fax, we would talk to other writers and we'd say, "Have you read this *Time* magazine thing?" and they'd say "Yeah, we were really disturbed by it too." And we'd say, "Well, we're doing this letter." So we started faxing it all around the country and we probably worked about a week on this letter. I'd like to read it to you.

To the Editors:

As African American artists, we were first shocked, then profoundly disturbed and ultimately deeply offended by your October 10th, 1994, cover story. Not only is it news to us that we are "Free at last," but it is truly frightening that the news is brought to us by the same people who on June 27th altered the image, and thus Niggerized, O. J. Simpson. The idea that black artists are now free seems to have been literally superimposed upon the artists' words like that five o'clock shadow on O.J.'s face—It does not come from any statements by the artists. We doubt that filmmakers Julie Dash, Charles Burnett, and Haile Gerima, for instance, who *Time* acknowledges, "continue to have a long, long way to go," consider themselves free.

Along with the notion that African American artists have reached the Promised Land comes a consistently stressed idea that these artists "arrived" as a result of making art that distanced them from African American culture, tradition and community. And if those artists' work used traditional European forms, so much the better: Is Bill T. Jones' chief significance that he makes works that "resist the aesthetic dominance of the late, great Alvin Ailey?" If Anthony Davis "steered away from overtly African American subjects," what is it that compels him to create works about Malcolm X and the *Amistad* slave uprising? You say August Wilson "sticks to black subject matter" but still "seeks to transcend racial limits." What does that mean? Has he not already proven that the lyricism of blues folk is the lyricism of humanity?

It is absolutely extraordinary to state that "today's African American artists increasingly strike themes that are racially and culturally universal." What is racially universal? An absence of reference to an African American context? Does "universal" mean "unraced"? And as Toni Morrison asks in *Playing in the Dark*, what does it mean to posit oneself as unraced "in the wholly racialized society that is the United States"? The assumptions here betray incredible ignorance: that work where race is submerged or coded is universal; that work which explores "the black experience" is not; and that our tradition has heretofore only produced race-relevant work. And with such assumptions, you have misread the work of the artists you've featured: all of these artists are grappling with the impact of difference in American life.

We also find inexcusable the absence of any number of significant women artists in every field, particularly in music composition and choreography, where none are named, and in the visual arts and theatre, where only two are included among lists of men. Despite their lengthy interviews with people in the art world, the writers stupefy us by characterizing Varnette Honeywood's work as "realistic portrayals," by using the term "serious music" to indicate classical forms, and by other reporting errors.

And, finally, we are deeply offended by the writers' conclusion that African American people do not support our art. Haile Gerima speaks for most of us, including the artists profiled, when he says, "without the support I've had from the black community, I would have been silenced totally." We all had black audiences before we had mainstream notice. Most of those discussed were also, like many of us, assisted by blacks at so-called "white" institutions, or black writers who brought them to public notice, black funders (particularly in film), or mainstream funders who have alert and informed black staff. Support may be more difficult to come by for those whose work is more avant-garde, but that is true for all artists; it says black people are like the rest of America.

It is a cheap shot to further this line with a statement that black people are not interested in art from Stanley Crouch, who is so well known for disparaging black artists' work that the term Negrophobe applies. From whence does so much African American art arise? White art schools? These artists have come from communities that not only gave them birth, but supported enough art to make possible this new black renaissance (and all the past renaissances), in a culture of deeply entrenched racism.

It is clear to us that *Time* approached this story with a thesis that could not be shaken by facts or reportage. You've produced a reductive piece full of generalities that attempts to encapsulate a complex universe. We take issue with your manipulation of the artists' work and words to conform to your notions of accomplishment. We support, and have always supported, unconditionally, the work of all those artists mentioned. Please note that a number of our signatories were mentioned in the article, in a way that surely your editors would define as favorable. The issue is our right to an African American context within which to define our art, ourselves, and our many years of struggle for freedom in America. As African American artists, we are, all of us, where we must be, in the vanguard of that struggle. When freedom is finally attained, we guarantee you'll be the second to know.

Signed:
Gregory Adams, producer
Elizabeth Alexander, writer
Harry Allen, writer
Jules Allen, photographer
Emma Amos, visual artist
S.E. Anderson, writer
Deborah Atkinson, filmmaker
Toni Cade Bambara, writer
Ifa Bayeza, writer
Derrick Bell, writer
Jacquie Bishop, writer
Deborah Bolling, filmmaker
Cecil M. Brown, writer
Wesley Brown, writer
Chris Burns, photographer
Steve Cannon, writer
Nick Charles, writer
Mamadou Chinyelu, writer
Michelle Cliff, writer
Michael Cummings, visual artist
Collis Davis, filmmaker
Thadious Davis, writer
Thulani Davis, writer
Bill Gaskins, photographer
Haile Gerima, filmmaker
Jewelle Gomez, writer
Hattie Gosset, writer
Cheryll Y. Greene, writer
Shirlee Taylor Haizlip, writer
David Henderson, writer
Jaribu Hill, singer/composer
David Hilliard, writer
bell hooks, writer
Arthur Jafa, filmmaker
Joseph Jarman, composer
Bill T. Jones, choreographer
Kellie Jones, curator/art historian
Lisa Jones, writer
Patricia Jones, writer
June Jordan, writer
Helen Elaine Lee, writer
Felix H. Liddell, writer
Benilde Little, writer
Louis Massiah, filmmaker
Robbie McCauley, writer/actress
James McBride, writer/composer
Rosemari Mealy, writer
Tony Medina, writer
E. Ethelbert Miller, writer
Marilyn Nance, photographer
Jill Nelson, writer
Stanley Nelson, filmmaker
Peter Nelson, filmmaker
Percidia Alice Norris, visual artist
Eleo Pomare, choreographer
Aishah Rahman, writer
Eugene Redmond, writer
Ishmael Reed, writer

Sonia Sanchez, writer
Ntozake Shange, writer
Judy Simmons, writer
Anna Deavere Smith, writer/actress
Barbara Smith, writer
Chuck Stone, filmmaker
William Strickland, writer
Sekou Sundiata, writer
Greg Tate, writer
Israel Tecuma, writer
Askia Muhammad Toure, writer
Quincy Troupe, writer
Colette Veasey-Cullors, photographer
Linda Villarosa, writer
Joe Wood, writer
Paula L. Woods, writer
Kalamu Ya Salaam, writer
Shay Youngblood, writer
Jawole Zollar, choreographer

Post Script: *Time* declined to publish the letter in full, including signatures. Thulani and I refused to allow them to publish their edited—and distorted—version.

Panel C2

BLACK LITERATURE: THE POLITICS OF PUBLISHING

Foreword

Brenda M. Greene

1995 witnessed a tremendous increase in the number of black-interest books brought to press by African American and mainstream publishers. Veteran black houses like Third World Press, Black Classic Press, Writers and Readers, Africa World Press, Just Us Books, and Noble Press continue to grow, restructure, or collaborate on projects with other black presses. Small presses, self-publishers, and single book start-ups increasingly make significant dents in the ever-growing African American reader market. . . . As a wider range of African American themes finds grace with mainstream publishers, the brain drain dilemma rears its head.

The writer of the above statement is Max Rodriquez, founder and publisher of *QBR, The Black Book Review*. Rodriquez wrote this statement on the editorial page of the 1996 May/June edition of *QBR*. It served as a context for a larger question: Do black authors have a responsibility to publish with BLACK presses? When Rodriquez posed this question to a group of black journalists, they either responded that blacks had a moral responsibility to publish with black presses, or they stated that this should be a last resort. Black journalists were, in general, concerned with issues of distribution. Because mainstream presses have access to wide markets and black presses do not, those presses that wish to ensure the wide distribution of their books often collaborate with mainstream presses.

The problem of distribution is only one of the dilemmas facing black publishers and small presses. Small independent presses were, at one time, the primary means by which black books were published. Now these presses, such as Third World Press, African World Press, and Black Classic Press, etc. have competition from mainstream presses who want to "grab" the latest black author. Those authors who address themes related to self-help and personal inspiration, male/female relationships (particularly those from the female perspective), personal success stories (particularly those whose protagonists rise above or are swallowed by a life of crime and drugs), stories which espouse middle class values, and autobiographies or biographies of successful black people, seem to be the ones mainstream presses immediately pick up. The alternatives for writers who do not address these kinds of themes are self-publishing or publishing with a small press; furthermore, these writers very often have to do their own marketing. Many of these writers pay tribute to those independent bookstores, such as Liberation Bookstore, Nkiru Books, Black Books Plus, and Isis & Associates in New York, who stocked their books and provided opportunities for them to read and sell their books.

The white publishing business, in general, is predicated on the number of books sold. Mainstream newspapers and journals such as the *New York Times, Publishers Weekly,* the *New Yorker*, and the *Atlantic Monthly* regularly review books of authors who in the past have generated a number of sales. If a book does not sell, it does not get reviewed, and before one knows it, the book is out of print. Hence, there are many black books that address themes which may be of interest to black readers but which never get reviewed. Panelists in this section argue that this is why it is important for black readers to support the efforts of a journal such as *QBR* which provides a high probability that a book will be reviewed, and at the same time provides mainstream presses with a comprehensive list of current black literary texts.

We are witnessing the effects of a resurgence in black literature in the black publishing business industry. Black publishing appears to be at a crossroad and must employ competitive strategies to ensure its survival. As Malaika Adero, a panelist for this conference, suggests, black publishers and black presses must do what many musicians have done in the music industry. They must collaborate with other presses and publishers. Furthermore, successful black writers should, as Walter Mosley suggested in his opening speech at this conference, make a commitment to publish with a small black press. Black writers, publishers, and distributors should also follow up on Amiri Baraka's suggestion and form various kinds of coalitions. Many small presses that were begun during the 1960s Black Arts movement have disappeared. In essence, the survival of black writers, presses, and publishers depends on the extent to which they reach out to their readers and create viable networks with other organizations and groups.

The essays in this section address the complex relationship between politics and the black literary publishing industry from the perspectives of a Pan Africanist scholar, a fictional writer, and persons in the publishing industry. Marimba Ani calls upon writers of "Afrikan" descent to adopt a paradigm that espouses an "Afrikan" worldview, one that is accountable to the community and rooted in one's familial, collective, and historical being. Malaika Adero calls for black publishers to expand their visions internationally and to support other black artists in publishing ventures. Paul Coates who describes the origin of his publishing company, Black Classic Press, calls on black publishers to "go out on a limb" and take advantage of the technology of digital printing. Susan McHenry, an experienced editor, draws on her experiences as executive editor of *QBR* and discusses why we need a venue for reviewing mainstream and emerging black writers. The final essay in this section by Terry McMillan addresses the issues of exploitation and survival in the publishing business. Citing herself as an example, McMillan cautions emerging writers to remember that the road to success is not easy; writers must be willing to pay their dues and find their own voices in their writing.

Writing as a Means of Enabling Afrikan Self-Determination

Marimba Ani

Writing and the dissemination of our writings are part of a process through which people of Afrikan descent are reclaiming their consciousness. There is a movement taking place within the world Afrikan community that is about the creation of a language of liberation. Afrikans on the Continent are beginning to return to their indigenous languages and/or to use colonial languages in Afrikan ways. We in the Diaspora are using Continental Afrikan languages to house new concepts which form and give expression to our thinking about the State of the Race: our historical circumstance and the healing and reconstruction that must take place within the Pan-Afrikan world.

This process involves reconceptualization, redefinition, creativity, imagination, and most of all, vision. This emerging tradition is (re) centering itself not only through Afrikan referents, but in an Afrikan consciousness. It is a spiritual movement where "intellect" is no longer understood as the denial of spirit or the elimination of subjectivity. We are repudiating conventional European conceptions of truth, being and reality. Our work seeks to transcend the lineal, sequential, objectified, rationalism of Western thought, which is not "large" or complex enough to encompass the multidimensions of the Afrikan world view. Reclaiming Afrikan consciousness in this way involves the creation of a new paradigm, drawing on ancient, ancestral modalities and themes. The construction of the paradigm is necessarily a collective enterprise, as the Afrikan ethos (*utamaroho*) is collective. This process of constructing the paradigm is itself healing as it implies renaming, reconceptualizing, and redefining reality from the center of our Afrikanness.

This literature is, of course, part of what Chinweizu, Ngugi, and others have referred to as "decolonization"; in this case we are talking about the decolonization of consciousness. For Afrikan people, this necessarily involves a reconnecting to the source of our strength. Ayi Kwesi Armah's writing, most importantly, *Two Thousand Seasons*, is a seminal work in this tradition. A central theme of the book is the process of disconnection, which means death to Afrikan people, while connected thought, hearing, and sight bring visions of victory, making it possible for us to "return to the Way." Relationships and reciprocity are the modalities of Afrikan cultural wholeness. We must destroy the "destroyer's arrangements." Many writer-thinkers in the vanguard of this movement have been inspired by the work of Armah. The film *Sankofa* by Haile Gerima visually expresses the concept of an Afrikan ancestral consciousness as a liberating and healing energy-force for our people. Our writing seeks to harness and manifest this force.

Sankofa is a concept that comes from the Akan tradition of West Afrika. It tells us that it is necessary for Afrikan people to reach back periodically into the wellspring of their ancestral legacy in order to gain the strength and direction with which to create an Afrikan-defined future. It is part of the process of cultural self-reclamation and of reality definition. This is an essential step in the liberation of a colonized people: the "freeing of the mind" from incarceration. The act of defining reality implies power. Bob Marley tells us that we can only do that for ourselves.

In *Let the Circle Be Unbroken: The Implications of Afrikan Spirituality in the Diaspora*, I introduced an Afrikan term, *Maafa*, to be used by Afrikan people in order to claim our history and to define reality for ourselves. The *Maafa* has come to refer to the disastrous occurrence that raped the motherland, kidnapping Afrikan people and enslaving them in New Europe. This was a systematic attack on our "spiritness" and humanity. The term or concept *Maafa* is now being used by Afrikan people throughout the world to refer to the phenomenon of Afrikan enslavement and to the effects of that historical circumstance. *Let the Circle Be Unbroken* argues that no matter where we find ourselves throughout the Diaspora, no matter what realities we have had to confront, we are still Afrikan in our essential being.

> *"We are Afrikan not because we were born in Afrika, but because Afrika is born in us"* (Amura Onaa, *The Promise, 1988)*.

Understanding the implications of our Afrikanness will allow us to use ancestral consciousness and to capture the political force of our "spiritness," a term used by Dr. Wade Nobles.

In *Yurugu: An Afrikan-centered Critique of European Cultural Thought and Behavior*, I have offered a new conceptual framework for the analysis of culture. The paradigm is inspired by principles inherent in the Afrikan world view and the axiology of Afrikan civilization. The conceptual model is presented in Kiswahili: *asili* being the core or seed of a culture; *utamaroho*, its energy, "will," or vital force; and *utamawazo*, its system of culturally structured thought. The work is helping to liberate us by giving our people a new language of analysis. It is helping us to "see" with Afrikan eyes. The *Yurugu* analysis identifies European objectifying epistemology as an expression of an *asili* which seeks power. The dominant themes and modalities of European culture become understandable as manifestations of this need to control the "object." Afrikan people, of course, are then made "objects" in the emergent system of European world domination.

This literature of Afrikan resistance, liberation, and reconstruction is enabling us to make our ideas known, to exchange ideas, to respond, and to create. Publishing, rather than a means of control, becomes a medium of call and response in the dialogue of Afrikan self-determination. The Afrikan worldview tells us that we are accountable to our community, to our antecedents, and to our children's children. We are, thereby, born into an eternal cycle of life and spiral of development. As Afrikans, we are responsible, even to the universal order (Maat). We must, therefore, help to establish ideological clarity concerning the destiny and needs of our people. This for me is the purpose of writing.

"Aesthetically" our goal is *Kugusa Mtima*, "to touch the hearts" of Afrikan people so that they may be inspired to live for us, the Afrikan family. The film *Sankofa* is an example of the use of an Afrikan aesthetic for the purposes of Afrikan healing and telling ourstory. The idea of value being rooted in one's familial, cultural, collective, cultural-historical being is expressed in the Zulu saying: *umuntu ngu muntu nga bantu*. "A person is a person because there are people."

My writing is a manifestation of reciprocity (Maat). I am bound to give back to that which gives me being. I do not consider myself a "writer" as such, but rather an organizer of Afrikan thoughts, a vehicle for the expression of ideas which come from our ancestral consciousness. Our people are desperately in need of healing and of cultural reconstruction. All Afrikan media and "aesthetic" expressions should reflect that truth, for we are, each of us, accountable to all of us.

The Challenges Facing Black Publishers in the '90s

Malaika Adero

Black Literature: the Politics of Publishing seems an obvious subject for focus at an conference like this, but it is a complex one, raising issues on so many levels. There is the relationship of black writers and readers to the mainstream publishing industry; the relationship between black publishers and the industry; the relationship of black publishers to their core markets, the relationship of the readership at large and the media; and the relationship of black authors and writers to independent black publishers, etc.

However daunting, it is necessary that writers think about and understand what is happening and what has happened in this industry that relies on us for marketable products. Our overriding problem in the publishing industry has been marginalization, just as it is in the larger society. Lately, though, we appear to have moved closer to the main arena, if not center. Why? Because more than a couple of black authors have made enough money for some major publishers to cause the industry-at-large to stand up and take notice. One of the consequences of this prompted one of the leading publishers, Random House, to assign Manie Barron, a senior marketing person, the title, African American specialist. This means that for the first time (that anyone I know knows about) a book publishing sales department is focusing on and viewing black book-sellers across the country as a territory unto themselves with special needs and concerns that are financially worthy of addressing.

Despite what you might think of the title African American specialist, this marks a significant and positive change. When I came into this business of publishing more than a dozen years ago, I was hard pressed to find colleagues who seriously considered the black readership as a market force, or projects by and about black people worthy of significant investments of time and money. They would either reject manuscripts and book proposals right out or pass them along to me, which more often than not added up to the same thing, because I would, at best, be given a sympathetic hearing in editorial meetings and, at worst, shot down quickly and painfully. Nowadays, my non-black colleagues keep the projects for themselves. This means that for black publishers and professionals as a group, our competition for the great projects is greater, but that is a good thing. It keeps us on our toes and aware that we not only have to offer top rate service to our authors but bring something unique to the publishing process with our African American sensibilities. And we most certainly do.

Most successful publishing professionals, trade publishers and generalists have one or a few arenas of special interest and focus. It is our job to identify books that would be of interest to an extremely varied and multicultural market. African Americans so inclined to enter the publishing field, enter with exposure to all kinds of cultural and class expressions and experiences; on the other hand, their colleagues tend to originate from the same socioeconomic and cultural place.

As the editors of the *Village Voice* described it, publishing is still "unbearably white." Despite the many best-selling authors who emerged from the black community, our power in publishing is unbearably faint. The politics of American publishing reflect the political climate of the society. Each publishing community, whether it be in England, France or America, has its own particulars, its own traditions.

The publishing industry in this country was first developed by a white Protestant élite in the days when blacks were confined to a racially based system of forced labor and legally enforced illiteracy. The 19th century publishing houses such as Appleton, Harper, and Scribner emerged largely for the purpose of reprinting the classics of English literature. The standard of cultural excellence for them remained European though American authors such as Washington Irving and James Fenimore Cooper were published in best-selling numbers in the 1820s.

Writing, reading and publishing for black people at that time was a revolutionary and, again, illegal act. But, as we know, it was done. Frederick Douglass, for example, not only learned to read and write but was published by 1845. Within a few months time, The Anti-Slavery Office which sponsored him sold 4,500 copies of his work and within five years sold 30,000 (with three European editions)—a respectable sales figure even today.

After the turn of the century and between the two world wars, while African Americans were moving from rural to urban life and to the North, the small American book publishing industry was growing with a new breed of publishers who had a different cultural orientation and politics. They were young and Jewish (and happened to have been, for the most part, graduates of Columbia University). Many of the companies that people are most familiar with today—Knopf, Random House, Simon and Schuster, and Viking—are institutions they built. Marc Aronson writes in his book *Editors on Editing* that this new generation of publishers were on a mission that went beyond promoting their literary aesthetic. They indeed challenged the American concept of First Amendment rights by embracing "a wider public that had been disdained or ignored." They did not follow in the practice of their predecessors in this book business who kept their eyes on Europe. "They looked toward Greenwich Village and Europe for authors." They also eventually took notice of African Americans who by now were creating exceptional literature and art with a newfound determination and confidence. The energy behind their efforts led to what we now call the Harlem Renaissance.

That was, I suppose, the first boom in the book world for African Americans. The next came during the Black Arts Movement of the 1960s and early '70s. The political climate of the times fueled the demands that black voices be heard and read and that we be represented in the ranks of those who worked behind the scenes in the industry. This is when the seeds of my desire to be a writer, editor, and publisher of books were planted. I wanted to do as people such as Amiri Baraka, James Baldwin, Toni Cade Bambara, Charles Harris, Marie Brown, and Toni Morrison did: write and publish and also further expand the notion of First Amendment rights, as well as what it means to be black, to be a free American, to have a life of the mind, to have meaningful and self-directed work—to be fully human.

That is why I remain in this business despite my impatience and frustration with it. I, like many others I know, black and white, are concerned that, like the larger society, the publishing industry is on a course that is dangerously market driven, right wing and ethnically repressive and polarizing. We are heartened by the progress that has been made by those who up-to-now represent the bottom of the social ladder, but we are alert to forces that counter our successes.

I recently heard Arthur Rosenthal, the publishing patriarch who ran Harvard University Press, say that "the founders of firms," such as the ones I mentioned before—Random House, Simon and Schuster, etc. and their compatriots in France and Germany—were outside of the society of their time, and their books and their passionate love of them were a means for themselves, their families, and particularly their children, to gain acceptance to the élite clubs, great universities, and the high culture of American life. Now the leadership of the firms are the members of the club and the guards at the gates that keep us out of the arenas of power in today's society.

Rosenthal's contention is that there was a moral center at the heart of the publishing process which has largely been eroded by the desire to win (profit), as opposed to the desire to do good work. In his words, the founders "are now gone and are replaced by the 'new owners' [in publishing], the large corporations who share the view that they, only they, will be among the few able to really publish in the 21st Century."

Rosenthal was talking to a group of twenty-nine men and women from Eastern and Western Europe, Canada and the United States that I was a part of, selected to be editorial fellows of the 17th biannual Jerusalem International Bookfair. The Jerusalem Fair has become, to the editorial side of publishing, what the Frankfurt Bookfair is to the foreign rights side of publishing and what the Bologna Bookfair is to children's publishing. People from all corners of the international publishing world assemble to do business, exchange ideas, and create and set agendas. People of African descent are rarely, if at all, represented in these arenas. I was the only and the first black editorial fellow for the Jerusalem bookfair. I sat and heard papers and reports being presented on the reading and bookbuying habits of people in various countries. I sat in seminars, awards ceremonies and forums organized by the Fair and the Aspen Institute and I saw no other brown face. It was a stark and profound reminder to me of how little access we have to the forces that move international and domestic publishing. (I might add that last year, right after the Arab-Israeli Peace Accord, was the first year that there was an "Arab" presence at the fair: representatives of Tunisia, Morocco and Egypt.) You do see more of an African presence at the Frankfurt Bookfair, but those of us here in New York can tell you that that "unbearable whiteness" in publishing referred to by the *Village Voice* editors is indeed a worldwide phenomenon.

Can we, black writers and publishers, live with this notion that "the new owners," the large corporations only "will be among the few able to really publish in the 21st Century?" Do we want the publication of our history, thoughts, arts, our books to be done only by the dominant cultures who control the large corporations? Do we want to continue to be excluded from the ranks of those who make the decisions about who, what and how to publish? Of course not. Our ancestors risked their lives for the right to read, write and publish. So, then the questions become, what can we do to cause black publishers to grow and become strong businesses, to cause the hiring of black professionals in mainstream companies, and to support each other's efforts as writers, artists, professionals?

I have some suggestions to make. Black writers need to learn more about the business and the economics of publishing. Black publishers and professionals need to expand their vision and business to the international arena, for example, by going to the international bookfairs in Frankfurt, Bologna, and Jerusalem. Some of us have begun: Amistad, Africa World Press, Writers and Readers; each has an international presence. We can pool our resources and experiences and expand the reach of the publishing and literary communities here. Those of us who have influence and resources must support and invest in publishing ventures and companies in the way that music artists use their influence and resources to produce other artists. Additionally, we need to organize on a national and international level to advocate our interest in a range of concerns including literacy, cyberspace and the information highway, privacy, first amendment rights, education, etc.

Good publishing of black authors is being accomplished more and more by black and white majority run companies; everyone is getting better at what we do. But we have far to go and so much to learn and catch up with, like the technology in the midst of quickly moving times. We need to help each other and in the process be helped by each other so that we are able not only to ride in the nice vehicle that publishing can provide, but to sit behind the driver's wheel.

Black people like us who write, who publish, who make literature, who document, who create access to the communication centers of the world, such as London and New York, are strategically placed to be of service to people around the world, particularly people of color, who remain ignored and ill served by the media in general and publishing in particular. I think it's time we acknowledged that and began some collective efforts to be of greater service. This conference is a great way to begin.

Out on a Limb: A Black Publishing Experience

W. Paul Coates

I want to begin by thanking the conference organizers, Dr. Elizabeth Nunez and the other people who have worked, who've really pulled together a very, very significant conference and have allowed us the opportunity, and actually provided an atmosphere for us to discuss black writing and the black experience, and black publishing and the black experience.

The one thing that I do want to emphatically deal with is the fact that I'm a black publisher, and I'm a black publisher first, and I've always been black. I shall leave this planet black. There is no confusion in my mind, none whatsoever. I'm very proud of that. I'm very proud of the fact that I have an opportunity to handle documents that my ancestors left here for all of us to share, for the universal world to share. I'm very proud to be a part of the process of sharing those documents and bringing those documents back and making those documents available. I'm very clear about this.

We publish books for, by, and about people of African descent. And we publish those books for an audience of black readers. That's our primary purpose. If other people read our books, and we invite other people to read our books, that's fine. But our existence really is based on publishing books for, by, and about people of African descent. That's our mission and that's what inspires me; that's what gets me up everyday; that's what makes me take days without pay; that's what keeps me going and I'm very proud of that.

I'm going to focus my comments on one of the major challenges that confronts our press at this moment. I think it fits within the context of this conference. It's the first time that I really have talked with people about this in a group, so this is sort of an announcement. Let's call it an announcement and a discussion.

The challenge I see that confronts our press is a challenge that really confronts not only Black Classic Press; it's a challenge that confronts the black community as well. Because we're a part of the black community, we come out of the black community, we live in the black community, and we deal with issues that affect the black community, the challenge is complicated. The fact is that there really are two things that are working with us today. On one hand, we have emerging technology, and on the other hand, we have our persistent companion, that is, the lack of resources, and we are required to capitalize and utilize that technology in creative ways that benefit and build our community and ensure our survival. That's the bottom line. That's why you publish. That's why I publish. So I want to direct my remarks to these issues in the few minutes that I have.

I want to share with you some of the points that other black publishers and I have talked about, so that you can keep them as a framework for the rest of the discussion. First of all, again, unapologetically, we believe in our community and we understand that black publishing is political; it has always been political and we like it that way. We like that we have an opportunity to speak as a voice in our interest. Second, we believe as publishers that our community supports us and we clearly understand that we should never abandon that base of support. Third, we're prepared to take leaps of faith (this is an important point) and go out on the limb, so to speak. Fourth, we understand that we usually don't have, and probably will never have, the resources that major publishers have. So what we lack in resources and what we lack in financial ability, we attempt, and very often successfully make up with mental agility.

Please keep these points in mind with the other comments that I will make. I also want you to keep in mind some comments by some futurists, Dennis Waitley and Robert Tucker. These are relevant and important comments also, and that's why I'm sharing them with you. Waitley and Tucker have said: " Those who have insight about change will prosper. Those who have an obsolete knowledge base will suffer the consequence."

On December 23,1995, Black Classic Press entered the age of digital publishing. We have acquired the most advanced digital publishing system available today: the Docutec 135. I know as I talk about this, some of this is going to sound like Greek and it's okay. You're going to hear these terms; you're going to hear these words as time goes on, because we can't get away from them. The technology is on us. A recent article in the *Baltimore Sun* commented on our newest foray as being out on a limb. Remember that point about being out on a limb? I considered that comment for about one moment, and I agreed, largely because it's true. And as I thought on it, all of the publishers, all of the black publishers that I have kept in my mind as models, all of them went out on the limb as they published. In fact, you can't do too much that's different, you can't do too much that's new, you can't do too much that's creative, if you don't go out on the limb. If you want to do the mediocre, you can stay on the ground. So these publishers stay in my mind and they serve as models to me, publishers like David Walker, who in 1829 published *David Walker's Appeal*.

David Walker was on the limb. He paid for being out on the limb with his life. But where would we be if David Walker had not gone out on a limb and published *Appeal*? Where would we be? David Walker (now some of ya'll may feel that Lincoln freed us in issuing the Emancipation Proclamation) was significant to militant abolitionists. Marcus Garvey was out on the limb when he and Amy Jacques Garvey published *Philosophy and Opinions*. He was on the limb when he published *The Tragedy of White Injustice*. J.A. Rogers, who published so many fine books for sixty years, self-published books on the limb, begged for support. He was on the limb. He couldn't even pay his rent most of the time; begged people to buy his books. He was on the limb but he still published and we're that much better because of it.

Drusilla Dunger Houston, my favorite queen, Drusilla Houston, was on the limb. Mrs. Houston died of tuberculosis, but before she died she worked for the better part of fifteen to twenty years putting together a multi-volume history of black people in the ancient world. People want to know why I published that old book. It was reading Drusilla Houston and realizing that the book was not available anywhere; that this black woman, working in 1926, self published this book while she had TB, and that this black woman died in obscurity in Phoenix, Arizona. That made me republish her book.

We owe. Amiri Baraka, Jihad Press in Newark, Kalamu Ya Salam with Ahideanna in New Orleans, Dudley Randall in Detroit with Broadside, and my friend and mentor, Haki Madhubti with Third World Press. Where would we be if these black Liberation Movement presses had not published, if they had not gone on the limb? So you see, when

I think about being on the limb and I talk about digital publishing press, I say that's fine because I'm in very, very good company, and I feel that I'm not going to get left on the limb. Remember what I said about the black community supporters; they supported them; they supported them all. David Walker is still revered.

What I want to talk to you about is central to being on the limb. In fact, our entry into digital publishing and into digital printing began really in the late '80s when I first began to understand that there was a technology emerging that people were referring to as, print on demand. I didn't understand that much about it and I was trying to understand why would somebody want to print a book on demand. Why would they want to print one book? It didn't make too much sense to me, but as I began to collect information on it, I began to fit it in and I began to understand the power of being able to print one book. You see, books aren't printed that way. Books are printed in thousands; everyone knows that. But there's a different power in printing one book on demand. One of the things that happened (I continued from the late '80s to follow the technology into the early '90s) as the technology went on, was the emergence of one company that actually had what I would consider to be, and what has emerged as the most superior system out there. That was the Xerox company. They manufactured a Docutec 135.

Now what are we talking about when we talk about digital printing and digital publishing? What we're talking about is a concept that really is fascinating because it's simple and complex at the same time. What we're talking about is the ability to take a document, almost any document, a flat document, a book or related document and scan that document or electronically enter that document into a publishing system. Once inside that system, the document can be manipulated; it can be merged; it can be stored; it can be left there for years and then brought back and printed at extremely high speeds to produce documents in quantities as low as one or in quantities as high as thousands. This is important technology. You actually print what you want and you print it when you need it, thus the term, printing on demand.

To make a long story short, it took until about late 1995 for me to get enough information together and to get close enough to sneaking up and finding out the price of this system. I knew it was very expensive and I knew that we had little money. So how do you deal with this? How do you deal with approaching technology that, for a full plan, runs in the range of a quarter million dollars to three hundred thousand dollars when you have little money, you're missing paychecks? Well, in our case, we approached it by dealing with, again, the mental ability, and that's a long story I'll save for another time. The point is that in understanding that we needed this, or understanding that we wanted this technology, we approached it and were successful in acquiring it at the end of last year.

Now, why is this important? When I heard about this technology, what I began to do (and as I said, black publishers are political), was to immediately apply this technology to what I did in publishing and to analyze how useful it could be in the black community. I saw that this technology, when applied to black publishing and small press publishing, literally could revolutionize how books and documents were produced in our community. And I don't use the word revolution lightly. Consider for a minute what we mean when we talk about revolution. Now consider that technology has the power to establish what we don't have. We have no black book printing companies in this country. Think about it. We have black publishers but whenever we wanted to get books published, we always have had to take them to white printers or other people. That's the name of the game because it's so expensive to set up a printing press. That's very important. We have none; we have companies that can print books, but they're not specifically set up to do it.

This is the reason why acquiring this technology can really change the equation. We can literally turn the whole thing around with this little piece of equipment. Think about all the things that we complain about being black: we don't have this, we don't have that, we can't do this, we can't do that. Literally, with one piece of technology you could put a price tag on, you can acquire this technology and change an equation around. That is a bold thought, and as I shared the idea with other publishers, we agreed that it was something that really needed to happen. The Docutec had to be moved on. We couldn't figure out how to deal with the money, but we still had to move on it.

This really is 21st century technology. Even though it's been around for five years and been out there for five years, very few people know about this technology. It's out there and the sad thing is, is that there are about seven thousand of these machines operating in the country right now and what we're talking about is one black publisher acquiring one. That's sad. It's sad and pathetic, but we have acquired it.

We have access to 21st century technology because the Docutec is more than a book printing system. In its network configuration, it can be, and is currently tied into computer systems worldwide. With this system, literally, you can communicate in live documents, in real time, and publish those documents around the world simultaneously. It's more than just a book printing system. This technology is in fact the cutting edge. Files can be sent around the world by the Internet or other communication systems and presented, downloaded and printed in an instant. Conference papers, like the papers that will come out of this conference, can be input into this system and printed out literally in minutes. I'm not talking about months; I'm not talking about weeks or days; I'm talking about printing the conference papers in minutes. And they can be done in such a way that they can be printed in different countries at the same time. This is tremendous technology.

Consider also, if you will, that this technology can be used to create books for students. I've talked with folks here at Medgar Evers. This technology can be used to create course-specific books for students at places like Medgar Evers College. With the brains that we have at Medgar Evers College, we can create course-specific books and culture-specific materials for people to utilize right here. In fact, we have a project in Baltimore with Sojourner Douglass College that is doing this exactly. There are 450 adult students and what we're going to do is print textbooks that the faculty will create and use right there. That school was founded on self-reliance.

I'm going to move this along a little bit, because I do want to tell you some of the interesting things about the Docutec. For example, its output is about 135 pages a minute, that is 8½ by 11, and about 270 book pages. You're talking about outputting approximately a book a minute. That's a pretty fast system. You're also talking about the ability to store and retrieve those documents and print them out when needed. The Docutec of the Black Classic Press publishing program will immediately expand the titles. We publish about 55–60 books now. We plan to expand our titles by the end of this year to 300 titles. Those books will only be published on demand, and will not appear in most stores. Additionally, this will allow us to create an African-American digital library. Books that we couldn't publish before because we just didn't have the economics will now be available on demand.

What does Docutec mean for self-published writers and authors such as yourself? What it means is that you have access to the technology. I was talking with a brother earlier and I was telling him about the technology and he was saying, "I can bring people to you and they could get published?" I answered, "Brother, you could set up a publishing company. You actually can do it yourself." We're talking about publishing books in quantities. One book may not be economical, but you could feasibly publish books in quantities as low as 50. You could also do 200 books or publish books when you want them.

What are we talking about in terms of other publishers? We currently are working with other publishers to do joint projects in order to produce titles on demand. And I think you're going to see more of this as time goes on. One of the things that we need to remember as we move towards the 21st century is that in this world, the methods of producing goods are changing. Everyone is trying to figure out how to produce things just in time. If you haven't heard of print on demand, you certainly have heard of the concept of just in time. It's the same thing; it applies to publishing and it's going to affect the way we get our books, the way people produce books. Technology has become less costly and it will be applied to everyday use for more and more of our books. Our publishers are looking for ways to cut cost and survive on demand.

I will draw this down to a close and tell you something about the financing. We're doing actually three levels of financing. We're currently in that first part of financing, which means that we've had to secure and we're securing loans within our community to finance the first level of operation of this system until we can bring it up to a point of profit. We put this project together after I talked with a number of people across the country, and one of the people I talked with was a sister named Emma Rogers. If you ever go to Dallas, check out *Black Images*. Emma is one of the most beautiful people in the country. I asked her what could we do as a community to put together money to get this technology. Emma said, "Paul, whatever you're going to do, count me in. I'm down for whatever amount of money you want." She sent me a card on Saturday. It was on Wednesday we talked. I want to read to you what this card says because this is the response that we are getting from people and the response we're going to continue to work to get.

> *Hotep Brother Paul and Sister Cheryl,*
>
> *Assante Sani for Black Classic Press. Continue to stretch to new heights. We believe in your work and commitment and decision to move forward. Please count me in the great number of supporters for your next expansion. Forward Africa.*

She signed it with her name and her husband's. The important thing about this is it came in a very, very nice card, with a thousand dollar check. Her check was the first check that we got. And do you know that was in November, a month and a half before the system came in? She didn't understand the technology, but she understood the significance. The point with all of this is, we still haven't cashed Emma's check. And I told Emma I'm going to try my damnedest not to cash her check because her check is simply a verification that black people will support you. It's like the way folks put dollar bills up on the wall. I want to be able to put a thousand dollar check up on the wall.

Remember that we are political and that I am political. Remember that the black publishers are political. The crux of all of this is that we're not talking about making problems. What we're talking about is getting more control of what we do; what we're talking about is self reliance. We're talking about being able to do for ourselves and that's what we want to do. Remember that the crux of this battle that we're fighting is like the battle that we should be fighting for civil parity and economic parity, and those battles must continue but on a world-wide level. The African community, and especially black publishers, must fight to acquire and stay abreast of existing technology that we can collectively support. We're talking about fighting a battle for informational parity and technological parity. We must look for opportunities to acquire that emerging technology and I, personally, don't care about being on the limb. My ancestors have raised some of the limbs from the finest trees of this country and we still survive and we're going to survive. They're the ones who called out to me; they're the ones who called out to each of you and our other readers and supporters to support this effort. And they're the ones that all of us must answer to if we allow ourselves and our children, in the midst of an information revolution and the computer age, to be computer illiterate, War Lords smart, and Windows dumb.

I'm going to encourage you to support our efforts and I want to let you know that I talked with Dr. Welsing [Dr. Frances Welsing] last week. She doesn't understand this technology either, but she understands the significance. Dr. Ben [Dr. Yosef Ben-Johannan] doesn't understand it either, but he understands the significance. Dr. Clarke [Dr. John Henrik Clarke] understands the significance; he's waiting for the books to come out. He wants to see the books. Later for the technology.

Editorial Considerations at *QBR*: The Black Book Review

Susan McHenry

Paul Coates further confirmed and contributed to the experience I've had at this conference since Thursday evening: I have really been to school, sustained by both inspiration and lots of practical knowledge. I'd like to join everyone else on the panel in thanking the organizers of this conference, Dr. Elizabeth Nunez and Dr. Brenda Greene, for providing this experience.

My remarks today actually continue Paul's theme of being out on the limb. I am a long time journalist and magazine editor, but the overall perspective that I'm bringing to our subject, the politics of publishing, comes from my last eight months. Eight months ago, I interrupted concentration on my first book to work with Max Rodriguez, the visionary founder and publisher of the then two-year-old *Quarterly Black Review of Books (QBR)*. Max is here today. I think I saw him in the back of the bleachers. At any rate, at that time Max invited me to bring my practical, editorial expertise, especially what I had learned from working with the late Wilmer Ames Jr., in the starting and running of the editorial operation at *Emerge* magazine. Max wanted me to contribute this knowledge to a task of long term planning for *QBR*. The challenge was to take *QBR* from its own promising but paralyzed start-up phase (again out on the limb) to a new level of visibility. Up to that point, Max had managed to sustain the publication issue by issue and in that out-on-the-limb fashion that Paul Coates was talking about. Now Max was asking my help to take *QBR* through a phase of professional management. His goal was to make *QBR* an enduring cultural institution, as our only national review of record for

African American letters. Well, the next thing I knew, I was out on the limb too: I was *QBR's* executive editor. My first issue was the November/December '95 issue, and the second issue I've edited, which carries the February/March '96 cover date, is currently available for sale over in the other building. I am now editing the copy that's scheduled for the May/June '96 issue.

What I have to say today especially reflects my experience so far as the roll-up-the-sleeves, hands-on editor of *QBR* and my observations about the constituencies I serve and the competing interests I must balance in order to do my job effectively. And this job has the potential of becoming a real hot seat. How hot begins to become clear if you simply think about the fact that not since Hoyt Fuller's *Black World,* which ceased publishing more than twenty years ago, has there been a national publication devoted to African American letters. In many ways, editing *QBR* is a precious, cultural stewardship. But then I also intend to heed the words of one *QBR* reader who wrote in response to the first issue I edited (This letter is published in the current February/March issue):

> I am happy about QBR's accessible, even colloquial prose style and its generally appreciative attitude toward books and the poor souls who write them. The overall tone of QBR is so kind and generous; it sometimes feels like you're being overprotective. Excessive praise gives me the nervous feeling that we black people are just hanging on to a literary presence by our fingertips and any cool breeze will blow us away. In fact, there is a robust market and tradition here.

Indeed, the tradition has never been more robust—a broad river, as Langston Hughes called it, and now more than ever with many tributaries. Indeed, what originally led Max Rodriguez to take the risk—going out on that limb—in founding *QBR*, was his dedication to the tradition and his belief as a black entrepreneur in the imperative that Amiri Baraka identified in his keynote address to this conference: to create for ourselves what we need.

What we needed in this case was a periodical that could be a vehicle to assist black publishers and black writers in making sure that our books were at least known in our own communities. But we also needed a periodical that could have a structural impact on the publishing community at large. And here I'll echo the opening remarks to this conference of Walter Mosley. He asked rhetorically: "Why don't we know more than we do about the gifted black writers in the African American tradition?" And his answer was: "Because white people didn't tell you about them." Walter, in making this observation, was ironically describing the facts of life about America's cultural hegemony.

Max's tag line for *QBR*—"Our lives, Our words, Our voices"—appeals to me because it codifies that need to redirect the flow of authoritative information about books by and about the life and letters of people in the black diaspora. The *QBR* I want to help construct is a vital forum in which African Americans can talk about books and ideas that reflect and define us—whether those images and ideas are recorded in fiction, nonfiction, poetry or children's books. There is no question that well-informed, critically skilled, black voices should be defining our cultural reality more often than we have had the opportunity to do it. Surely we are as well, if not better, equipped than most of the overwhelmingly white critical voices enshrined by the mainstream media to define the cultural realities of the black diaspora.

And quiet as it's kept, we have many illuminating things to say about the world and culture of white folks too. After all, it's our legacy and leverage as African American people who live and work among the people with power in society. We know more about the folks in power than they ever considered asking about us. And as Paule Marshall pointed out in her address last night, we are the descendants of Olaudah of the loud voice and well-spoken.

To be sure, there are a few black critical voices who deserve their propers for having survived the mainstream's one by one tokenism. To name a few of the high profile people, there's Pulitzer Prize winning Margo Jefferson at the *New York Times*, Henry Louis Gates Jr. at Harvard and David Nicholson, the only person of color who's at the *Washington Post Book World* and the only person of color on the board of the National Book Critics Circle, until he recently and unhappily resigned from the NBCC board.

Nicholson's unfortunate resignation may be a prime illustration of the fact that these black critical voices that have penetrated the mainstream are always in need of experienced colleagues of color—back-up who can both confirm and elaborate upon their fine critical insights as well as challenge their sometimes not so well founded conceptions. Hence, you have the role of a black-owned publication that serves as a forum for black cultural commentators and cultivates a community of its own. Critical voices and community are both something I take very seriously as *QBR*'s chief editor.

You may ask, as many white people invariably do, does that mean that *QBR* only uses black reviewers? My answer to that is our mission is to cultivate a community of black critical voices, but that doesn't necessarily mean we won't occasionally use a white reviewer when that person does add something to our community because of his or her cultivated knowledge of African American letters and expertise in a particular creative genre or nonfiction subject matter. But, in truth, white reviewers are rare in *QBR*, and yet this still probably occurs more often than the equivalent opportunity for black reviewers to comment on books by white authors on non-black subjects in comparable white-owned publications. In any case, the few white reviewers we have used are insightful enough to consider writing for *QBR* a privilege.

What's exciting about editing *QBR* in 1996 is not only the increasing variety of new books about people of African descent being published today and deserving the attention that only *QBR* can give it, but the vital and visible presence of an audience of readers who clamor for these books and clamor for *QBR* to help them keep up. Max should certainly be given credit for starting *QBR* before the industry really noticed this active black readership and began to document it. According to a Gallup survey commissioned by the American Books Association and conducted in 1994 and 1995, some 9.9 million African-American adults purchased about 39.7 million books in any given quarter. The black-owned marketing research firm Target Market News estimates that all this amounts to our spending $297 million on books in 1994 and $350 million in 1995.

Through Max's dedication to non-traditional marketing and outreach, I have had a valuable opportunity as an editor to be able, personally, to meet a cross section of the black reading public at these *QBR* author events that we have. And I'll tell you one story that actually happened at the opening reception of this conference. I was enjoying myself, greeting old friends and acquaintances, and meeting new folks, when my friend Michelle Wallace said to me: "So Susan, is this like the book parties *QBR* gives?" So I looked around and I said: "Well, it's certainly as much fun as any party we've given. But this is a room full of literary professionals; our parties are filled with readers, with black reading fans who buy the books." I had only to recall the folks who came to the *QBR* party ten days ago for E. Lynn Harris. By the way those fans let me know in no uncertain terms that E. Lynn Harris is the Luther Vandross of commercial fiction. And, Terry [McMillan], you're Oprah.

In these kinds of personal comments, in the snail mail and e-mail, readers tell me exactly what they like in QBR: the variety of the books featured, the variety in the quality of the reviewers we have writing about the books, and the clean and stylish design of the publication. They let me know what they don't like, especially when they think we've neglected a favorite author of theirs. I listen to what they say because as an editor, my main job is to fashion an editorial mix that will attract an audience of a size and quality that will enable the publisher to sell advertising. And I'm happy to report that we've more than doubled our subscription base since November '95, which means we are well on our way to our ambitious, long term goal of getting our paid circulation up to 50,000. And believe me, we're dancing as fast as we can to stretch our modest resources and build the kind of business infrastructure that we're going to need in order to absorb this growth that we want to attain.

The arena in which *QBR*'s founder and publisher has determined he wants the quarterly to succeed is in the commercial marketplace. National publications typically get 60% of their revenues from their advertisers and 40% from circulation (that's both newsstand and subscription). Now, black publications typically take a much longer time than their white counterparts to put all the elements of this magic formula together, and we're no exception to that rule. When *QBR* was originally conceived, its advertiser rates were set with small independent, black-owned presses in mind. However, because these firms, like *QBR*, are often undercapitalized and have to strive mightily to pay their bills on time, small presses, whether black-owned or not, are not a sufficient advertiser base to sustain *QBR*, or maybe I should amend that to, not *yet* a sufficient advertiser base to sustain QBR. But again, we're talking about here and now survival issues, not rosy scenarios.

Of course, the mainstream publishers have the fatter advertising budgets, but the challenge is getting them to see the benefits of advertising in black publications, especially for the most successful black authors. *QBR* has to contend with mainstream advertisers that figure black readers will see the ads in the *New York Times* with the general market and that they will buy the books anyway. After all, it's the white readers that these mainstream publishers are going after now. The good news is that these same mainstream advertisers are just beginning to recognize the value of a vehicle like *QBR* to advertise their upcoming black authors who have not yet commanded a wide audience. But still there's a lot of work yet to be done to mine that particular vein.

Now those of you who were fortunate enough to hear Walter Mosley on Thursday night realize that Walter, this very highly successful novelist, is very seriously considering an idea that *QBR*'s publisher proposed to him many months ago on a panel—that is, that black authors who have enjoyed the kind of mainstream success he has, occasionally publish their work with a small black-owned publishing house. In other words, make a kind of investment in black presses, which, after all, are taking to print a lot of writing talent that mainstream publishers aren't knowledgeable about enough to publish and market. [In 1997, Mosley published *Gone Fishing* with Black Classic Press.]

Here's another suggestion, a baldly self-serving one for *QBR:* that such writers and their agents encourage their mainstream publishers to place ads for their books in *QBR*. This will thank their core audiences for their continuing support and thus ensure that *QBR* is around as a vehicle to help up and coming black writers to find their core audience. After all, it is only a $1,100 investment to take a full-page premium ad in *QBR,* compared to $20,000 for the *New York Times Book Review*.

Now, you may ask, "Why is an editor talking about all these advertising concerns?" I can understand why this might be making you nervous. You're wondering, "Do these issues have an impact on the way books are assigned and reviewed in *QBR*?" Let me be frank: Editing a young publication that is trying to grow beyond bare subsistence level, I am always acutely aware of what's going on with the advertisers. Those revenues generated are the cash flow we use to pay the issue cost, and this includes paying the reviewers. And as many of you whom I've been fortunate enough to work with on my first two issues at *QBR* know, we are paying subsistence level wages to the reviewers—or less than subsistence levels, really. And we're slow to actually pay, so we need those revenues. I am aware of what's going on with the advertisers, but my allegiance is first to bringing *QBR*'s readership the smartest and most readable critical judgments and truly accurate information on which they can rely for making consumer choices in the bookstore.

Now editors make important choices that determine the tone and sensibility of the book review. At *QBR*, I decide what books are to be assigned for book review, but I do have people looking over my shoulder, holding me accountable for giving adequate coverage not only on books from mainstream houses, but, more importantly, on books from small independent presses, black-owned presses and even self-published books. My special strength as an editor draws from my wide range of contacts over the last eighteen years among writers I have worked with. This has enabled me to very often match the book that I assign with a reviewer who'd give it the smartest, best-informed, well-written consideration. At least that's what I strive for anyway, and there are always surprises, believe me.

Experienced periodical editors will all tell you that as carefully as you plan each stage, from the book selection through working with the writers on the assignments, to working with the reviewers on the copy they turn in, there are always surprises and tough decisions before you close the issue and send it to the printer. There are bloodlettings, I call it, often changes at the last minute when the copy is all in and all edited and somehow *QBR*'s 48-page book can't accommodate it all. I was looking this morning at the lineup for *QBR*'s May/June issue, and I assigned for review 34 nonfiction books, eight major novels, five books of poetry, and eight books for young readers. Those are all the major books about people of African descent that we've managed to get the publishing houses to send us in time to assign the reviews, in time to meet our production deadlines. That doesn't count capsule reviews of two dozen additional nonfiction books and one dozen fiction books written by *QBR*'s young staff and interns, and now under consideration for "Books Worth Noting." But ultimately I decide what has to be re-edited to run at a shorter length or cut entirely from the issue. With me these decisions are never arbitrary or capricious but always quality driven, although there are tradeoffs to be considered—impossible tradeoffs like running a pedestrian review of a book everyone expects to read about, or an absorbing review of a new discovery no one has ever heard of. Now, ideally, of course, you want to read absorbing reviews of both kinds of books, but sometimes this is not an option despite all valiant efforts.

What I never do, and never want to be in a position of doing, is killing a review simply because I don't agree with the opinion it expresses. If the review is logical, compelling, well constructed, if the reviewer makes clear her or his major assumptions, critical imperatives, personal and ideological predispositions, then my job as an editor is done. I do not edit opinions, and sometimes I publish opinions I don't personally agree with, as long as the review does not insult *QBR* readers. That's where I would draw a line. It's my personal and editorial stance that diversity of opinion enhances the quality of our discourse, as well as the vitality of the publication and of the black critical community I hope it reflects.

So I think I've at least suggested to you some of the many detailed considerations that come into play at editing this unique book review publication. It is a precious stewardship and a hot seat, and I relish the challenge.

I'll end with a challenge to you, and here I'm flying the flag, Paul Coates, as you advised me to. Again, this is a bold and somewhat self-interested appeal to this conference. If you think it's important that we have a black-owned and -operated literary review, support it with your subscription dollars. Get your friends and relatives to subscribe. Give gift subscriptions to schools and libraries and community centers. For all the kudos, good will, and enthusiasm we have received, we have, as a main challenge, the need to make strides as an undercapitalized black-owned business. Your dollar support is vital to the kind of growth, the strides that *QBR* needs to make if we are going to become the kind of institution we aspire to be. In the politics of publishing, the name of the game is the economics of survival and growth. There is no room for complacency.

A Renaissance? Beware of the Backlash

Terry McMillan

I just want to say it's nice to know there's some smart folks in the world. I want to thank Elizabeth Nunez for inviting me here. I'm really pleased. I learned a lot today. Did you guys learn a lot? First of all, I guess I'm here to sort of present the writer's point of view in terms of the politics of publishing and I will be brief, not that they have been.

First of all, I would like to say my publisher is Viking. Years ago, we, as African American writers, were just so pleased to be published that we almost didn't care who published us. And that, in some cases, is still true. One of the things that I think that we do pride ourselves (and I know I pride myself on it) is on the presence of African American bookstores. These stores all over the United States of America have grown since the seventies. When I started going on book tours, one of the conditions was that wherever there was a black bookstore I had to go. Now, that's true not just for me, but I think for many writers too. No matter how small the store, I want to go there.

In many ways, we as writers, for whatever reason, have not had access to, or have not been able to have our works published through African American publishers. Years and years ago, it seemed that the problem was distribution and that printing thing that Paul Coates was talking about. There are a whole lot of different reasons and I'm not apologizing. I will say this; I'll make sure Viking takes out an ad in the *QBR: The Black Book Review*. They're not cheap and I'm making them a lot of money.

I like what Walter Mosley said. I wasn't here Thursday. I would be more than happy to publish through a small, African American press. You'll be surprised at the writers who would be willing to do that.

Alice Walker started years and years ago. As writers, even though we may appear to be in a position to support black publishers, people don't ask you. I just never heard anything.

Years and years ago, I wrote Diana Ross asking her if she could pay my way through college. I never heard from her, but I think that there's something to be said for that. If you appeal for the right reasons, a lot of times you will get support just like Emma Rogers from Dallas gave Black Classic Press. As writers, this is important to us.

Over the past few years I've noticed that people have sort of made me out to be the one who has had something to do with all this stuff that's going on with writers, and I don't necessarily take credit for it. One of the things that I have seen happen, and that I find very, very scary, is a lot of young writers out here who are hoping to get their first novel, or whatever, published with half million dollar advances and they get pissed when they get offered only eighty thousand for their first book. I mean there's an incredible amount of this stuff going on out here and I just really, really worry because I've heard some stories about folks publishing books who were really poets, and publishing novels (not to say that poets can't publish novels, don't get me wrong) and getting a half a million dollars for books that haven't been finished. I've said to myself: You know, they just don't get it.

There are agents out here saying, Hey, my writer, she's desperate; she's hungry; she needs to pay her rent; she's got bills and all this stuff. The problem with that is that there is always a backlash, just like we had this proliferation of African exploitation films back in the sixties and everybody was making money and stuff and then all of sudden. . . . Do you realize what happened to them? I see a danger in this, because now you have a lot of these young writers out here getting two and three hundred thousand dollar advances. This is not to say that they haven't paid their dues, but where do you go from there? If you jump out of college and get a million dollar job, where do you go from there? What kind of stress and pressure do you have?

Basically, and I'm here to testify. I wrote a seventy-five hundred dollar book and then a forty thousand dollar book and then a two hundred and fifty thousand dollar book and now a multi-million dollar book. Okay, the sh-t is hard. You know, people are bugging you about stuff and when it's your first book, your very first book, and you've never even done it before, I don't care how good you are, or how good you think you are, it's a lot of pressure out here, and it puts a lot of pressure on everybody else too. I'm not saying that you're supposed to turn down a half a million dollars. I'm not suggesting that at all, but there's this whole thing going on and I feel like in some ways we've become like pawns. It's as if they're using us again and we're letting them do it just because the money is good. But that's like what a prostitute does.

I think that we're getting bad advice from people who, in some cases, just want to take the money and run. I have not done it, and I suggest that for those of you out here who are struggling to maintain a sense of integrity, do not do that. You can sell your soul short for a dollar and end up paying big time in the long run. And there's a whole lot of folks out here, if you look around, who had first novels, and you never heard from them again.

Doris Jean Austin went through all kinds of changes trying to finish her second book. She got a ton of money for her first one, but it was just pressure. I was her best friend. Our books came out at the same time. My second book sort of went off and I started selling a lot of copies. She was still struggling with hers and I was doing all that I could to try to be supportive, to be her girlfriend, her sister and say, "Doris, you can write your butt off, Girl." She could write better than me, everybody knew it, but she couldn't finish it. She just couldn't finish it, for whatever reason. Then when she did finish it, they didn't want it. Talking about the politics of publishing, you know it's true, Malaika. And then her editor had the audacity to send me a book last week, called (I'm not going to say the name of it. Let me shut up) by this sister. It was about three African American women and their love lives and she wanted to know: Would I give it a blurb? I read the first five pages and I just wanted to grit my teeth and say, "What I look like, a fool?" She was sending me a different version of my own book for me to comment on. And I'm not dogging the sister out who wrote it. That's not the point. The sister can write, but my plea to you also is, young writers, find your own voice. We already got a Terry McMillan. You know what I'm saying? We got a Toni Morrison; we got a Alice Walker; we got a Bebe Moore Campbell. We don't need another me. There're some young sisters and brothers out here who have voices and stories to tell. Tell them.

And you sister, Marimba, what you said that I really, really liked was about this whole idea of reinvention and this whole spiritual movement in literature and how we need to recognize our illness. The things that we write about as writers, myself included, are the very things that we get criticized for. What I write about is what I like to think of as our illness, our ill treatment of each other. The bottom line is that you can do that in your very own words, with your very own heart, and you bring to it what you already have. Sharing that is about health; that's the way I look at it. And years and years ago, what's his name? Chekov said, " A man will only become better once you make him see he has light." And, of course, that's true for all of us. I believe it, and that's what we do in our work. We share it, and, hopefully, you can get healed by what hurts as long as you're not the one that's necessarily inflicting the pain.

We need to continue to show each other support. I appreciate everybody who spent their hard earned money on my books, and, again, if there's a black press out there that would approach me and say, "Hey Terry, you got a few stories or whatever . . ." Yes! I don't have that kind of contract. White folks don't have me locked up, you know. I don't have that kind of contract.

About the Contributors

Malaika Adero is Executive Editor at Amistad Press. Previously she was editor for Fireside (Simon and Schuster), Editor for the Southern Christian Leadership Conference, and Editorial Assistant for the New American Library. Among the books that she has edited are *Up South: Stories, Studies and Letters of This Century's African-American Migrations; The Beautiful Nubian Baby Book; Miles, the Autobiography* by Miles Davis with Quincy Troupe; *She's Gotta Have It* by Spike Lee; *Mo' Better Blues* by Spike Lee and Lisa Jones; *Gone with the Wind: The Book, The Movie, The Legend* by Herb Bridges; and *In the Spirit: The Inspirational Writings of Susan L. Taylor* by Susan L. Taylor. Adero is the recipient of the Tony Godwin Award for Editors and was a 1995 Jerusalem International Book Fair Editorial Fellow.

Marimba Ani is author of the essays: "The Ideology of European Dominance," "European Mythology: The Ideology of Progress," "The Nyama of the Blacksmith: The Metaphysical Significance of Metallurgy in Africa," "The African 'Aesthetic' and National Consciousness," and two books, *Let the Circle Be Unbroken* (1980) and *Yurugu: An Afrikan-Centered Critique of European Cultural Thought and Behavior* (1994). Ani holds a BA degree in Philosophy from the University of Chicago and the MA and Ph.D. degrees in Anthropology from the New School for Social Research. She is a professor of African Studies at Hunter College in New York City and the Director of the Afrikan Heritage Afterschool Program in Harlem.

Houston A. Baker, Jr. is an Albert M. Greenfield Professor of Human Relations and the Director of the Center for the Study of Black Literature and Culture at the University of Pennsylvania. He received his undergraduate degree, magnum cum laude, from Howard University, Washington, D.C., and his graduate degrees from the University of California at Los Angeles. Baker is the author, editor, and co-editor of several books: *Long Black Song, Essays in Black Literature and Culture; Singers of Daybreak: Studies in Black American Literature; Reading Black: Essays in the Criticism of African-Caribbean, and Black American Literature; Blues, Ideology, and Afro-American Literature: A Vernacular Theory; Modernism and the Harlem Renaissance; Workings of the Spirit: A Poetics of Afro-American Women's Writing*, and *Black Studies, Rap and the Academy*.

Amiri Baraka , a Newark, New Jersey native, has had a long storied career as an activist and writer. He first gained national attention in 1964 with his powerful dramatic play, *Dutchman*. This was followed by a series of major productions over the next eight years, which included *The Toilet* (1964), *The Slave* (1965), *The Death of Malcolm X* (1968), and *Four Black Revolutionary Plays* (1969). Baraka's volumes of poetry included *Black Art* (1967), *It's Nation Time* (1968), and *Afrikan Revolution* (1973). His nonfiction publications include *Home* (1965), *Black Music* (1967), *A Black Value System* (1970), and *The Autobiography of Leroi Jones/Amiri Baraka* (1984). He is currently working on two new books, *Jesse Jackson and Black People: Essays on Jackson and the Afro-American Political Movement since 1972*, and *Eulogies*, a book of eulogies he has given in the last twenty-five years for people like Miles Davis, James Baldwin, Dizzy Gillespie, Sun Ra, William Kunstler, and people in the Newark community.

Bebe Moore Campbell is the multi-talented author of *Singing in the Comeback Choir, Brothers and Sisters; Your Blues Ain't Like Mine; Sweet Summer: Growing Up With and Without My Dad*; and *Successful Women/Angry Men, the two Career Marriage*. Her writings can be found in many publications including: *Ms., Working Mother, Ebony, The New York Times Magazine, The Washington Post, The Los Angeles Times, Seventeen, Parents* and *Glamour*. She is a recipient of numerous awards including the National Endowment for the Arts Literature Grant, the Mayor's Certificate of Appreciation (from Mayor Tom Bradley of Los Angeles), and the 1994 NAACP Image Award, in the fiction category, for her novel, *Your Blues Ain't Like Mine*. She is a regular commentator for *Morning Edition* on National Public Radio.

Barbara Christian is Professor of African American Studies at the University of California, Berkeley, where she has taught since 1971. She is the author of *Black Women Novelists: The Development of a Tradition 1892–1976*, which won the Before Columbus American Award; *Black Feminist Criticism: Perspectives on Black Women Writers* (1985); and Monarch Notes on Alice Walker's *The Color Purple*. She co-authored the prize-winning *In Search of Our Past; Six Units for the Teaching of a Multi-Ethnic Women's History*. Most recently she has published essays on the state of theory, "*The Race for Theory*" and "*Fixing Methodologies: The Case of 'Beloved.'*"

Paul Coates is founder and director of Black Classic Press (1978–present). Coates was formerly the African American Studies reference acquisitions librarian at Howard University's Moorland-Spingarn Research Center. He is the co-editor of *Black Bibliophiles and Collectors: Preserves of Black History*. He is a founding member and chair of the National Association of Black Book Publishers. He is currently an adjunct instructor of African American Studies at Sojourner-Douglass, Baltimore, MD. Coates is the publisher of Walter Mosley's most recent novel, *Gone Fishing*.

William W. Cook is the Chair of the English Department and Israel Evans Professor of Oratory and Belles Lettres at Dartmouth College. He is the author of *Flight to Canada* and *Hudson Hornet and Other Poems*. His critical works include *Writing in the Spaces Left; Ellison's Modern Odysseus; The Black Arts Poets; Mom, Dad, and God: Sex Roles in Black Drama; Swim: Cultural Separatism in Contemporary Black Literature;* and *What Rough Beast: Modern African Novelists*.

Stanley Crouch is author of the collection of essays and reviews, *Notes of a Hanging Judge*, that was nominated for an award in criticism by the National Book Critics Circle and was selected by the Encyclopedia Britannica Yearbook as the best book of essays published in 1990. In 1993, he was the recipient of both the Jean Stein Award from the American Academy of Arts and Letters and the MacArthur Foundation grant. His most recent publication is *The All-American Skin Game*. He is currently working on a biography of Charlie Parker, a collection of jazz essays and reviews. His epic novel, *First Snow in Kokomo*, should appear in 1998. He is presently writing the scripts for an eight-part television miniseries entitled *Jazz: The Music, The People, The Myth,* and he has served as Artistic Consultant for jazz programming at Lincoln Center since 1987.

Selwyn Cudjoe is a Professor of Africana Studies at Wellesley College where he teaches Afro-American Literature, African Literature, Black Women Writers, and Caribbean Literature. He obtained both the B.A. and the M.A. degrees in English and American Literature from Fordham University in 1969 and 1972, and in 1976 he received a Ph.D. in American Literature from Cornell University. Cudjoe is the author of *V.S. Naipaul: A Materialist Reading* (1988), *Movement of the People: Essays on Independence* (1983), *Resistance and Caribbean Literature* (1980), and *the Role of Resistance in the Caribbean Novel* (1976). He has also edited *Caribbean Women Writers* (1990), *Eric Williams Speaks* (1993), and co-edited *C.L.R. James: His Intellectual Legacy* (1994).

Thulani Davis is the author of the novels, *1959,* and *Maker of Things,* and *Malcolm X, The Photographs.* She published two volumes of poetry: *Playing the Changes* and *All the Renegade Ghosts Rise.* Davis wrote the librettos for the acclaimed operas, *X, The Life and Times of Malcolm X,* and *Amistad* by Anthony Davis. Davis's other work in theater and music collaborations include the 1990 adaptation of Bertolt Brecht's *The Caucasian Circle,* and the libretto for Anne Lebaron's opera, *The E. & O. Line.* Her most recent theater works are the plays, *Miss Ruby's Blues: Story of a Murder in Florida* and *Ava and Cat in Mexico.* From 1993–1995 Davis was a PEW/TCG Resident Fellow with the New York Shakespeare Festival.

Arthur Flowers, a Memphis native, attended Memphis State University and the City University of New York. He has taught writing workshops at the City University of New York and New York University. He is a Vietnam veteran, blues singer, and co-founder of the New Renaissance Writers Guild, NYC, and he is currently the Director of The Griot Shop, Memphis, Tennessee. His works include *De Mojo Blues* (1986) and *Another Good Loving Blues* (1993). Works in progress include *No Rest for the Weary* and *The Hoodoo Book of Flowers.* Flowers is a recipient of a National Endowment for the Arts fellowship award.

Cecil Foster was born in Barbados and moved to Canada in 1978. His novels, *No Man in the House* and *Sleep on Beloved* were published to critical acclaim in the United States and Canada. Since leaving his position of senior editor at the *Financial Post*, Foster has worked for CBC radio and television and has written for several leading magazines.

Marita Golden is the author of the classic memoir, *Migrations of the Heart*; the novels, *A Woman's Place, Long Distance Life*, and *Do Remember Me,* and the book *Saving Our Sons: Raising Black Children in a Turbulent World*. She is editor of the anthology *Wild Women Don't Wear No Blues: Black Women Writers on Love, Men, and Sex* and co-editor with Susan Shreve of *Skin Deep*, a collection of fiction and nonfiction on the subject of race by black and white women writers. Golden holds the position of Senior Writer in the MFA Graduate Writing Program at Virginia Commonwealth University in Richmond, Virginia. She is also the founder of the Zora Neale Hurston/Richard Wright Award for emerging African American college fiction writers, underwritten by HarperCollins Publishers.

Lorna Goodison is a poet and fiction writer whose work has been included in anthologies and collections of Caribbean poetry published in the West Indies, Europe and the United States, including *The Norton Anthology of World Masterpieces*. Goodison opened the Association of Commonwealth Literature and Language Studies Conference in 1989 in England with Derek Walcott. She was the only anglophone Caribbean writer at the Celebration of the Arts in Latin America in Montreal in 1990. And in 1992, she was the keynote speaker at a special celebration of Haitian Art and Culture-Espoir d'Haiti in Detroit. Her works include *Baby Mother* and *The King of Swords* (short stories), *Tamarind Season, I Am Becoming My Mother, Heartease*, and a volume of *Selected Poems*. Her latest book of poems is *To Us All Flowers Are Roses* (1995).

Karla FC Holloway, a Professor of English and African American Literature at Duke University, is the author of three books: on Zora Neale Hurston (*The Character of the Word*), Toni Morrison (*New Dimensions of Spirituality*), and her most recent work on black women writers in West Africa and the United States, *Moorings and Meta-*

phors. Both *New Dimensions of Spirituality* and *Moorings and Metaphors* were awarded Outstanding Academic Book by Choice Magazine. Her work in literary theory focuses on black women writers, especially their uses of language, the cultural connections within their works, and their poetic re-creations of a woman-centered ancestry. Her book, *Codes of Conduct: Reflections on Ethics and Ethnicity*, blends autobiography, literary theory, and cultural studies, and considers the way in which our contemporary culture both challenges and encourages ethnic identity.

Kevin Christopher James was born in Trinidad. He holds a B.S. from the University of the West Indies and a doctorate in science education from Columbia University. His short stories have appeared in *Between C&D, BOMB, American Letters and Commentary, Quartro, The Portable Lower East Side, The Literary Review,* and *Les Jungles d'Amérique*. In 1989, he won a New York Foundation for the Arts fellowship in fiction. His books include *Jumping Ship and Other Stories* (1992) and two novels, *Secrets* (1993) and *A Fling with a Demon Lover* (1996).

Yelena Khanga, now a TV Talk Show host in Russia, served as a general assignment reporter covering a wide range of political and economic issues for the Moscow News. Ms. Khanga was selected as the first Soviet journalist in an exchange program between American and Soviet Media. She has appeared on "Vsglyad" (former Soviet Union), "20/20," NBC's "Today Show," "Posner/Donahue" (CNBC), PBS's "McNeil/Lehrer News Hour" and CNN's "Sonya Live" and "International Hour." She has authored *Soul to Soul . . . The Story of a Black Russian American Family 1865-1992* (1992). In it she traces her family roots spanning three continents, America, Europe and Africa. Her other publications include "No Matreshkas Need Apply" (*New York Times*, November 1991), and "Overrun by Ugly Americans" (*New York Times*, August 1994).

Paule Marshall. one of America's leading black women writers, is the author of *Daughters; Praisesong for the Widow; Brown Girl, Brownstones; The Chosen Place, The Timeless People; Reena and Other Stories*; and *Soul Clap Hands and Sing*. A recipient of the prestigious MacArthur fellowship, she is professor of English at New York University where she holds the Helen Gould Sheppard Professor of Literature and Culture Chair. She lives in New York City.

Stephanie Martin was born and raised in Jamaica. She is a visual artist and co-founder of Sister Vision Press, the first and only women of color publishing house in Canada. Ms. Martin lives in Toronto.

Susan McHenry has been a key editor at magazines that have pioneered reaching new audiences of sophisticated readers among women and among African Americans. She spent nine years as an editor at *Ms.*, where her own cultural commentary won a Newswomen's Club of New York Front Page Award for best magazine column. In 1989, she anchored the start-up editorial team of *Emerge* as its first managing editor. Most recently, McHenry was a senior editor at *Working Woman*. She is now completing a book, *Do Your Work: African American Women Professionals as 21st-Century Role Models.* McHenry earned a B.A. with honors in American history and literature from Harvard-Radcliff, a master's degree in literature from Boston University, and was a 1987–88 Knight-Bagehot Fellow in Business and Economics Journalism at Columbia University. She was executive editor of *QBR: The Black Book Review.*

Terry McMillan received her B.A. in Journalism from the University of California at Berkeley, and attended the MFA Film Program at Columbia University. McMillan's first novel, *Mama*, published in 1987, received a National Book Award by the Before Columbus Foundation. She has been awarded a 1988 National Endowment for the Arts Fellowship in literature, a 1986 New York Foundation for the Arts Fellowship, and the Doubleday/Columbia University Literary Fellowship. She was a three-time fellow at Yaddo Artist Colony and The MacDowell Colony. She has been a Visiting Professor of English at the University of Wyoming and Stanford University and an Associate Professor of English at the University of Arizona in Tucson. Her second novel, *Disappearing Acts*, was published in 1989. She has also edited and compiled an anthology of contemporary African-American fiction entitled *Breaking Ice*, published in 1990. Her novel *Waiting to Exhale* (1992) was recently adapted to the much-acclaimed movie of the same title. *How Stella Got Her Groove Back* (1996) is her latest best-seller.

Walter Mosley has earned critical acclaim as well as dedicated fans stretching from Southern California all the way to 1600 Pennsylvania Avenue. His quartet of Easy Rawlings novels, *Devil in a Blue Dress,* which was adapted to the much-acclaimed movie starring Denzel Washington, *A Red Death, White Butterfly* and *Black Betty*, has provided a unique perspective on American life. His mysteries have brought alive the multi-racial reality of postwar Los Angeles in all its richness, sprawl and divisiveness. Last August he published his first non-mystery, *RL's Dream*, whose hero, Soupspoon Wise, is an aging Mississippi Delta bluesman who once played with the legendary "RL" or Robert Johnson. His latest works include *A Little Yellow Dog* and *Gone Fishing*.

Jill Nelson is a native New Yorker and a graduate of the City College of New York and the Columbia University School of Journalism. A journalist for almost twenty years, her work has appeared in numerous publications including *Essence, The Nation, Ms., The New York Times*, and *The Village Voice*. She was a staff writer for *The Washington Post Magazine* during its first four years of existence and was named Washington D.C. Journalist of the Year for her work there. She wrote the highly acclaimed memoir, *Volunteer Slavery: My Authentic Negro Experience* and has authored a collection of essays, *Straight, No Chaser (1997)*.

Hugh Pearson is the author of *The Shadow of the Panther: Huey Newton and the Price of Black Power in America* (1994), a book about the life of Huey Newton and three former black Panthers who were rank and file members of the party. His book received rave reviews in the *New York Daily News, Newsday*, and *The New York Times Book Review*. Pearson currently resides in New York City.

Eugene Redmond is a Professor of English at Southern Illinois University at Edwardville. He was named a 1993 winner of the American Book Award for excellence in multi-cultural literature for his poetry collection, *The Eye in the Ceiling*. Redmond has several published books of poetry, including *Sentry of the Four Golden Pillars, Consider Loneliness as These Things*, and *River of Bones and Flesh and Blood*. His publications include criticism, notably *Drumvoices: The Mission of Afro-American Poetry*. He is the editor of *Drumvoices Revue*, Associate Editor of *Literati Internazionale* and *The Original Chicago Blues Annual*, and permanent contributing editor of *The Pushcart Prize: The Best of the Small Presses*.

Ishmael Reed grew up in working class neighborhoods in Buffalo, New York. He attended Buffalo public schools and the University of Buffalo. As well as being a novelist, poet, and essayist, he is a songwriter, television producer, publisher, magazine editor, playwright, and founder of the Before Columbus Foundation and There City Cinema, both of which are located in Northern California. Two of his books have been nominated for National Book Awards, and Reed has received numerous honors, fellowships, and prizes, including the Lewis H. Michaux Literary Prize, awarded to him in 1978 by the Studio Museum in Harlem. He has taught at Harvard, Yale, and Dartmouth, and for twenty years he has been a lecturer at the University of California at Berkeley. He lives in Oakland, California. Two albums of his songs, *Conjure I: Music for the Texts of Ishmael Reed* and *Conjure II: Cab Calloway Stands In for the Moon* have been released by Pangaea Records. His works include three collections of essays, *Writin' Is Fightin'*, *God Made Alaska for the Indians, Shrovetide in New Orleans*; novels such as *Mumbo Jumbo, Flight to Canada, The Free-Lance Pall Bearers, Reckless Eyeballing,* and *The Terrible Threes*; and the poetry volumes, *Catechism of D Neoamerican Hoodoo Church, A Secretary to the Spirits, Chattanooga, Conjure*, and *New and Collected Poems*.

Brent Staples has a Ph.D. in psychology from the University of Chicago and writes editorials on politics and culture for *The New York Times*. His memoir *Parallel Time: Growing Up in Black and White* (1994) was on *The New York Times* best-seller list. Staples has also published works in *Reporting: The Chicago Journal, The Reader, Chicago Magazine, Downbeat Magazine, Jazz Hot-Paris, The Museum of Contemporary Art,* and *The Chicago Sun-Times*.

Carlyle V. Thompson is Assistant Professor of African American and American literature at Medgar Evers College of the City University of New York. He is currently completing a book on the literary and social phenomenon of black individuals passing for white in the novels of Charles Waddell Chesnutt, James Weldon Johnson, Nella Larsen and William Faulker. He received his M.A., M.Phil. and Ph.D. degrees in English from Columbia University.

John A. Williams is the author of twelve novels, eight nonfiction books and editor or co-editor of ten other books. He is a Distinguished

Professor of English and Journalism at Rutgers University's Newark Campus. Among his novels are: *!Click Song, The Junior Bachelor Society,* and *The Man Who Cried I Am.* Williams, who lives in Teaneck, New Jersey, is completing his thirteenth novel, *There Will Come Thunder*, and is mid-way through yet another, *The Book Without Title.*

About Medgar Evers College

MEDGAR EVERS COLLEGE was founded in 1969 as a result of the collaborative efforts of community leaders, elected officials, the Chancellor, and the Board of Trustees of the City University of New York. Named for the late civil rights leader, Medgar Wiley Evers, the College was established with a mandate to meet the educational and social needs of the Central Brooklyn community.

Though still committed to the fulfillment of the founders' dream of quality higher education for the diverse population of Central Brooklyn, the college has expanded its scope. Today its students represent over seventy nations of the world. They come from different socio-economic and academic backgrounds and have diverse personal and professional interests. However, they share one common goal: the pursuit of self-actualization. To help them realize this goal, the College offers a number of programs tailored to their specific needs.

Medgar Evers College awards both baccalaureate and associate degrees. It also provides certificate programs and non-credit courses for those seeking personal enrichment or enhanced career opportunities. A host of services, including counseling, tutoring, career planning, veterans' affairs and health care, ensure that students receive the academic, financial and personal support they require for a successful learning experience. Additionally, the Women's Center, Head Start Program, Ella Baker/Charles Romain Child Development Center, Middle College High School, Adult and Continuing Education Program, Caribbean Research Center and the Center for Law and Social Justice provide valuable resources for the students and the Brooklyn community. Yet the greatest resources the College provides to the community are its graduates. The alumni of Medgar Evers College return to the community as doctors, dentists, lawyers, politicians, teachers, accountants, businessmen, nurses, artists, social workers and civic teachers.

Under the able leadership of its president, Dr. Edison O. Jackson, Medgar Evers College continues to seek excellence in its academic programs, its administration, faculty, staff, students, alumni and the community it serves.

About the Editors

Elizabeth Nunez is Professor of English at Medgar Evers College of the City University of New York. A native of Trinidad, Nunez has published articles on Caribbean writers including Jean Rhys, Phyllis Shand Alfrey, Jamaica Kincaid, Merle Hodge, V.S. Naipaul, and George Lamming. She is the author of the novels *When Rocks Dance* (Putnam) and *Beyond the Limbo Silence* (Seal). She directed the National Black Writers Conference sponsored by the National Endowment for the Humanities in 1986, 1988, 1991, and 1996. She received her M.A. and Ph.D. degrees in English from New York University.

Brenda M. Greene is Professor of English Studies at Medgar Evers College, CUNY, where she chairs the Department of Literature, Languages, and Philosophy and teaches composition and literature. Her research interests are in the areas of composition, multicultural literature, and writing across the curriculum, and she has conducted workshops, presented papers, and published in those areas. She is coeditor of *Rethinking American Literature* (NCTE, 1997). Professor Greene is currently conducting research on the literature of contemporary women of color. She was Conference Coordinator for the Fourth National Black Writers Conference.

